The Good Old Days

THE GOOD OLD DAYS

AN INVITATION TO MEMORY

Edited and compiled by R. J. McGINNIS
in cooperation with the staff of
The Farm Quarterly

F. & W. Publishing Co., Inc., Cinn. Ohio

CONTENTS

The Day's Work

Lore & Myth

Special Events

Transition & Destiny

Dedicated to the memory of

LOUIS BROMFIELD

who knew and loved the way of life of the oldtime farmer and sought to preserve his homely virtues in our modern world.

"*I dreamed constantly of my home country, of my grandfather's farm, of Pleasant Valley. . . . I would find myself returning . . . going back again to the mint-scented pastures of Pleasant Valley or the orchards of my grandfather's farm. It was as if all the while my spirit were tugging to return there, as if I was under a compulsion. And those dreams were associated with a sensation of warmth and security and satisfaction that was almost physical.*"

LOUIS BROMFIELD from *Pleasant Valley*

INTRODUCTION

Although a man's life may be well ordered, there will come moments when the realities are too stern, the business of life too demanding, the daily battle for survival too frustrating. In these moments he looks beyond the horizons, or goes back in memory to a better day when man seemed more free, when the pursuit of food and shelter was uncomplicated and direct, and all had peace and security. ¶ This he finds, in looking back, on the farm of his grandfathers, where indeed there was peace and security, and the good life. The way of the farmer satisfies an elemental yearning in all of us. The planting and the harvest, the lowing of a cow at evening milking time, the cock crow at dawn, are part of our immediate heritage. ¶ Plagued by cold wars and hot wars, high velocity living and constant fears, we escape to this dream world when we can. And the more our sophistication, the more we yearn for the simple life as it was lived by our rural ancestors. ¶ To our farmer forefathers nature was both an ally and an antagonist; and that's the way he wanted it, for he gloried in the battle with nature. As an ally, the soil and the sun and the rain brought his crops. Nature fed, clothed, and sheltered him. When nature became an antagonist, he met the issue with confidence. His tight barns were built of shaped red oak framing timbers, joined with second growth hickory pegs; his creek stone house had walls a foot thick; he stored his fruit cellars with food for the long winter and piled the firewood high; he fought frost and drought, flood and insect pests. When he won, the victory was sweet; when he lost he kept his dignity, for he had lost to a respected foe. He could always say that he fashioned his own security. He won and lost his own battles and this is why he considered himself an independent and free man. ¶ The old-time farmer was self-sufficient; he needed little from anybody or anything outside the limits of his own farmstead. He built his own A frame harrow, and he bred and fed his own horse power. He saved seed from the best of his grain and his livestock supplied the only fertilizer he used. His wife carded and spun the wool from his sheep, made the clothing for the family. ¶ This way of life was good, we believe, but it was not to endure. The revolution in the industrial world set up pressures felt at last on the farm, and these too caused a revolution. The revolution in farming was the most explosive in all history. Almost overnight, as historical time goes, a way of life disappeared. The turn of the twentieth century saw the beginning of the end of farms and farming as they had been known for a thousand years. Twenty years later, when the world was picking up the pieces after World War I, the old-time farmer was in precipitous retreat. Mechanization and science rewrote his text books. ¶ His old barter economy gave way before cash and credit and he lost that singular feeling of responsibility for his own security which had been bred into the poor subsistence farmer. The press and force of great numbers of people all about him, international markets for his crops and livestock, and government controls over his harvests made him aware of his obligations as a member of a world society. ¶ This book describes life on the old-time farm, fading into memory and never to return. It is the history of ordinary people as they once lived in their self-sufficiency and the spurious freedom of isolation. History such as this is rarely written; it is preserved only in the memories of people who, like the veterans of old wars, will eventually pass away. We seek to preserve these memories in The Good Old Days. ¶ Memory can play us false. We can easily forget the utter isolation of the old time farm and the intolerance and selfishness which it bred. We can forget too, because we want to, the cruelty to man and beast that went unpunished, the sins and transgressions of unlettered people. ¶ Freedom, too, was often abused. One was free, it is true, to buy a bottle of elixir guaranteed to cure everything from cancer to hangnails; one was free to make a slave of an orphan, or beat his mule. ¶ But these things, fortunately, are overlooked and soon forgotten. It is well that we think of the good old days as an era of serenity and comfort. There was the warm kitchen, always perfumed with the aroma of new-baked bread; the fruit cellar with its bins of apples and turnips and potatoes; the fields and the barns; the animals and the simple tools of the farmers' trade; the days work with its triumphs and defeats. ¶ Here is a way of life that we will not know again. In retrospect it seems a little bit of heaven; and that is how we should feel about the dead, be they people or just days and years.

THE VILLAGE AND COMMUNITY

The first settler, like the first man to eat an oyster, was a man of courage, and a gambler too; he took a chance. He cast aside the precedents of the Old Country to make a new way of life. His ancestors had lived in a tight groove. They were born into a class above which they could not rise; their social life was rigid, the routine of everyday living long since stabilized by custom and tradition. ¶ Now, a new man in a new world, he made his way from scratch; he had to be self-sufficient, make his own decisions, write new laws for a new society. Liking his fellow man, he walked over the hill to visit the second settler and the two of them sang a song and traded labor at harvesttime. Then others came, and crowded upon each other and they found they needed a set of laws, a police force, and a court. ¶ They needed, too, a place to trade, for self-sufficiency vanished with the coming of others. They brought in a man of God to interpret the Word, and built a temple. They had hopes their children would go beyond what they were, so they banded together and built a school. ¶ These things grew into the crossroad village, with its church, its school, its blacksmith shop, and its trading post. The village became the big wheel that turned the smaller wheels of outlying farms. Like arteries feeding the limbs, roads threaded out from the village to the farms; over them their crops went to market, their children to school, and their families to church. And eventually telephone lines followed them, and the R.F.D., the free delivery of the daily mail. ¶ This was the village and the community, almost as self-sufficient and isolated as the settler's farm had once been. But this, too, passed with the twentieth century, when wheels and good roads knit the whole world of America into one community.

THE LITTLE RED SCHOOLHOUSE

THE little red schoolhouse, like the buffalo and the horse and buggy, is becoming a dim historical memory. Once upon a time it was the hub of the community, the haven of learning, and the wellspring of all the virtues. Our forefathers there learned the three R's and the lessons of life that made them the leaders of America for a century and a half.

They were of a pattern, clapboard or brick, painted red, four-square with a row of high windows on two sides, a small cupola with a bell to call the pupils in from the farms. Two outhouses, one for the boys and one for the girls, stood in opposite corners of the schoolyard. The schoolroom was not designed to make rosy the road to learning—a big pot-bellied stove in the center aisle, a row of desks or benches on either side, the teacher's desk up front on a little platform, with a blackboard behind.

There were hooks along the back wall for clothes and a shelf for the lunch boxes. There too was the water pail, with long-handled dipper—all drank from the same canteen. There was a McGuffey "ABC Chart" near the teacher's desk, a map or two on the wall, and a globe to show that the world was round.

The smaller pupils sat up front and progressed by age to the rear of the room. The rear desks were occupied mostly by boys, for only a very daring girl would care to be a part of the horseplay that went on there when the teacher's back was turned. One of the pastimes was shooting paper wads at the ceiling. Making a paper wad of the right consistency was an art. A scrap of paper was chewed until it became a pulpy mass and then propelled to the ceiling by the thumb. If it were expertly done, it stuck, dried out, and in time was covered with fly-specks and dust

and became a permanent part of the décor. There were only a few wads in the front of the room, for here the small boys were under close surveillance, and usually lacked the technique and strength of thumb.

Ages ranged from a precocious five to sixteen and up, the latter ambitious lads who wanted all the learning they could get, or came in during the winter months when work was slack on the farm. The school was a clubhouse for them, and an opportunity for juvenile courting.

The ability to read determined, roughly, the class you were in. Some schools took you to the sixth reader. A bright reader of eight might progress through two or even three readers in a year and find herself (for some unknown reason the good readers were always girls) reciting with classmates twice her age. On the other hand, a lazy or dull reader of sixteen might not have progressed further than the third reader. Learning was a mark of the sissy in those days and the star pupil had to endure a good deal of teasing and ridicule.

The curriculum was simple—reading, writing and arithmetic, the old stand-bys, and history and geography. Fancy subjects, like science, were unknown. There was no library and the school with a fat Webster's was considered lucky. Every pupil had a slate, for paper tablets were expensive and were used only on special occasions, like essays to be done at home.

The best-remembered teachers were the old maids, dedicated to teaching, loving youngsters, but too often ill-trained and poorly educated. The men teachers were usually serious young men who resorted too frequently to the birch rod. They boarded at a farmhouse near the school, went early to start the

fire, sweep out, and clean the blackboards. A good one with a long tenure was paid as much as thirty dollars a month; a beginner started at twenty dollars.

The midmorning and midafternoon recesses, and the lunch hour, were the high spots of the day. The half-hour recess afforded just enough time for a game of three-corner-cat. In marble season the boys, and the occasional tomboy, smoothed off a place in front of the door and played for keeps. Some teachers regarded this as gambling, and forbade the game. There was crack-the-whip, the biggest boy at one end, the smallest, who was the cracker of the whip, at the other. In winter the hardiest played fox-and-rabbit in the snow; the girls and the small boys played parlor games around the hot stove.

Those who attended a country school may have forgotten in time the sums and the history they once learned there, but they never forget the full-bodied aroma of a schoolroom on a cold winter day, with the stove glowing red-hot. This aroma was compounded of the wet jackets drying out on the woodbox, the remnants of bygone lunches, the dust and cobwebs on the ceiling, the musty tang gathered in the tight room during the summer. All these added up to an unforgettable mixture that forever remained in memory.

Unforgettable too was the long walk. Fortunate were those who lived on farms adjoining the schoolhouse. Some walked through winter rain and snow over miles of muddy roads. In winter darkness fell before the home farm was reached. This was one of the reasons why the products of the little red schoolhouse were so successful. Education came the hard way, you didn't take it lightly, and it stuck with you.

THE WARRIORS

WHEN I was a boy there were many Civil War veterans scattered around the community. They formed a tight little group which the stay-at-homes referred to, on the sly, as the Liars Club. I thought of them as warriors and heroes. They got special consideration at family reunions and picnics, and on the Fourth of July and Memorial Day they put on their old campaign caps and paraded behind the band.

They were great storytellers and when they got together and began to brag about their exploits a boy would leave his favorite game to sit and listen.

My favorite was old Gus Scherr. Gus was not much force as a farmer, but he was an unsung rural Homer when it came to spinning yarns about The War. His stories got longer and taller with time. He liked boys and there was always a gang following him around, begging him to tell them a story. One of them who was getting along in his history book once pointed out to him that he couldn't have been at the Battle of Shiloh and the Battle of Fredericksburg, since they were both fought on the same day. Gus was not disturbed by this, claiming that history books have a way of being wrong about dates.

Gus had other talents. He was the best fisherman in the country, and if he especially liked you he would invite you along to his favorite pool. He was a great squirrel hunter too, and could take off warts by rubbing them with his thumb and reciting some mysterious words.

The middle finger on his right hand was missing,

lost, Gus said, at the Battle of Gettysburg. "I was layin' there behind a rail fence," he said, "and I see this Johnny Reb sneakin' up on me, ready to shoot. I drawed a bead on him and we both fired at the same time. I hit him right between the eyes. His bullet took off this finger, clean as a whistle."

He lived comfortably on his pension and what he took off his little farm. Since he never allowed his work to interfere with his hunting or fishing, his corn patch was not the most productive. Most of his year-round food came from his kitchen garden, which his wife tended.

To Gus the Civil War was not only the greatest war in all history, but the greatest event of all time. It never really ended for him, just tapered off into a sort of passive cold war. Once when he was picking potatoes the smaller ones kept falling through his hand at the missing finger. It had been fifty years since Gettysburg, but Gus straightened up, spat a stream of tobacco juice into the wind, and shouted, "Consarn that Rebel!"

The small boys who followed in his wake and idolized him may not have learned sound history from him, but they'll tell you today that any boy who hasn't had an old soldier to tell him stories has missed one of the great experiences of life.

THE MEDICINE MAN

ON A ledge behind the horse stalls, along with the currycomb and brush, Grandfather kept an assortment of bottled goods bought from peddlers. These peddlers drove about the country, making regular calls. Those that represented the larger patent medicine houses generally had a bright red or yellow buggy and a spanking team of horses. Others carried a variety of salves, ointments, elixirs, and liniments in a suitcase and got about in a hired rig from the livery stable in the village. They were personable characters with what was known as "the gift of gab," and they could smell a chicken dinner for miles.

One of the standbys on the ledge was Sloan's Liniment. Grandpa wouldn't have thought of farming without a bottle of this marvelous panacea. Let a bump, swelling, cut, bruise, spavin, fistula, or sprain appear on a horse, and Grandpa brought out the Sloan's. He didn't hesitate to use it on himself or the hired man. It was, and is, a potent concoction, and applied to the bare skin was a counterirritant powerful enough to make you forget anything less than a compound fracture.

Sloan's Liniment was for the exterior surfaces of man and beast. There were other and equally universal remedies for the inner ills and pains of livestock. The label said a dose would cure colic, scours, bloat, abortion, and constipation. They were effective, too, in relieving undiagnosed ills commonly referred to in humans as the miseries, but in animals as the epizootic.

Regardless of what the label on the bottle or the gay posters hanging in the blacksmith shop said, Grandfather wouldn't buy until he had sniffed the contents. If his snifter made him reel and raised his hat off his head, then it must be good. If it wasn't more than a dollar he bought it.

Veterinarians were scarce and poorly trained and not very popular. Grandfather preferred to make his own diagnoses and do his own doctoring. If, by any chance, the bottled magic failed to do the work at hand, Grandfather was not stumped. He had a lot of superstitious hocus-pocus at his command in an emergency. For example, chewing tobacco and kerosene, taken internally and rubbed on, was good for tetanus, or lockjaw; an old sock, smeared with grease and forced down a cow's throat, cured bloat and indigestion; if a dog had mange, a copper wire hung around its neck soon checked it; and if a horse got stubborn and lazy, Grandfather laid a board across his head and gave it a smart whack with a hammer. He also treated for diseases that never existed, like hollow tail and hollow horn.

When the Foods and Drugs Act came in the patent medicine people had to back up their claims for the universal powers of their goods. Most of them went out of business. The colleges began turning out well-trained veterinarians; grandfather's grandson took four years at the state ag college, and now runs the farm. Livestock therapy is more complicated today, but the livestock are better off.

Prof. FLINT'S HORSE AND CATTLE RENOVATING POWDERS

are in our opinion, the best article known for all diseases of the horse and cattle, arising from impure blood.

For COUGHS, HEAVES, EPIZOOTIC, PINK-EYE, HIDE-BOUND, ROUGH COAT, Etc., THEY HAVE NO EQUAL.

PRICE, ONE POUND PACKAGE, 50 CENTS.   HALF-POUND PACKAGE, 25 CENTS.

For full information, see our "Treatise on the Horse and his Diseases." Price, by mail, 25 cts.   For sale by all Druggists throughout the United States and Canada.

R.F.D.

W. Levi Clough, rural mail carrier, Queen Annes County, Maryland, saw the red flag up on the Enoch Sloan box. He stopped his horse at the box, opened it, and took out an alarm clock, with a note attached. The note read: "Pa's watch stopped. Will you please set our clock?"

It would appear that delivering mail to 30,000,000 people would be a big enough job for our 32,546 rural mail carriers without the added duty of setting clocks. But to the families lined up along the thousands of miles of rural routes in this country, the mail carrier is just another neighbor, willing and glad to help out with little favors.

The carriers themselves feel the same way about it. The service has a fine tradition of helpfulness and neighborliness back of it, built up during its relatively short life. The rural mail delivery service will observe its fifty-eighth birthday this year.

It all started back in the middle 1880's when a pert little farmer's wife got to her feet in a Grange meeting out in the Grand Prairie region of our Midwest and complained bitterly about having to drive eight miles over bad roads for the mail. "People in the cities have their mail delivered to them," she said. "Are they any better than we are; why can't we have a rural free delivery?"

The idea swept the country like a fire on the Grand Prairie. Politicians were quick to see its virtue as a rural vote getter. By 1891 there was sufficient pressure back of the idea to induce Postmaster General Wanamaker to suggest a bill in Congress to create such a service. The bill failed, but the next year Congress appropriated $10,000 for an experimental rural delivery route. Mr. Wanamaker was annoyed at the stingy appropriation and stated that it was inadequate for a full exploitation of even an experimental route. The appropriation was on an annual basis and by 1896 enough had accumulated to justify a start.

On June 9, 1896, the first R.F.D. route was started at Charles Town, West Virginia, and a little later in the same year two more routes were established in the same state. The service spread like the green bay tree. At its peak there were 45,382 routes serving the rural areas.

The name, Rural Free Delivery, is a misnomer, and although it was used officially for a time, the "free" was dropped in 1903, no one knows why. The official designation now is simply Rural Delivery. It is not now, and never was free.

Rural mail carriers are a race apart. Theirs is a lonely life. They go their appointed rounds, day after day over the same routes, with no company but their thoughts. They watch the snows of winter melt off the hillsides, the tender green of spring appear, merging into the lush summer and then into the painted autumn. They get to know every stick and stone and puddle along their piece of country highway. Some of the people along their routes remain only names on the mailboxes; others, as lonely as they, become friends and neighbors, coming to the end of the lane in sunbonnet and apron, to exchange a few words with the outside world. They see children grow up and become fathers and mothers and then grandparents. From the very nature of their duties they become helpful neighbors, and their chores stretch beyond their official duties of carrying the mail, making out money orders, selling stamps.

W. Levi Clough, who set the clock, has been carrying the mail over the same route for forty-seven years. His total mileage would reach twenty times around the earth. He wore out more horses and buggies than he can remember, and nine automobiles. For thirteen years after he started his route in 1916 he drove a horse. Sometimes, when the bottom fell out of the dirt roads in winter, he rode horseback, taking short cuts across the fields. A runaway horse once dumped him, with all his mail, into a wet ditch. He once wrote a letter for an illiterate farmhand to his best girl. The letter, a proposal of marriage, was so convincing she said yes.

The Post Office Department learned very early that it could not restrict the extracurricular activities of its mail carriers. There are a few things they cannot do—they cannot solicit on their routes, and they cannot make deliveries for business firms. But there is nothing in the regulations to prevent them from matching a spool of thread for a patron or stopping at the blacksmith shop for a sharpened plowshare. They

The delivery hack was standard about the turn of the century. It was a tight,
weatherproof box with sliding doors. This one operated out of Crawfordsville, Ind. Carriers
at this time wore an unofficial heavy, blue-gray uniform and cap.

As roads improved, carriers gave up the horse and took up the new automobile.
Here is one, vintage of 1906, with a mail rack in the dashboard, one-lung engine
in the rear, and clincher tires.

have delivered babies, put out fires, helped round up strayed livestock, taken splinters out of fingers. Walter Hansen, of Vermont, found this note in a box: "Will you please stir my applebutter. I'm taking Lafe his dinner."

The telephone, radio, and daily paper have not seriously threatened to displace the mail carrier as purveyor of news, rumor, and neighborhood gossip.

The hazards of driving more than a million miles would seem to be a strain on the law of averages. Yet John Stansbury, who has carried the mail in Vermillion Parish, Louisiana, for thirty-two years, has never had an accident—"never even bumped into anyone," he says. The carriers have a remarkable safety record.

The department permits carriers to operate sideline businesses as long as they do not interfere with the delivery of the mail. Stansbury has a little farm, gets up at four o'clock, feeds his stock, and goes to the post office to sort his mail. He says that he always looks forward to his daily thirty-mile drive, for like all carriers he believes the people along his route are the best. "Why," he says, "I'm always finding a bunch of new onions or a length of sausage at butchering time, or a cup of hot coffee on the cold days."

If a carrier wants to stop and chat, there's nothing in the regulations to prevent it. He is not confined to a time schedule, but is expected to cover his route regardless of storm or heat or cold or gloom of night. If he finds a bridge out, he is permitted to take alternate roads, but otherwise he cannot take short cuts even though he has no mail to deliver.

When the service was started in the late nineties the routes were shorter than they are now. Up to the early twenties routes were laid out on the basis of the distance a cavalry horse could walk in eight hours. As automobiles replaced the horse, the length of routes has been increased. Very often when a carrier retires, his route is combined with another. The longest route today, 104.1 miles, is out of Edinsburg, Texas. The shortest is out of Robbin, Illinois, and is 6.25 miles in length. The standard route is 30 miles, and it is on this length that the basic salary is computed. The first carrier was paid $200 per year. Through the years the salary has been gradually increased. Today the maximum salary a carrier can draw is between $4,000 and $5,000, depending on the length of service, length of route, and the population served. He furnishes his own car, but is paid depreciation and maintenance. Carriers are required to retire at the age of seventy. A few reach this age with fifty years of service behind them. These veterans are regarded as the royal family among carriers.

A carrier is chosen from the area he will serve. When a vacancy occurs, a Civil Service examination is held and the highest man, usually, gets the appointment. The qualifications are simple—a citizen, must know postal rates and regulations, be able to read No. 4 print at fourteen inches, be sound of wind and limb. Both sexes are eligible, but the calling has scant appeal for women. Out of the 32,000-odd carriers, only 348 are women.

"Miss Lutie" Mayfield, Morely, Missouri, retired last year on her annuity at the age of seventy, one of the few women carriers to achieve that distinction. She became a carrier after the death in France of her husband in the First World War. She had previously been a schoolteacher.

Rural mail has been delivered from about every sort of contrivance that moves—buggy, motorcycle, sled, sleigh, wagon, bicycle, automobile, by foot, and from the back of a mule. About the turn of the century the Post Office Department authorized a standard delivery wagon, a boxlike affair, painted white, with the inscription, U.S. MAIL, and the route number. The mail was filed in a slotted shelf in front of the driver. The reins came through slits above the shelf. It could be closed tightly against the elements, but the windshield could be dropped and the sliding doors opened in pleasant weather. During the winter the carrier usually placed a lighted kerosene lantern

between his legs to keep him warm. His lunch reposed under the seat. In those days the more elegant carriers wore a uniform, somewhat reminiscent of what was worn by the boys in blue during the Civil War. It was a trifle stuffy for hot July and August days, and was gradually discontinued.

The standard mail "hack" in turn gave way to the automobile. Fred. J. McKeown, Giddings, Texas, started carrying the mail on pony back in 1903 and retired in 1953 after fifty years of service. He acquired a two-wheel cart which he used when the Texas roads dried out. "During the winter rains I often had to swim my pony across streams and if I wasn't careful he could drop into a mudhole."

He thought a Model T Ford could get around as the roads improved, and he bought one in 1917. But he had to be pulled out of so many mudholes by friendly farmers that he went back to his pony for a few years more.

He passes daily the one-room schoolhouse which he attended, and four of his schoolmates are on his route. In the early days, before telephones were common, he was often asked to send the doctor after he got back in town. He still does a brisk business toting packages from town and to neighbors.

The old-time mail carrier periodically had a very knotty problem—what to do with his horse once he was through with him. A horse which had been used for any length of time by a mail carrier was ruined forever after as a driving animal. He wanted to stop at every mailbox along the road, and what was more frustrating, slowed up as soon as he saw one; he was reluctant to travel any road other than his old mail route. No one ever got anywhere on time with an old R.F.D. horse. The daily twenty to thirty miles of an average route soon took the ginger out of a horse, but he was still good as a family horse long after he was unfit for a mail route. Gypsies or traders usually bought the mail horses, at a very low price, and peddled them to suckers in strange neighborhoods.

A growing number of special cars are being made for the rural mail carrier. These have a right-hand drive which permits reaching the mailbox without sliding across the seat. They are equipped for easy and convenient storage of mail and packages.

When parcel post came along, the duties of the carriers were more than doubled. Packages up to seventy pounds were handled. The Post Office Department adopted a larger mailbox, capable of handling the larger packages, and asked the carriers to push them. However, there are still many small rural boxes. When the carrier has a package larger than the box will accommodate, he may deliver it directly, if it is convenient. Otherwise, he leaves a note asking the patron to call at the post office for it, or to meet him at the box the next day. He cannot leave it outside. A carrier dare not take mail from a home which is quarantined. He must deliver a special delivery letter up to half a mile off his route. The department requests that he not leave his mail out of his sight, although it is doubtful if there would be a prosecution should a carrier be invited into a home for a chicken dinner.

A carrier gets 13 days' vacation a year for less than 3 years' service, 20 days up to 15 years' service, and 26 days after that. He is allowed 13 days' sick leave per year with pay.

Rural mail delivery blankets the country today. There is scarcely a family, however isolated, that doesn't get its mail delivered regularly. Some isolated mountain communities are still served by pony express. In the bayous of the South, where there are no roads, the mail is sometimes delivered by boat. Claude Underwood is one of the carriers down there. His route, in Baldwin County, Alabama, is served entirely by boat. He starts at Magnolia Springs, going through Weeks Bay and up the Fish River. He moves from one side of the river to another in his six-cylinder boat, "Jeanetta," stopping at docks, boathouses, and at boxes nailed on trees. He sometimes has to dodge alligators, and keeps an eye open for snakes. His route is a little over twenty-two miles long, with sixty-eight families.

Rural carriers have an exuberant national organization, The National Rural Letter Carriers' Association, with headquarters in Washington. Their patriotism takes no back seat, even to the D.A.R., and they have a zealous pride in their organization and membership. Each state has its own tight little association. The carriers have a death benefit association, the Rural Carriers' Provident Guild, and a social organization known as the Retired and Pioneer Carriers' Club.

In Washington the politicians come and go, but the rural mail carrier, oblivious to everything except the prompt and regular delivery of his mail, goes his appointed way. There are few who would challenge the statement that no government worker does a better job of serving the citizen.

THE
HAY RIDE

It was hot, dusty, and slow; the hayseed got down your neck, the wagon jolted the fillings out of your teeth, and you couldn't get very far out of town, for a yoke of oxen, at high speed, traveled less than five miles an hour. It wasn't horsesense for the women to wear corsets and the men to wear coats, but you suffered because it was the mode of the time. Then, when you got to your destination, the bank of a creek or a shady dell, you found that the watermelon was warm and someone had put his foot into the lunch basket and the sandwiches were full of ants.

But it was a hay ride, and you had fun in a desperate sort of way. Coming home in the cool of the evening you could hold hands and cuddle a little when the chaperon wasn't looking. The cost to each gentleman was not more than twenty-five cents. It was cheap entertaining and courting and it got you out of town to faraway places.

You look back on those hay rides with a sentimental nostalgia, yet you know, right down deep, they were pretty poor excuses for a good time.

23

THE HUCKSTERS

THE huckster wagon, which at one time linked American farms to the crossroads store, has passed into limbo along with the buggy, the buffalo robe, and the bustle. In its heyday, during the century preceding the early 1900's, it was indispensable. While it brought the goods of the general store to isolated farms, and was run for profit by the storekeeper, it was much more than that to the lonely housewife tucked away among the endless fields.

There may be a few tough survivors—in the Tennessee hills, or in the Ozarks—but most children today would not recognize a huckster wagon if they saw one. There are modern grocery stores on wheels, luxurious vehicles on rubber, stocked with everything the inner man can desire. But these effete equipages are not to be confused with the old-time horse-drawn wagon piloted by a rugged, versatile individual who was more than a peddler—he was an institution, a cog in the wheel that brought America from the pioneer's log cabin to greatness. The roads he traveled were either ankle deep in dust or they were knee deep in mud. Through heat and cold and storm he made his appointed rounds. He was resourceful and hardy, and he had hair on his chest.

Such a huckster was Matt Fichter of Fichter Bros. General Store. The Fichter store was, and still is, the hub of the little universe of Reily, a quiet village among the rolling hills of Butler County, Ohio. The Fichter Bros. at one time operated huckster routes six days a week and kept three teams, which they used on alternate days, in their stables.

Matt, the younger of the two Fichter brothers, was the huckster. On huckstering days he'd roll out of bed at three in the morning. The night before he stocked the shelves of his wagon and filled the special orders from the previous trip. The wagon jolted out of Reily before dawn and drove into the first farmhouse before the morning milk pails stopped rattling.

When Matt's wagon turned in at the end of the lane the housewife put on a clean apron, slicked up her hair, and went out to the barnyard to meet it; the children appeared out of nowhere, the dogs barked, and father tied his team to the fence at the end of the corn row and walked up to the house.

Matt knew what was expected of him. He was a talkative and gregarious man, and as he wrapped the reins around the whip and climbed down from his seat, he began a discourse on the state of crops on the other side of the county, the health of the neighbors up and down the line, the arrival of new babies, national and local politics, and what to do in case of sunstroke in the hayfield. He passed along the gossip he had collected along his route. He was in a hurry, for he had to cover a ten-mile circuit before dark, but he knew that if he didn't throw in a bonus of gossip his customers would be disappointed.

He weighed the week's butter, loaded the egg crates, and stuffed a half-dozen culled hens into the crate hung beneath the tail gate. He dived into the dark recess of the wagon and filled the grocery order, drew a gallon of kerosene from a tank beneath the seat, and made a memo of next week's wants. As a parting gesture he gave each of the kids a stick of

candy, climbed into the seat, and clucked his ponies into a trot. The wagon disappeared down the road in a cloud of dust.

Matt's morning passed with trading and talking from kitchen to kitchen. He made his noonday stop at a big elm tree beside a creek on a solitary stretch of dusty road. In the deep shade at the side of the road Matt ate the lunch prepared for him at home. He fed his horses, and watered them from a bucket filled at the creek. Then he readied his accounts and set out on the afternoon run.

His bookkeeping was important, for most of his customers paid their bills just twice a year—when the hogs were sold in the spring and when harvesting was over in the fall. The farmer and his hired hand were carried on credit. If a bad year came along, the accounts were carried for the next year. Most people paid as soon as they got the money. Sometimes a ne'er-do-well took his family and skipped the county, but these risks were expected. Honest folk could not be penalized.

The liberality of credit during the huckstering days of the Fichter Bros. is written through the pages of their heavy, leather-bound ledgers. Scarcely anyone was refused if he asked to be "put on the book for a spell." There was no high-pressure collecting. Back in 1929 Jim Wilkes had a bad year, like so many others. His bill mounted to several hundred dollars as one streak of hard luck followed another. Jim made a slow recovery, but Matt continued to stop at his place every week. Finally he was paying his bills regularly again, but nothing was ever said to him about his 1929 debt. Twenty years passed; the 1929 ledger had a thick coating of dust on it, and the paper was already yellowed. Then one day two years ago Jim walked into Fichter Bros. store and put down the money he owed. It was correct to the penny.

Matt Fichter was more than a huckster. He played cupid for a hired girl and a bachelor farmer for several years, and not only carried their love letters but helped compose them. When the wedding day came the groom rode to the bride's house in the huckster wagon.

Matt dosed out simple medicines for the sick, wrote letters for those who had never learned the art, cashed the checks of Civil War veterans, diagnosed the ailments of cows and horses, and settled line fence feuds; he found jobs for workers and workers for jobs. Some folks set butchering day for Matt's visit, because he knew how to sledge a hog between the eyes and when to take off the kettle of lard. He was an expert at seasoning sausage and mixing the sugar cure for hams and bacon.

It was surprising how many of the day-by-day wants Matt's light wagon held within its crowded interior: the staples—sugar, coffee, flour, spices, salt; drugs such as Castoria, Epsom salts, cough syrup, castor oil, camphor, liniment for man and beast; small items of hardware, nails, hinges, buckles, scythe blades, horse collars; dry beans, rice, corn meal, breakfast oats; overalls, candy, bolts of muslin and calico, clothespins, a bucket of salt mackerel, a jug of turpentine, machine oil, straw hats in season, oranges at Christmastime, plug tobacco, cheese.

There was a seasonal variety too. In the spring he loaded up heavy with onion sets, garden seeds, and seed potatoes; in the summer there were big grocery orders for the threshing rings and Mason jars with extra lids and rubbers; in the autumn there were husking pegs, double-thumbed gloves, and sausage seasoning. He was a keen merchandiser. If there was a shelf-worn item at the home store he carried it along on the wagon and moved it as a special; he usually added a sale or two in the luxury class—a hair ribbon for the little girl, a bag of marbles for the small boy, or a bottle of toilet water for the young lady. Father got his Sunday afternoon cigar from Matt, either a Pittsburgh stogie, three for a nickel, or even, when the hogs had been sold, an expensive five-cent panatela.

His books show that fifty years ago he paid 10 and 12 cents a dozen for eggs and 20 cents for an old rooster; fryers were 7 cents a pound; butter was 15. He sold a pound of sugar for 5 cents, salmon for 10 cents a can, and calico for 5 cents a yard. Bologna and salt mackerel were 10 cents a pound.

A great deal of the trade was barter. When the hens were laying well and the cows freshened, the housewife paid for the week's supplies with chickens, eggs, and butter, and had some change left over to drop into an old sugar bowl on the top shelf of the pie cupboard. Then the wagon usually carried more weight on its homeward trip than it carried out, for the huckster was the sole channel through which country produce moved from the farm to the city markets. Refrigeration being what it was fifty years ago and before, city people had only a vague notion what fresh country butter was actually like, and their eggs had often lost the bloom of youth.

The huckster wagon was a light-wheeled rig, either with roll-up canvas sides or with wood sides which supported shelving. It was usually drawn by two horses, light enough to make good speed. The so-called Western ponies were favorites, for they were tough and could trot along all day without tiring.

In the early days of auto trucks the progressive storekeeper sold his horses and bought a Reo or a Mack. This improved his speed and widened his territory, but the farmer no longer could set his clock by the huckster, for the engines in the early trucks were cranky and unreliable.

Fichter Bros. invested in a red Reo, which was known far and wide as "The Red Truck." The Red Truck was retired scarcely twenty years ago, when huckstering finally withered on the vine. About this time Fords, Maxwells, Essexes, and other passenger cars came within the reach of the farmer's pocketbook, roads were improved, and the huckster went into a swift decline. The whole family went to town on Saturday night to do the week's shopping and get an ice cream soda. The days of huckstering were numbered; the tempo of country life quickened, and horizons widened to the modern-day supermarket.

SWEET MUSIC

The old-fashioned brass band has done more, to my way of thinking, than any other one thing to make our country the great nation that it is. The yeast of democracy never bubbles harder than when two dozen barbers and grocery clerks and farmers tear into "Dixie" or "Columbia, the Gem of the Ocean."

In my day a brass band marching down Main Street on a Fourth of July and bursting forth with "Yankee Doodle" was positively the grandest sight on earth. On it marched, with firecrackers popping all around. I remember once when a small boy tossed a cannon cracker into the bell of a bass horn. It made the loudest and most explosive note ever to come out of a horn.

The more runaways a band caused, the better it was liked. In my home town every Fourth of July parade caused an average of three runaways. When the band came abreast of a skittish team of geldings, they would rear up on their hind legs, and then amidst the screams of women and the cries of children the

terrified horses would plunge down the street. I know of nothing that gave a person more downright wholesome excitement than a team of runaway horses.

Parents who exercised careful and profound judgment in assisting their sons in choosing a band instrument were well rewarded. If a boy had buck teeth and a receding chin, a wise father steered him away from a horn. Squint Peabody was a perfect case of matching the boy to his instrument. Squint had a mouth that puckered like a black sucker's, giving him a perfect down-draft for a piccolo.

Of course, a two-hundred-pound man looks a bit ridiculous as he clutches a piccolo against his bosom and waits through almost an entire musical selection until it comes his turn to blow a few tweets. He feels that life has sort of passed him by. But on the whole, piccolo players get as much fun out of life as anybody. In our band we always ranked the piccolo player as a panty-waist. We thought he blew a little more into a piccolo than he ever got out of it.

There was an old axiom that the village innocent always played the bass drum. But I wouldn't say that. My Uncle Pod Goodwin was a bass drummer—and an excellent one. He wasn't really deficient; he just looked dumb as he sat on the edge of the bandstand and banged away on his drum. He didn't know any music and he didn't have to know any, and since he wanted to be in the band we thought he would do less damage beating a drum than blowing a horn.

Picture in your mind's eye the town park on a balmy summer evening with the bandstand gaily lighted and with the gold braid and the gold buttons of the musicians' uniforms reflecting little beads of light. There comes a dramatic pause in the music— and then the cornetist rises and points his horn heavenward. With bated breath the audience follows the silvery notes until, finally, the band director's baton drops to his side. The cornetist resumes his seat amid a thunderous wave of applause.

Any man who can remember back to the time he played a silver cornet solo need never feel that his life has been lived in vain.

Not far behind the cornetist in prestige was the trombone player. You could spot a trombone player's wife any time because she was so thin and pale and nervous. Any woman who had to listen to her husband practicing a trombone smear night after night for weeks was bound to have bulging eyeballs and the whim-whams.

In the good old days a town was rated by the number of musicians in its band and by the elegance of their uniforms. A brass band with an oboe and a French horn was considered very de luxe.

Financing a band often was a serious problem. Some bands had to play in the red year after year. But loyal boosters of a really progressive town took it upon themselves to raise a band fund every year. It was understood this fund was to be used to buy uniforms; then, if there was a balance remaining, that, according to well-established precedent, was to go for an oyster supper.

Unfortunately, for some reason, band players were very fond of oysters. I remember our band boys once voted to treat themselves to oyster suppers very early in the season. Nobody seemed to keep in mind the exact amount of the surplus, and it turned out the boys ate so many oysters that the new uniforms, figuratively, went down their throats.

It's my firm conviction that when the small town band went out, treason, disloyalty, and subversive activities came in. I just can't imagine a subversive band member; he blew all his primitive urges right out through his horn. And it was hard for the bystander to feel anything but complete loyalty when the boys got wound up and ripped into Sousa's March. Rural life lost something fine and honest when our band played its last concert; we haven't been the same since.

29

HE SCARED GRANDFATHER

At first thought it would appear pretty difficult to teach anything with a duck, much less draw a moral from her life and habits. Yet William Holmes Mc-Guffey did it, and he did it so convincingly that every time Grandfather heard a duck quack, he became a better man.

At least he learned the virtue of loving and obeying his mother. For in the First Reader, Professor Mc-Guffey told him, "The ducks must love their mother, and do all that she would have them do. And I dare say they will do so, for God has made them know that they must."

In fact, Grandfather had the devil scared out of him by Professor McGuffey. In every McGuffey story, Fate, or God, or society steps in to punish the wrongdoer, and there is no escape. In "The Truant," one of the boys playing hooky is almost drowned on his day of stolen freedom. In the Third Reader story, "True Courage," the boy who couldn't refuse a dare threw a snowball at the schoolhouse door and got a whipping for his foolish act. The lesson points the moral that the boy should have had the courage to say no to the dare. "This would have been real courage," the story concludes. "You must have this fearless spirit or you will get into trouble, and will be and ought to be disliked by all."

Many of the lessons, especially in the first three readers, were used by the author as instruments for teaching the wild frontier youth that crime doesn't pay, that vengeance is the Lord's only, and that only the good become rich and happy.

McGuffey's message to mankind was wrapped up in a primer, six readers, and a spelling book. The primer and the first three readers were written at Miami University, where McGuffey, fresh out of a Paris, Kentucky, schoolroom, had gone as professor of ancient languages in 1826.

Robert Hamilton Bishop, president of Miami University, which was then little more than twenty-five years old, hired William McGuffey from a backwoods schoolteaching job in Kentucky, where he was holding classes in a made-over smokehouse. He rode into Oxford with all his possessions in his saddlebags—a few homespun garments and his precious books in Latin, Hebrew, and Greek, and texts of books he had borrowed and hand copied. Behind him rode his ten-year-old brother, Alexander, whose upbringing and education William had taken over following the illness of their mother, who died in 1829. Alexander was to become a prominent Cincinnati lawyer. He also had an important part in the development of the readers, compiling the speller and the Fifth Reader himself, and contributing to others.

William Holmes McGuffey, or M'Guffey as it was sometimes spelled, was of Scottish ancestry. His grandfather, an uncompromising Calvinist, was born in Scotland, emigrated to Pennsylvania, and fought in the Revolution. William's father, Alexander, known as Sandy the Scout, achieved some fame as a spy and scout in the Indian Wars immediately following the Revolution. Sandy's close friend and scouting companion was Duncan MacArthur, distant kin of General Douglas MacArthur and later governor of Ohio. Sandy and Duncan were with General St. Clair in his ill-fated campaign against the Indians which ended in his defeat and rout. Later they scouted for Mad Anthony Wayne, who defeated the Indians at the Battle of Fallen Timbers in 1794. Later Sandy married and bought a farm in western Pennsylvania, near his father's home. William Holmes was born here in 1800.

When he was two years old the family moved to the Ohio county, following the example of Duncan MacArthur, who had bought land near Chillicothe, Ohio. The McGuffeys bought a farm near Youngstown and it was here that William Holmes grew up.

For the most part, he was self-taught. His mother tutored him and in his late teens he attended a school in Youngstown conducted by a Presbyterian minister, the Rev. Mr. Wicks. After failing to pass the Yale entrance examinations, he entered Washington College, near his father's old home in Pennsylvania. Pressed for money, he left Washington and became a roving teacher. Here he was found by President Bishop, who offered him $600 a year to teach languages and philosophy. McGuffey received his degree from Washington *in absentia*.

Legend has it that McGuffey had the manuscript for a school reader in his saddlebags when he rode to Oxford in 1826. Certain it is that he had been considering a new type of textbook.

The readers and spellers then in use were usually archaic and foreign to the new Western mind. Most of them were of English or New England origin, deadly dull in content and as far as the poles from reaching a common ground with the settlers' children. The best known of the lot was "The New England Primer," which opened with the dour warning, "In Adam's fall, we sinned all." McGuffey envisioned a reader with lively narrative about everyday life which would stimulate and interest, as well as instruct. There would be a moral in almost every lesson, thanks to his Calvinistic turn of mind.

He knew well the state of literacy in the new Western world. There were few books and few schools, and many a substantial man signed his name with an X. McGuffey probably knew that one of the greatest men of his time, Daniel Boone, had carved on a tree in Kentucky, "I ciled a bar on this tree." Parents could study his readers with their children.

McGuffey probably had no immediate plans for publishing his reader, but, like many a great new idea, it had germinated elsewhere. Winthrop B. Smith, junior partner in the publishing firm of Truman and Smith of Cincinnati, was also working on the same idea, but with a commercial rather than an educational angle. Schoolbooks were expensive in the Western country, and would have a better chance for sale than stock items of literature.

Smith took his idea to Miss Catherine Beecher, who, with her sister Harriet, had opened a school for girls in Cincinnati. Catherine's great talents were later shadowed by those of her sister, Harriet, author of *Uncle Tom's Cabin*, but she was a great woman in her own right. She was a leader in the feminist movement of her time and had advanced ideas on education. The Beecher home in Cincinnati was a center of literary life and culture, and William Holmes McGuffey, in nearby Oxford, was soon a member of the circle.

Catherine Beecher knew of McGuffey's plans and when Smith came to her with his project, she suggested McGuffey. McGuffey was delighted. He contracted with Smith for four readers, for which he was to receive $3,000. Later he received a small gift from the publisher, but no actual royalty. Alexander received $500 for the speller.

It is not known how great a hand Smith had in shaping the content of this first edition. As an important part of his teaching method McGuffey asked for

pictures, and Smith obliged with stock items from his files. Many of these were of English origin, and the characters and scenes were distinctly out of character with the frontier. But they were pictures, achieved their purpose in no small way, and were greatly improved in time.

The First and Second Readers appeared in 1836 and were followed soon after by the Third and Fourth. Sales were slow. Truman and Smith apparently failed to work in double harness and were never quite solvent. They parted company in 1843, Smith taking the McGuffey property as his part of their meager assets.

Smith was an energetic salesman and the readers were soon the leaders in the Midwest. He engaged Alexander McGuffey, who was practicing law in Cincinnati at that time, to write a Fifth Reader. This was at first called "The Rhetorical Guide" and was later expanded into the Fifth Reader.

From 1834 to 1890 seven publishers brought out McGuffey books. Smith expanded into W. B. Smith & Co. in 1853. In 1863 Sargent, Wilson & Hinkle took over the rights. They were followed by Wilson, Hinkle & Co. in 1868, Van Antwerp, Bragg & Co. in 1877, and the American Book Co. in 1890.

The last edition was printed in 1901. In 1880 an edition called "The Alternate McGuffey Readers" was brought out in an attempt to meet a demand for more than one reader in the schools. There was nothing of McGuffey in these readers to justify the name except an effort to duplicate their purpose.

It was under Van Antwerp, Bragg & Co. that the readers reached their peak of popularity. Constant revision had been made, partly by McGuffey, partly by his brother Alexander and others. The 1879 edition, under the editorship of Henry H. Vail, is regarded as the greatest in artistic excellence. It was during the tenure of Van Antwerp, Bragg & Co. that a group of prominent artists were commissioned. Among them was Henry F. Farny, a Cincinnatian, who was to become famous as an illustrator and Indian painter. Others were George Wharton Edwards, Mary Hallock Foote, William Hamilton Gibson, Will H. Low, Thomas Moran, Charles S. Reinhart, James Carter Beard, a brother of Daniel C. Beard of Boy Scout fame, and Howard Pyle. Pyle's first published work appeared in a McGuffey Reader.

In the heyday of the readers, between 1870 and 1890, 60,000,000 copies were sold. They were the basic schoolbooks in thirty-seven states, exclusive in many. From 1836 to 1901 there were more than 122,000,000 copies printed.

They went west in covered wagons, crossed the Pacific and were translated for Japanese schools. Spanish translations were used in the schools of Puerto Rico and Spanish America.

Yellowed, dog-eared, patched, they were handed down in the family, and on to the next generation and the next. With Ray's arithmetics they were often the only textbooks in the log schoolhouses of the pioneer, and in the middle years, when the little red schoolhouse came along, they were its bulwark and foundation stone.

What was the secret of the readers' success? For one thing, they were as American as the one-room schoolhouse. The scenes and characters which McGuffey projected into the schoolroom were familiar to all—a world of farmyards and fields, streams and hills, peopled by a new species, the American, fast evolving from Englishmen and Irishmen and Germans. Known intimately to all in this new Western world were the horse and the cow, the duck, the dog and the cat. McGuffey wrote for a farming population, for in those days most people were either farmers or farmers once removed. The work of the farmer, his animals, his simple pleasures, his problems of adjusting himself to a new and strange society— these supplied much of the subject matter for the first three readers.

M'Guffey's Eclectic First Reader.

THE

ECLECTIC FIRST READER,

FOR

YOUNG CHILDREN:

CONSISTING OF

PROGRESSIVE LESSONS

IN

READING AND SPELLING;

MOSTLY IN

EASY WORDS OF ONE AND TWO SYLLABLES.

BY W. H. M'GUFFEY,
PRESIDENT OF OHIO UNIVERSITY, ATHENS.

ENLARGED AND IMPROVED.

TWENTY-FOURTH EDITION—150,000 COPIES.

CINCINNATI:
PUBLISHED BY TRUMAN AND SMITH.
::::::::::::
1843

McGuffey used the idiom of the people; his simile and metaphor were taken from everyday life. He was a purist in his use of language and as articulate as Lincoln. And when the Primer and the First and Second Readers were conquered and the learner no longer dreaded the printed page, he gave him a heavier, but no less appetizing, diet. In the upper Readers, Third to Sixth, he introduced a discriminating variety of poetry, oratory, and essays, so well tuned to rural minds they were read from the pulpit and around the fireplace.

The McGuffey Readers gave the pioneer his first dash of culture, his first exposure to learning. Here

was the flamboyant oratory that had stirred revolutionary America, Patrick Henry's immortal "Give me liberty or give me death" speech; here were the homespun rhymes of Longfellow, "The Village Blacksmith" and "Paul Revere's Ride"; the thoughtful, mystical "To a Waterfowl" of Bryant; Hamlet's soliloquy; Chief Logan's reply to Dunmore.

McGuffey's reputation, however, is anchored to a far greater concept than the catholic literary selections in the upper readers. His method of teaching reading and spelling was revolutionary in its time. Under the traditional method the young pupil was taught spelling—months and months on end—before he was permitted to read. McGuffey plunked him right down to reading his first day of school. "A stands for Ant" was his introduction to education.

McGuffey also introduced illustration as a device to teach reading by association.

Each lesson was a drama, complete with suspense and almost invariably with a happy ending. McGuffey's young characters were always getting into trouble, or were faced with problems, or were the victims of unsympathetic grownups. But good always triumphed, and virtue was always rewarded. He was not mawkish; his greatness lay in his ability to teach morality in a simple, friendly, and dignified way.

McGuffey was one of the most celebrated teachers of his time, but he was an even greater moralist, a reputation he apparently did not seek. He was never quite sure whether he was a teacher or a preacher. Moralizing came naturally to him. He just couldn't bring himself to write so many good words solely in teaching to read—the same words would point a moral, so a moral he pointed.

Although he spoke from many pulpits (he was ordained a minister in 1829) McGuffey rarely invoked the dreaded tools of his contemporaries, hell's fire and brimstone, to frighten the pioneer bad boy into

being good. While the virtues he sought to inject into the pliable youth were mostly Biblical, God was not pictured as a stern avenger of the wrongdoer. Rather, McGuffey went right down to the seat of the boy's pants to make a good citizen out of him. In "True Courage," the backwoods delinquent who threw a snowball at the schoolhouse door was not promised punishment in the hereafter. Not at all—the schoolmaster emerged, birch rod in hand. McGuffey knew boys—God was unseen, the hereafter was a long time away—the schoolmaster was flesh, all too solid flesh.

The virtues which McGuffey sought to cultivate in the young reader ran the gamut from abstinence to zeal. Bravery, honesty, truthfulness, fear of God, parental obedience, pity for the unfortunate, kindness, generosity, were hammered in, lesson after lesson.

While patriotism was an important theme in the readers, by intent or happy coincidence the explosive subject of abolition was avoided. McGuffey knew the issues, and as a minister and a Northerner one cannot doubt where his sympathies lay. He had been a teacher in Kentucky, where slavery was a household subject, and he had been a member of the Beecher circle, which was widely known for its championship of abolition. He could not have been admitted to that circle, and certainly Catherine Beecher would not have recommended him to Winthrop B. Smith had his views on abolition run counter with their views. It may have been that Smith, looking forward to a Southern market, had a hand in keeping this delicate subject out of the readers. There is no record of any public expression of opinion on McGuffey's part of his stand on abolition. He made many speeches, appeared in numerous pulpits, but, unlike most of his colleagues in the pulpit, he did not "thunder against slavery."

This restraint bore fruit in his later years when he went to the University of Virginia as professor of philosophy. He taught there through the Civil War, and, according to his biographer, Dr. Harvey C. Minnich, "Though a Northerner, no hint of disapproval of his views has been found. He was much beloved by the Virginians and was especially kind to the Negroes and the poor."

McGuffey went beyond the Bible to the realities of his time to teach the value of thrift and the inconvenience of poverty. The Scots in his ancestry gave him a healthy respect for this world's goods and he

more than hinted that being the richest man in the county had its good points. He was fully aware of the new American cult of success and was careful to point out that being a good boy was not only spiritually rewarding, but goodness also brought success and riches. "Grateful Julian," a Second Reader story, closes with this fine sentiment: "The rich man sent Julian to school, that he might have a good education. He grew up an intelligent and industrious lad. Everything prospered with him; and when other parents wished to teach their children to be grateful, they told them the story of Julian and his rabbit."

McGuffey fell short of practicing what he preached, however, and never became wealthy. His books made several millionaires among publishers in their time, but very little of the millions filtered into McGuffey's pockets. He received $3,000 for his first three readers from Truman and Smith. After paying him a pittance for one of his later editions, the publisher had an annual attack of conscience, and for many years sent him a barrel of hams for Christmas. He did not seem unhappy about his small returns, for big money from royalties was not common in the textbook field.

Although McGuffey's reputation today rests upon his readers, in his lifetime he achieved the stature of a giant in education. After ten years at Miami as a teacher he served three years, 1836-39, as president of Cincinnati College, and the four years following as president of Ohio University. He was not happy, however, as an administrator and in 1843, when Ohio University lacked funds, he went back into the classroom at old Woodward College in Cincinnati. In 1845 he went to the University of Virginia as professor of philosophy and taught there until his death in 1873.

No one could ever forget McGuffey's face—it was so prodigiously homely. His features seemed to have been picked at random and thrown together around a particularly unhandsome nose. He wore a top hat to classes to the day of his death and stuck to knee britches long after they were found only in museums.

After McGuffey's death in 1873, the readers went on through a number of editions. The last regular edition came out in 1901, but popularity was waning, and by 1920 the time of the readers was past. A reprint of the 1879 edition is still in print and one occasionally hears of its use. The revised readers, known as the Golden Rule Series, have been adopted by Texas.

THE VILLAGE SMITHY

The blacksmith is another of a vanishing race. Victim of the automobile and the tractor, he has become a symbol of the past. His forge is cold and his sons have become garage mechanics. The old-time blacksmith, in addition to his specialty, was a mechanic of no mean ability. His chief skill was that of an ironworker. He re-tired the wheels of buggies and farm wagons, repaired the metal parts of farm machinery, and in his spare time built sleds and an occasional wagon, painted buggies, repaired kitchen and barn utensils, and did odd jobs of welding and ironmongery. The blacksmith shop was the horse trading center of a community, the clearing house for farm gossip and farm labor. Empty nail kegs supplied the seats for the village patriarchs. There the community wag and the inevitable town bum had their hangout. Here the village fool paraded his ignorance, the village wits traded their lewd banter, and the young bloods boasted about the speed of their horses or their girls. Small boys sometimes earned money for marbles by switching flies from restless horses.

The blacksmith shop kept all senses alert. There was the sooty forge, the sparks that flew from glowing metal under the hammer, the ring of the anvil, the pungent odor of a burning hoof under the heat of a hot shoe. There was the hiss of steam from the tub of water used for cooling hot shoes, and the sharp, animal smell of a sweaty horse; the blacksmith himself, with his bulging muscles, his hands so careless of the heat of a hot shoe; the pile of old iron, buggy wheel and wagon wheel rims, worn-out horseshoes, metal parts of this and that. Stomping at flies in the shade of a nearby tree were horses awaiting their turn.

The clientele of the blacksmith shop was strictly stag. To the men of the rural community, it was a truly masculine, comfortable, satisfying place.

MANNERS, MORALS AND THE FREE LUNCH

DR. C. V. GIRARD'S GINGER BRANDY

"A CERTAIN CURE for Cholera Colic Cramps Dysentery, Chills & Fever, is a delightful & healthy beverage.

FOR SALE HERE.

Sinning in the old days was not easy. For the men there was the county fair peep show, cigarettes, profanity, cheating in a trade, and drinking out of season. A swig out of the jug to prevent pneumonia and at threshing time to "cut the dust" was acceptable. But to have a bottle hidden in the barn, as Grandpa did, was one of the worst sins imaginable. Chewing tobacco was not even regarded as a dirty habit, much less a sin, but cigarettes, especially for the growing boy, were said to spring directly from the devil.

Only a daring man like Grandpa, who was a regular devil when he got away from Grandma, could enjoy what little sin there was. He ate the forbidden fruit right down to the core every time he went to town with a load of grain or a fat steer. I liked to go with him, for there was sure to be action when he was around.

Grandpa made it a point to arrive in town with his load of wheat or corn about noon. After unloading at the elevator, he tied up his team at the hitching rack in front of the courthouse and we headed for McCarthy's Saloon, regarded in those days as a den of vice and a trap for the unwary.

Behind the swinging doors it was dark and cool. The odors were earthy but not offensive, a curious mixture of sawdust, stale beer, pickled pigs' feet, sauerkraut, and cigar butts. Grandpa made a beeline for the free lunch, at one end of the bar in the back.

The saloon-keeper knew just what men liked—roast beef, baked ham, pigs' knuckles, sauerkraut, baked beans, pickles, cheese, and smoked herring. Grandpa ordered a large beer for himself and root beer for me. We loaded our plates with the free lunch and took them to a table. Grandpa plunked down a dime on the bar and assured the bartender, "There's more where that came from."

While we were eating our lunch several of Grandpa's cronies pulled up chairs and Grandpa ordered another beer. Then they started a game of Seven-Up, or High-Low-Jack-and-the-Game, at two bits a game. Along midafternoon Grandpa had won seventy-five cents, but he kept looking at the clock and I knew he was thinking up a good story to tell Grandma, and was uneasy.

On the way home he cautioned me to keep my mouth shut about the saloon and the beer and the Seven-Up, but you couldn't fool Grandma. She had a sort of sixth sense when it came to sinning. When we came into the kitchen, where she was peeling apples for applesauce, she sidled up to Grandpa and got a whiff of his breath. "Did you take that child in a saloon again!" It was not a question, but a reprimand, and the fat was in the fire. Grandpa got Hail Columbia.

We got out of the house as soon as we could "to do the chores." Grandpa chuckled, "She sure ain't easy to fool, but it's fun tryin', ain't it?"

THE LAST BUGGY FACTORY

On the Ohio River edge of Lawrenceburg, Indiana, is a ramshackle factory which by all the rules of the business world should be dead. The Standard Vehicle Company, maker of buggies for two generations, however, refuses to die, although malnutrition has long since set in.

The world has for forty years been gradually but surely moving away from this buggy factory. Ed Knapp, owner of the company, with one foot in the present and one in the past, refuses to admit that his is an unnatural or uncomfortable position. He insists that he can bridge the gap. His small staff of multi-skilled workmen still turn out more than three hundred buggies a year for customers in all parts of the nation. His factory is the last relative of buggy plants which in 1914 included well over eight hundred competitors.

When you go to Lawrenceburg looking for the Standard Vehicle Company it is wisest to stop in town and ask directions, for a stranger would have trouble finding the factory and trouble recognizing it when he did find it.

Time has dulled the red brick walls of the rambling three-story building and smoke and soot from the rail-yards across the street have blackened them.

To find Ed Knapp you climb the darkened stairway to the second floor and wind your way through piles of buggy wheels and heaps of iron. Knapp will be talking over the phone to a distant manufacturer of buggy wheels, writing letters to buyers of ordered but as yet unmade buggies, or working over a stack of bills and invoices on his ancient roll-top desk. Or he may be out in the factory checking his workmen.

But he will still take time to talk. Perhaps he will let his work wait, because, as he says, "The buggy business isn't quite what it should be." He thinks the slump is only temporary. "No reason to think the buggy business is dead," he says. "Horses are more popular today than they have been for years. Why, we're getting orders from all over the country—from parts of the country we haven't had orders from in years. That's encouraging."

At sixty-five Knapp can look back on more than fifty years in the buggy business, for his father started the business and young Ed joined him at a tender age. As he sits on his desk, his feet dangling a few inches above the darkened floor, he will sketch in those years, his quiet voice stopping occasionally as he mentally places each episode in its proper sequence. Around the factory he wears a pair of gray work trousers, a blue and white striped shirt and a brown tie with somber-colored leaves falling across it. His rust-colored felt hat has a brim that time has styled into an amazing wreck.

"My father," Knapp says, "was a blacksmith until he got into the buggy business. A lot of blacksmiths went into buggy making in those days. My father started a buggy factory in Cincinnati, but it burned down. Then he came over here to Lawrenceburg and bought this factory. This place was a buggy factory at the time and before that it was a furniture factory.

"We didn't think anything of taking orders for carload lots of buggies. We could get an order for sixty-five new buggies, go to work, and have them on their way in three days. Any more, we just ship them one at a time.

"I started out working for my father as a salesman. I traveled in the South a lot. Our best market was with the Cajuns in Louisiana. I used to go down there a couple times a year. I would ride a train, then hire a buggy to take me around to the towns. One trip I visited forty towns and sold buggies in thirty-seven of them. Hardware stores used to handle them for us because everyone needed buggies then and the hardware stores were a good place to get them.

"Things have changed, though, in Louisiana." Knapp shakes his head a little as though he has trouble understanding people who no longer want good buggies. "Those Cajun farmers don't use so many buggies any more. Cotton brings a high price in the South today and farmers buy secondhand cars.

"Well, sir, some people ask me why I don't take some trips to Louisiana and try to sell some more buggies there. But there's a reason. Just isn't any use, cotton being as high as it is. But if they start talking about gasoline rationing they'll flock in here to buy buggies. Guess I'd rather never sell another buggy than see another war though."

Business was good for Standard during the Second World War. Orders for buggies came in from all parts of the country and especially from the South. "Why, they took buggies out of here," says Knapp, "with one black wheel and three red wheels. We had more than twenty people in here building buggies."

It was during the war, too, that Standard for a short time faced a shutdown order from the War Production Board. The Board was prepared to classify the buggy factory as a nonessential industry until circumstances proved that even a horse-drawn buggy can contribute to a World war. A large oil company was working in back-road country of Louisiana where cars and trucks couldn't plow through the brush and mud. The company ordered a dozen sturdy buggies from Standard and the War Production Board changed its verdict. "If we hadn't been in business," says Knapp, "where would they have found those buggies?

"The Amish and Mennonites," says Knapp, "have always been good buggy customers for us. Their religion frowns on using automobiles, so they still use buggies. They're particular customers though," he adds. "Their buggies have to be very plain, no stripes on the wheels, and no fancy stuff. They usually order them without tops. When the young people get married they make their own buggy top."

The show horse world also provides a fraction of Knapp's buggy orders. And children who get new pony carts may never know it, but the carts usually come from Lawrenceburg.

Knapp is not a man to bear a grudge and consequently has no hard feelings about the fact that it was the automobile that pushed the hard-working, hard-riding and rattling road buggy up to the edge of oblivion. He admits that he would much rather ride an automobile than a buggy, but points out that a growing number are buggy riding for pleasure.

It was shortly after the First World War that the automobile business grew big and bustling at the expense of the time-tested buggy. That was the time, too, when buggy makers all across the country were deciding whether to switch to automobile manufacture or go down heroically with the buggy. William Knapp, Ed's father, thought about the new enterprise too, but young Ed talked him into staying in the buggy business. "Lots of buggy makers went broke trying to make cars," he recalls. "The only one that made the switch successfully was Studebaker."

The buggies turned out at Standard are all custom-made vehicles. The purchaser can take his choice of more than half a hundred models of buggies, carts, and wagons. Knapp keeps no stock models for imme-

diate shipment. He waits until he has an order for a buggy, then puts it into production. About ten days later the buggy is ready for shipment.

During those ten days Knapp's six buggy makers have fashioned various parts of the vehicle from wood, leather, and steel. Each of them has worked on several parts of the buggy because, as Knapp says, "There isn't work enough to keep them all busy at the same jobs all the time."

The various departments are scattered over the three floors of the factory, with one or two workmen to the floor. There are stockpiles of raw materials all over the place. The floors themselves are parallel to nothing in particular, not even each other, but Knapp declares that the building is still serviceable.

One of the oldest and most popular models in Standard's line of vehicles is the Blue Grass Special, a one-seated runabout that was common on the country roads a half-century ago. Standard sells this model for $156. Knapp points out that buggy prices have not gone up in proportion to prices of other commodities. You can still buy a good buggy for slightly more than it cost a decade ago.

The hickory-spoked wheels for the Blue Grass Special are made in a wheel factory in the Pennsylvania Dutch section. The wheels are shipped to Lawrenceburg without tires and steel tires are attached to them by Elza West, the blacksmith who joined Standard the day it started operations in Lawrenceburg. The wheels are then painted to please the buyer.

The bed for the buggy is made of oak by Louis Hunter, who has been making buggies for over half a century. His is an old craft and he does his work as carefully and thoroughly today as he ever did. The buggy body, fifty-six inches long and twenty-three inches wide, is designed and built to stay together over several thousand miles of rough country road.

On either end of the body is a spring to hold the buggy above the chassis and help absorb the bounce. At the front end of the buggy is the dashboard to keep the horse in the shafts from throwing mud into the face of the driver. The driver sits on an upholstered seat wide enough for two and no softer than a buggy seat ever was. The iron work that holds the top is handmade in the blacksmith shop on the first floor of the factory. The top itself is made of leather and rubber and there is a flap that hangs down to the back of the seat behind the passengers. Then for an extra price the buggy purchaser can order side curtains to keep out the cold wind and the rain or snow. He can also get oil lamps to equip the rig for night riding. Knapp thinks all this is a bargain at $156 and he is probably right—if you happen to need a buggy.

There is no show room at the Standard Vehicle Company. Most of the orders come in by mail. Knapp makes no special effort to show potential customers how his buggies look behind a horse, and the chances are good that he would have trouble finding a horse if asked to do so. This may be due to the fact that he doesn't like horses. "No more than I care for working horses or riding in a buggy. I sometimes wonder how I got into the business I'm in. Horses scare me."

In addition to building buggies, Knapp does a small business in repairing them. He recently rebuilt a stagecoach that once belonged to the old Wells Fargo line. The coach is owned by a rancher in New Mexico and the rancher hauled it to Lawrenceburg on a truck. He ordered new upholstering, and repairs in the wood and iron work on the body. When it was finished he came back to Standard and loaded his stagecoach onto his truck for the trip back to the Southwest. He still uses it to haul visitors around his ranch. The citizens of Lawrenceburg, who see nothing unusual in loading yesterday's buggies on today's freight cars, were well represented, however, when the stagecoach was pushed out of the factory and loaded on the truck.

Knapp will make a pony cart or buggy as fancy or as plain as the customer wants it. He still builds basket carts for ponies and fancy surreys for show horses. He says that he has never made dog or goat carts because he considers these somewhat out of his line. Neither does he make racing sulkies.

Knapp thinks his toughest days in the buggy business are past. He doesn't see how there could be tougher days than those he knew during the thirties. "Father," he recalls, "was a man who thought everyone was honest. He thought everyone was as honest as he was. When the depression came after the First World War, dozens of his debtors lost their money and eventually left him with a debt of $262,000. Instead of going into bankruptcy he stayed in the struggle. Year by year we paid the debt off, but progress on it was mighty slow."

It was so slow that William Knapp died an old man a couple of years before the last of his debts were paid. He died after a hard day's work at the factory, where he spent most of his time in the blacksmith shop and not in the office. Then came the Second World War and even the buggy business prospered. Ed Knapp paid off the last of the debt after almost twenty years of nibbling.

Even though Knapp still makes a good living, the gross income of the factory is down now. "People are not buying buggies like they should," he says. "But times will get better. Why, we had an order from Iowa this week for a new buggy, the first order we've had from Iowa in years. Now, if that happened to you wouldn't you think you still had a chance?"

Knapp has one regret that clouds his life. "As I get older," he says, "I keep thinking that it's too bad I never had a son, somebody to carry on this buggy business after I'm gone. If this factory closes I don't know where people can go to buy their buggies."

THE WATER MILL

One of the first business enterprises in a pioneer community was the flour mill. Corn could be ground at home, but the milling of flour took more skill and machinery than was ordinarily found on the farm. The early settlers sometimes pooled their capital and labor to build a mill and construct the race, subsidizing the mill owner. The trip to the mill was a regular chore, with the sacks of wheat thrown over a pack saddle or stacked in the bed of a farm wagon.

The grain was run between two millstones, made of a special type of granite and weighing more than a ton each. If the granite was not available in the neighborhood, the millstones were transported from long distances. Some of the early millers brought their stones across the mountains on ox wagons.

A site near a stream with the proper fall was selected and a mill race dug to conduct the water to the wheel. The wheel was either "overshot" or "undershot," depending on the fall of the stream. Metal was scarce and many of the older mills had no metal in machinery or construction. The cogs which turned the stones were made of wood and the timbers were held together with wooden pegs. Hog fat was used to grease the moving parts.

After the grain was ground the bran was separated by screening, and bagged separately. This was used as stock feed. There was no effort made to refine the flour, which retained all the germ and a good deal of the bran, or outer covering of the grain. Bread made from this flour had a flavor and body not easily obtainable today.

The miller kept a portion of the grain as his fee and usually sold flour to traders and the village grocery. There is some scientific support of the belief that grain ground by metal burrs loses some of its flavor because of the heat generated in grinding. Stone-ground meal is today regarded as superior to all other. Certainly our memory of homemade bread fashioned of potato yeast and stone-ground flour supports this pleasant conceit.

TO THE LORD'S HOUSE ON SUNDAY

On Sunday we put on our best clothes and went to church. This was an ordeal for the entire family, for "Sunday-go-to-meeting" clothes were no joke, especially to us kids. We went barefooted all week and when we put on shoes our feet burned like fire all during the trip to and from church, and during the services. Mother put on her corset, which cut her freedom to near zero, but made her stand very straight and dignified. Father got into his broadcloth suit, which he'd had since his wedding. It was fine for winter, but a veritable Turkish bath in summer.

All our skirts and dresses were starched as stiff as sheet iron, and everybody walked around like knights in armor. We were cautioned to "keep nice and clean" for it was a disgrace to appear at church with even a ruffle mussed.

To us children Sunday church was genuine torture, and it was not much better for the older people. We endured it because we were told to; the oldsters because they thought it was good to suffer a little.

The church was in the village at the crossroads, under a spread of trees. There were hitching racks in the rear, near the little cemetery. Father tied up the horse there, throwing a blanket over him if it were cold; in summer he tried to find a shady place.

We saw everybody we knew at church. The men liked to arrive a little early, gathering in knots outside under the trees and talking crops. The women eyed the new dresses and talked cooking and canning. We stood around miserably, not being allowed to shout or muss our clothes.

The sermon was too long for most everybody, but the choir sang well, and the notes from the pump organ were sweet. The word of God was good for men and women who had been isolated in fields and lonely farmhouses.

In summer the ride home was dusty and hot, in winter cold and bleak. But when we got home there was a big Sunday dinner, and the blessed relief of getting in our everyday clothes again.

CRIME
AND
PUNISHMENT

Bob Hinton farmed a parcel of Luke Parker's land. They fell out over a crop matter and there was bad blood between them. Both were big men, but cowards, and everybody said their quarrel would never come to a fist fight, the usual way to settle such things.

Then one day in August, during the Dog Days, Parker got out of his rig in front of the village store and saw Hinton sitting on a bench in front, whittling on a piece of soft pine. It was the Dog Days, they said, else Parker wouldn't have reversed his buggy whip and aimed a blow at Hinton's head. Without getting up, Hinton reached out and thrust the six-inch blade of his knife between Parker's third and fourth ribs.

They took Parker home, where he bled to death, and someone rode for the sheriff. The grand jury said it was an open-and-shut case of self-defense, but for the rest of his life Hinton brooded over the blood on his hands.

This was the worst crime we ever had in our neighborhood. Our little farm town was two hundred souls, two grocery stores, a blacksmith shop, three churches, and a schoolhouse. The law was a justice of the peace and a constable, both farmers, in some distant part of the township, and the sheriff at the county seat. You didn't see a law officer from one year end to the next because people were generally law-abiding and feared the law. The sheriff was a burly man with a nickel-plated star on his chest; mothers frightened children by the mere mention of his name. He was seen twice in our village, once when he came for Bob Hinton, and once when he passed out cigars at the grocery store before election.

On the other hand, people were not saints in our community. There was a little petty theft now and then, and once or twice a horse was stolen, a crime almost worse than killing. There was a good deal of bastardy, too, especially among the hired hands and the hired girls. A word from the justice of the peace was usually sufficient to bring the erring couple to the altar. An illegitimate child in our community carried a stigma through life. Although they were children of love, and the girls were sometimes comely, no young man would dare approach them with honorable intentions.

There was one pleasant exception. A roving harvest hand came in one summer and began to date the love child of one of our more prosperous farmers. One afternoon the blacksmith, who was a blunt man, said to him, "Floyd, I hear you're going to marry old man McCoy's daughter. Don't you know she's a bastard?"

Floyd was calm. "Yes, I'm going to marry her and I know she's a bastard. You see, I'm a bastard too."

This was about the extent of our crime. It wasn't that we were so virtuous; it was just that we were always too darn tired, working our farms, to get into mischief.

LIVERY AND FEED

I grew up right across the street from a livery stable and I remember it with nostalgia and affection. My parents' hotel, the Union, faced Mr. Oscar Hudgins' livery stable on Main Street. Each building had a long passageway running from front to rear, and we and our guests were acutely conscious of the establishment across the street. Once Mr. Oscar Hudgins was sitting on our big front porch when a city-bred cousin of mine remarked that she didn't imagine our traveling men enjoyed the smell of horses very much. Mr. Hudgins replied, without rancor, that perhaps horses didn't like the smell of traveling men.

A livery stable, for the benefit of those who never heard of one, was an establishment which catered to horses. It boarded them, doctored them, and bred them, whenever any of these services were required. It also furnished "rigs"—a horse and buggy or perhaps a team—for anyone who wished to ride, rather than walk, about the town or countryside. This arrangement was about the same as the "U-Drive-It" system for automobiles nowadays. It was a popular service for traveling men who came into town on the railway train and wanted to call on customers in crossroad communities. Young swains who couldn't afford a rig themselves rented them to take their best girls for a spin in the country. Father used to hire a "surrey" or carriage, with fringe on top and two shiny black leather seats, and take us all on a picnic or to call on relatives. He always brought his own buggy whip, a resplendent article of whalebone with gilt stripes and a mother-of-pearl handle. When he placed it in the whip socket it meant we were ready to start.

The Hudgins' livery stable was conveniently located for our traveling men and other transients. I don't know whether Mr. Hudgins erected his place of business across the street from our hotel or whether we erected our hotel across the street from the livery stable. This egg-or-chicken argument between Mr. Hudgins and my father was never settled, but each establishment was a perfect adjunct to the other.

As was so often the case with people in small towns in that beautiful age, Mr. Hudgins had several sidelines. Besides being the only veterinarian for miles around, he owned and drove the only hearse in town. He also had three de luxe equipages commonly known as hacks. These were low-hung carriages with doors and plate glass windows which could be raised or lowered. The driver rode on an elevated seat behind the horses. They were used mostly for funerals and weddings.

The hearse, however, was the show piece of the stable. It was a marvelous equipage indeed. Mr. Hudgins "ordered off" and had it made in St. Louis. It had a high seat in front, from which Mr. Hudgins managed the pair of white Percherons, Dot and Dolly, which might easily have been circus horses of the type which Mr. Poodles Hanneford and his illustrious family have made famous. The hearse actually looked more like a circus wagon than a bearer of the dead. When Mr. Hudgins drove it, he wore a top hat which he had bought from a vaudeville supply house. He was a big, red-faced man with a goodly growth of mustache under his big, red nose. Sitting in a commanding position on the hearse, which was painted a bright gray, he made a funeral procession something of a parade. To add to the illusion, there were golden tassels inside the hearse, and carved cherubs at each corner. For funerals Mr. Hudgins bedecked the Percherons with harness which he had made especially for him. This special set of harness was decorated with brass "spots," red-white-and-blue rosettes, and tall rust-colored pompons between the horses' ears.

Since my father, in addition to his duties as host at the Union Hotel, was the local undertaker, the location of the livery stable across the street was very convenient. Father owned no funeral vehicles and that end of burials was given over to Mr. Hudgins for a slight commission. He was often called to other communities and made quite a nice thing out of his gay hearse and his hacks.

Lonzo Brizzalara, a local boy who joined the circus and worked his way up to general manager of the biggest show on the road, tried to hire Mr. Hudgins to be his horse-boss but Mr. Hudgins said he wouldn't work for anybody but himself. He enjoyed the sense of power and importance which his seat on the hearse gave him and he always carried himself with becoming dignity. He preserved this dignity even under trying circumstances. Once, one of Mr. Hudgins' hens made a nest on the cushions of the driver's seat, and having failed to hatch her brood by the time the next funeral came up, rode all the way to the church, to the cemetery, and back to town beside Mr. Hudgins. Not an egg was broken.

When a new traveling man alighted from the train at the S. W. & W. station on the outskirts of town, he had no trouble locating Mr. Hudgin's place of business. It had its own aroma, as unmistakable an identification as the painted sign over the doorway, and far more effective at a distance. It was a blend of manure, harness oil, old and new leather, Sloan's Liniment, and hay in all stages of ripeness; occasionally there was an overtone of wagon paint and pine shavings, which were sometimes used for bedding instead of straw.

On summer evenings when Mr. Hudgins sat out in front in a chair brought from the office, the unforgettable odor of his amazing pipe dominated all other smells. This pipe was well known in the neighborhood, and feared and respected. Once when my little sister had an earache, mother called over Mr. Hudgins who blew smoke into her ailing ear. This produced an immediate cure, and the patient started sucking her thumb and soon fell asleep.

Besides the regular help, there was always a number of loafers hanging around the stable. It was a favorite haunt of small boys, but was forbidden ground for most of them. Mothers warned their sons to give its doors a wide berth and it was generally believed that a livery stable was second only to the poolroom as a sink of iniquity. Traveling men usually gave their stories a rehearsal there before starting out on their routes and it was from the livery stable that they spread all over town by the usual grapevine. Sports and fast young men liked its informal atmosphere.

A room in front of the building was partitioned off as an office. It was furnished with a littered desk, a potbellied stove, a cuspidor, and a half-dozen wooden chairs. During the slack season in winter, the hostler slept in one of the chairs during the day. Tramps usually made the livery stable their first port of call when looking for a free bed. If they could convince Mr. Hudgins that they wouldn't smoke or make off with one of the horses, they were allowed to sleep in

49

the haymow or on the bales in an empty stall. Some of the more respectable gentlemen of the town, it was said, bedded down there when they knew it was dangerous to go home. Mr. Hudgins had two old army blankets which he gave to his more prominent guests.

One of the important functions of a livery stable was to serve as a headquarters for horse breeding in the community. In this, Mr. Hudgins took an active interest. He rented box stalls to owners of stallions, who "stood" their animals there during the breeding season. He himself owned two jacks. Jacks are curious beasts, given to whims and vagaries. Experienced jack keepers can spend hours telling of their idiosyncrasies. For example, one will develop a dislike for running water and will neither drink it nor cross it. Another will refuse to have anything to do with still water. Some develop claustrophobia and won't enter a stall that has no windows. Unlike his highly bred cousin, the race horse, a jackass cares nothing for mascots, like bantam roosters, goats, or Shetland ponies. He lives alone and he seems to like it.

Jackasses bray when the notion strikes them. They all have this in common. Now, Mr. Hudgins' barn was made of tin, or sheet iron. There is no sound which is quite as startling as that of a jack braying in a tin barn. This is especially true when the barn is strongly built, and on a good foundation. A good barn gives good resonance, like a good horn. If the barn is full of cracks it will leak compression and won't carry the sound very far. There is danger, too, of the jack blowing his own house down.

Mr. Hudgins' two jacks were known as Little Windy and Prince Albert. The latter was named after a highly respected smoking tobacco. Little Windy came by his name because he was believed to be the windiest jackass in the state. Prince Albert was a tall, baggy-kneed Black Mammoth jack; he had a barrel chest, and was an uncommonly stout brayer. But Little Windy, a gray animal of Spanish descent and not nearly as large, had it all over Prince Albert. Besides unbelievable volume, he had an engaging huskiness in his bray which gave it quality as well as power. When he brayed, he shut his eyes, dug his feet into the earth so he would not be carried away with his own wind, stretched out his neck and put every ounce of his body behind his effort.

Besides their sporadic brayings, which occurred whenever they felt like it, Prince Albert and Little Windy were on a pretty rigid schedule. They were self-appointed town clocks, and kept the town strictly on its toes. My home town had several business establishments beside the Union Hotel and the livery stable. There were besides the stores, two lumber mills, three grain mills, and an ice plant. It was customary for the planing mill to blow its whistle at five in the morning to let the mill hands know they had an hour to get up, eat their fatback and eggs, and get on the job by six. There was also a noon whistle and one at six in the evening. The planer, being the senior business, would start its whistle first. Then the heading mill, the ice plant, and the three grain mills would follow suit—respectfully of course. When all the whistles were blowing it made a "right rousin' racket," as Mrs. Hudgins used to say.

Aside from these scheduled tootlings, it was the custom for the ice plant to serve as a fire alarm. The ice plant had to keep a man on duty all night, and when a fire alarm was phoned into the girl in the telephone office, she would call the ice plant. The fire signal was a series of long, low blasts, a mournful and ominous sound that never failed to rouse the bucket brigade as well as everyone else in town.

There was also the curfew, which the ice plant sounded at nine every night. It meant that all minors, unless with their elders, had to start for home forthwith, or be accosted by Rainey Sleight, the town marshal.

Each and every time a whistle blew, Prince Albert and Little Windy would join in with wild and complete abandon. What with six steam whistles and two jackasses going full tilt, my home town really announced itself on these special occasions.

It is well known that animals have a more precise feeling for time than humans have, and this was demonstrated when the new night man at the ice plant forgot to blow the five o'clock whistle in the morning. His embarrassment was tremendous when he heard the two jacks, nearly a mile away, start reminding him in brassy notes that he had forgotten his duties.

Prince Albert and Little Windy have long since been hauled off to some forgotten glue factory, leaving behind them a multitude of hard-working offspring.

After their demise Mr. Hudgins decided that mule breeding was falling off so much that he wouldn't replace them. A few years later his livery stable followed the jacks into oblivion. He sold it to a young fellow who wanted to start a repair shop for a new contraption called an automobile.

[TACK ME UP]
What *the* Papers said *of* 5A Horse Hats

These Cuts appeared in the leading Papers of New York. Chicago and other large Cities.
The demand for 5A Horse Hats will be active. Order some.

The Giddy Girl.

Horse Beaters, Beware.

Just Arrived from Mexico.

Fedora Hats are Popular.

The Old-Fashioned Horse.

Ready for the Field.

Our Country Cousin.   A Rusty Politician.   In the Military Parade.   Golf is Still Popular.   Clean as the Bread we Eat.   The Old Sport.

WON'T GET SUNBURNED.

"Until I Got This Hat, I Freckled Horribly."

Slipped on a Sunshade to run to the Grocer's.

One *of* the "400"

"Do you Sunburn?"
"Not since I got this Hat."

"Go right away and get your Hats.
You'll get sunstruck."

"IS MY HAT BECOMING?"

The Dandy Police.   A Popular Jockey.   A High Stepper.   The Beautiful Widow.   Old Salt.   Rural Police.
They Smoke While on Duty.

GROCERIES & NOTIONS

Julius Caesar Taylor's general store in West Concord, Vermont, looked pretty much like any other of the eighties. The front of the white frame building with upstairs living quarters gave on an open porch and faced the packed dirt of Main Street. The back dropped down a banking above Higgins' sawmill.

Push into its warmth on a sub-zero morning and you breathed the fragrance of calicoes, ginghams, challies, flannel sheeting, denim, heavy silks (even velvets), along with stronger odors from leather boots, kerosene, coffee beans lately pulverized in the big red hand-grinder, rich country cheeses, pickles in an uncovered keg, and chunks of hardwood burning in the big cast-iron stove.

These mingled aromas greeted me New Year's Day of 1888 as I began my service in the Taylor store, unaware of the course in public relations I was about to take. At nineteen I boasted no storekeeping experience. I measured only five feet four, but I was a cordy little fellow for all that.

A fellow needed to be husky to work in a country store in an era when produce came mainly in barrels or hundred-pound bales. Clerks had to maneuver these without the sissy's aid of moving belts or rubber-tired trucks—muscle did it.

Barrels of flour, barrels of red McIntoshes, barrels of "West Indy" molasses—or, on occasion, huge hogsheads of dark syrup. Barrels of potatoes from back-hill farms; of pickles, salt pork, sugar, and coarse salt. Barrels of flaky, round St. Johnsbury crackers baked in the next town, ready for chips of butter out of some farm wife's firkin. Bales and kegs of dried salt codfish to vary the West Concorder's diet of perch, pickerel, and horned pout taken from Hall's Pond.

All too often I found I must face up to a slippery green barrel of kerosene—a 300-pounder—which must be hoisted to a box top or rough horse, a kerosene can's height above the floor. Then I must pierce it for the flow which would fuel lamps to set Concord's hillsides asparkle at lighting-up time.

The uncounted hundreds of flour barrels I loaded into—then out of—J. C. Taylor's Dry Goods and Grocery Store! Almost every farmer's order began with, "I'll take a barrel of flour."

Mr. Taylor, father of six, had been previously served by my second cousin, Elmer Reed, and our business arrangement was much the same as that between him and Elmer. My pay would be in the form of room, board, laundry (with which went some mending), and a salary of a hundred dollars a year.

A hundred dollars a year meant a full year. Vacations, summer or winter, were not in style and not even expected by a country store clerk of the period. A year was a year was a year. But once, out of my fifteen months' service, I did get off for a two-day fishing trip to Cow Pond, an unheard-of lay-off.

Puttering round the yard goods section my first week of employment, I overheard Mr. Taylor talking with a farmer out front.

"I can say one thing for Elmer Reed," he said to John Pratt, "and I can't say it of any other clerk. At the end of the month he always had his full pay coming to him."

"Old Man," I silently promised my fifty-year-old boss, "you're going to say that of me, too." Accordingly, every month I received intact, with not one penny deducted, my wages of $8.13.

J. C. Taylor sensibly closed down at 9:00 P.M. Thus my hours ran roughly from 7:00 A.M., when I came to sweep the floor and light a fire in the hungry box stove, until the Town House clock in its thin, slow chime struck the conclusive hour of nine.

That gluttonous stove I must feed daily ate up sixteen-inch-long sticks of hardwood with rapid gulps, and following the second winter of my employment, every last stick fed into the iron creature was cut by me.

Youthfully confident, I made brags in spring that I would saw all the logs in the yard below Taylor's store within the space of one week. This would be twenty cords of wood. Release me from store duties; let Charlie Dowse, a good hand at filing saws, keep mine keen at all times, and I would do the rest. Mr. Taylor understood boys. On assuring me that I could never fulfill my brags, he knew the woodpile was already as good as stacked.

It was April, frost out of the ground, trees budding into tremulous green, our little Moose River splashing boisterously under the rainbow arch of the covered bridge my Temple uncles had helped build.

I picked up my razor-sharp saw and selected a piece

of four-foot wood from a forbidding pile. All too soon I discovered that every log was as thick around as a stovepipe—some thicker. Others defied a full cut, unless I turned them over. Twenty cords in one six-day working week! Over three cords of hardwood a day, each piece cut twice in two, a pile four by twenty-four feet in size. Charlie Dowse better be good with his filing.

Word got out that Jim Frye was in back of Taylor's, sawing and sweating. Idlers came to gape and advise, friends to mock Little Jim desperately and publicly busy. Like an artist on a street corner, I must not glance up at spectators and become distracted. In silence, I sawed. Across the river in his frame house, Charlie filed. Harry and Fred Taylor were caring for their father's little roan in my place— I had a stove, not a horse to feed.

Early mornings, when plump robins were scuttling about our small common looking for grubs and bobolinks were calling from meadows nearby, I was at my saw horse. Late twilight found me still sawing, while the sun disappeared in a wedge of gold between two hills over Waterford way. It was a very weary lad who triumphantly flung down his tools on Saturday night and a grateful one when his boss said, "Don't touch another stick; the boys and I'll stack it." But I'd kept my word; sawed every last piece.

A shy stripling early in my employment, I was at some confusion if waiting upon the womenfolks, fitting them to ladies' high button boots; rolling out bolts of yard goods while trying not to rumple chambray and print with my clumsy hay-rube hands nor muss the handsome poplins; snipping off eighteen inches of satin for a hair bow; measuring scrim and buckram; displaying whaleboned corsets nested in deep, slim boxes.

Townsfolk, at first, generally asked for Mr. Taylor to wait on them. Yet, slowly, I began to learn. When I was hired, deep red and blue, such as my sisters, Sabiny and Maryann, knit into mittens and mufflers, were about the only colors I could identify. Presently I could glibly recommend ashes of roses, indigo blue,

54

garnet, pistache green, and the popular seal brown. Once customers came directly to me, I knew I had caught on.

By then, I could deftly flip over a length of ribbed silk or bombazine or select the box of tortoise shell hairpins some woman needed for pinning on her Sunday-go-to-meeting switch of hair. I could advise a maiden as to a gold-plaited breast pin or locket that lay, with small wares, displayed in one of two glass cases.

Over these cases I daily fluffed my chicken feather duster. They were chockablock with a conglomeration of small items as divergent as penny candy and shaving mugs. The list of goods carried by a country storekeeper was astronomical. Cuff buttons and scythe snaths; common pins and mop pails; seeds and jackknives—on and on it went. Whips, brooms, ax handles, herd's-grass, oil lamps—to believe in such variety, one needed to see the stock in its odd juxtaposition.

All day, townspeople and farmers, their wives and children, drifted in to buy or gossip. But after the early supper hour enjoyed at West Concord, six or eight men would settle down on a pair of simple benches, light up pipes or take out quids, and a chewing match (conversation and tobacco) would begin. Always the stove was a focal point of the gathering in the wintertime—but winter or summer, the sawdust box set on iron feet was in demand by tobacco chewers.

When I became a storekeeper in Concord years later, I had had enough of wood cutting, so I installed a towering affair for stove coal that had a round wooden drum to use as a warming oven. The stove taught me several lessons—first, that the fiercely independent aged just won't admit that they forget—to do so is to admit to old age.

Orville Lawerence was a regular customer, an old man at the time I became a proud young storekeeper. One bleak day he tied his piano buggy to the nearest hitching post, stamped in shaking snow from his leg-boots, and placed his mittens on the stove drum to dry. When he left, carrying his groceries but not his mittens, I called to him as he opened the door.

"Mr. Lawerence, haven't you forgotten something?"

"I say—have I?"

"Your mittens, sir."

For a second he hesitated, glancing at the stove, then realizing this as a confession of forgetfulness, moved on out.

"I say—I'm not ready for 'em yet," came the face-saving reply. Extra steps to return and recover the mittens were worth proving he'd not forgotten.

On the lighter side was my experience with Cousin Elmer's young wife Ella, who lived just over the store. Because my stove's damper had not been properly adjusted, gas built up inside the heater. One morning the gas blew up without warning, and following the course of the stovepipe, decided to explode right in the middle of Ella's neat bedroom. She came down at once to confront me as belligerently as a naturally gentle soul could.

"What have you done to my bedroom?" she cried out in dismay.

All I could do was offer to pay for removal of the coating of black soot showered from floor to ceiling—and watch my damper thereafter.

By the time I owned a store my cousin Elmer owned one also and there was a third merchant in town, H. F. G. Branm, who ran a store somewhat above us. All three of us inevitably stocked the long heavy woolen undergarment in two sections then favored by both men and women for winter wear. From this stock I was to learn a lesson in discretion. As a husbandly gesture, Harve Judevine elected to take home a set of nether garments from all three stores—perhaps planning to compare the merchandise. Wifelike, Mrs. Pratt repudiated the choice of her spouse. But not until months later—in a hurried trip to each storekeeper—did the buyer redistribute the goods. And then, not to rightful owners.

Elmer got a top piece of Branm's; this had become moth-eaten in places. I got the corresponding moth-eaten lower piece and a shirt of Elmer's while Branm got my full set.

Now I'd always kept a civil tongue in my head, as a young man should, while serving Squire Judevine, but I had no particular love for him. To accept moth holes along with belatedly returned goods was asking too much.

I confided to Elmer that unless I got my own garments back, I'd sue. Elmer must have quoted me and word been taken back to Judevine for he came in one day to say in farm-frank language it did not lie in me to do this. We parted coldly. Next day Branm brought back my rightful set, but with lofty righteousness I said, "Trot those down to Judevine—*he* bought 'em and *he* can return them *himself*."

An old doctor in the store, and my sponsor when I joined the Masons, spoke up. He advised against my act as Mr. Judevine was a man of influence; I listened, accepted the underwear from Branm—but not until years later did I fully appreciate the wisdom of his counsel.

J. C. Taylor, my first employer, had never trusted out. Nor Curt Stacey, a small storekeeper who had above the top of a time-silenced clock in his store the warning, "No tick here." But as I expanded, I began to let folks charge what they bought. Cleveland's panic lay on the land. Income began to fall below outgo. I had made a practice of presenting a trifling gift when a bill was paid, a bag of candy, a fat cigar. As the panic grew these gifts were infrequent.

"Give me a barrel of flour," a customer would say. Then as I loaded it into his wagon, "I'll pay ye later."

With hop farmers in the vicinity this had been a familiar way of doing business, "Pay ye when I sell my hops" was as good as a bond. But this Cleveland panic was different.

Was Uncle Charlie, village blacksmith, really a prophet when he uttered his dictum against the Democrats on Cleveland's election? A die-hard Republican, he sat down to read the day's news in tipped-back comfort. One glance at the news—Cleveland had actually been elected! Whang! Down came feet and chair legs as Uncle roared, "The country's gone to hell; and I can't help it!"

Certainly it seemed so to me as bills rolled in and wholesalers in Boston and Portland began pressing me. A backer wanted cash on his loan. Contributing as usual to both Methodist and Universalist church funds was impossible. Store-keeping, once my delight, was now my nightmare. "Never Trust Out"—why hadn't I heeded Mr. Taylor?

Farmers still drove round with no cash but "pay-ye-later" promises. Men still perched on countertops in the late evening to gossip and argue. If I turned out the lamps to be rid of them, it being summer, they kept on with their talk, seated outside on the family-size barrels of flour ($4.25) strung out from the store door in a long row. Plenty of goods went out over my counter—but no gold in any form seemed to come back.

There arrived a heart-breaking period of forced inventory and settlement, and the humiliating public auction of my goods. "Finis" was written to my career as a storekeeper.

At last I locked my door for good. It was dark. Pleasant summer quiet lay upon West Concord. To-morrow was only another day.

Four down trains from Portland would whistle at the crossing by the grist mill as usual. Four up trains would whistle in reverse. Horses from Ed Joslin's livery stable would clomp past to Uncle Charlie's for treatment for interfering. Farmers from the corner would drive up with their wives' grocery lists— kerosene—flour—stick cinnamon—a nipple for baby's bottle—but not to Jim Frye's store; he was done for—done!

I stuck the door key in my pants pocket for the last time—like a freed slave flung my hands high.

"Thank God, that's over!" I cried.

Yet I've always been glad I first tended, then owned, a country store for it taught me many valuable lessons I could never have learned from books.

THE CHURCH SUPPER

The church mouse did not achieve his legendary reputation for leanness from mere accident. He was no doubt the inhabitant of a country church in the days of our grandfathers when he sometimes ran a poor second to the minister.

The underpaid, and often unpaid, ministers to the souls of our rural forefathers were often reduced to a polite form of begging and few of their families rose above genteel undernourishment. Their parishioners had no illusion about how much food and clothing the eighty or a hundred dollars a year, an average salary, would buy. The customary supplement to this starvation wage was the church social, given as a benefit for the preacher and his family.

Church socials were held on the lawn of the church on summer evenings. Members of the church donated cake, platters of fried chicken, canned preserves, fruit, and other delicacies of the season which were served at plank tables laid on wooden sawhorses. Food was served family style and the usual cost of a church social meal was twenty-five cents for all you could eat.

Ten cents was charged for children, who usually ate twice as much as their elders. Society leaders of the community presided at the cake table, where the work was easy and where they got a chance to compare the baking skill of their neighbors. The preacher's wife and the lesser members of the congregation washed dishes and served the hot food from a brick stove or kerosene range set up for the evening under a canvas. It was a gala time for the children of the community, who could play on this rare occasion when neither Sunday school nor public school cast a shadow on their spirits.

The swain who squired a girl at a church social dinner was a marked man, for this was understood by all as an open and public declaration of serious intentions. There was no trifling with tradition.

The minister's family was richer by twenty-five or thirty dollars, everybody had a good time, and every housewife gathered up enough leftovers to feed her family the next day, a phenomenon of the fish and loaves sort that was very mysterious and wonderful.

COVERED BRIDGES

On the sultry afternoon of June 14, 1877, the old covered bridge at Northampton, Massachusetts, lurched from its foundations, sailed crazily through the air, and crashed a thousand feet away into the bed of the river.

Like the Bridge of San Luis Rey, it carried with it a burden of human and animal freight. Eleven persons with six teams of horses had taken shelter under its roof when a black and ominous cloud had risen out of the north, and when the tornado had struck they became airborne with the bridge. One woman died in the twisted and splintered wreckage; six men were cut and bruised. It was the wonder of all that only one person died in the destruction of the bridge.

Most of the covered bridges of the country are doomed to destruction, not by act of nature like the Northampton bridge, but by the hand of man to make way for progress.

The covered bridge is a link in yesterday's highways, and yesterday's highways and bridges were designed for the horse and buggy.

Scattered across the country there are still some two thousand covered bridges, most of them doing daily duty, their plank floors rattling beneath the wheels of trucks and automobiles. Ohio alone has more than one-fourth of those still in use. The state claims 563½ covered bridges, splitting ownership of a bridge on the state line with Indiana.

In New England and the Pacific Northwest trains still thunder through a few covered railroad bridges. In California there are a handful of covered foot bridges.

58

The origin of the covered bridge is lost in antiquity. It is not unique to America. There is one recorded as having been built in Babylon in 783 B.C. No one is quite certain when the first one was built in this country. Some antiquarians say the bridge that Timothy Palmer built over the Schuylkill River at Philadelphia in 1804 was the first in this country. Early settlers were skeptical about their durability, and wherever one went up in a community it was freely predicted that it would vanish on the crest of the first spring freshet. By 1810, however, the covered bridge was accepted as the most modern structure with which to span a stream.

In the early days the bridges were built either by the villages which they were expected to serve, or by private individuals. In either case toll was collected to pay for the structure. Some towns conducted lotteries to raise money for bridgebuilding. Several bridges were financed in this manner until local church leaders pronounced the method "sinful gambling," and public pressure brought a stop to the practice, although churchgoers usually crossed free of charge on Sunday morning.

When the erection of a bridge came up for debate, the town hall was crowded with local citizenry and out-of-town bridge engineers.

In the Midwest most of the bridges were erected by the counties, on county roads.

The bridgebuilders were carpenters with a flare for engineering. When bidding for a bridgebuilding job they carried with them a model of their bridge. The models were elaborately painted and decorated. One bridge engineer who aimed at making his bridges working structures rather than works of art was Lemuel Chenowerth. He showed up one night at a bridge-planning meeting in Richmond, Virginia. He watched the other engineers give their sales talk on their fancy bridges and display their models. When it came Chenowerth's turn he brought out a sturdy, unpainted model of his favorite bridge. He gave no sales talk, but silently placed two chairs in the middle of the floor and rested one end of his model on each chair. He then straddled his model with his feet dangling. He got the contract.

The minor specifications for a new bridge were usually left to the builder. The town selectmen decreed only that it reach from shore to shore, and be wide and high enough to accommodate a load of hay.

There were always those among the townspeople who considered thrift a greater virtue than progress. It was about a hundred years ago at a town meeting in Vermont that a farmer stood and asked for permission to speak. "We've built four bridges in this town, four bridges within two miles," he said, "now we're asked to build a fifth. Mr. Moderator, I move we bridge the whole damn creek—lengthwise."

Once the site was chosen, the bridge planned, and the price agreed on, the engineer moved in with his construction crews. With the aid of ox teams, and the free advice of a crew of pioneer sidewalk engineers, he cut timbers and hewed them into beams. The beams and timbers were fastened together with wooden pegs instead of nails.

One of the most famous of the early bridgebuilders was Theodore Burr. One of his bridges, built at Waterford, New York, in 1804, carried traffic until

1909, when it met its untimely end because a poorly insulated electric wire set it afire.

Burr was a shrewd showman. When he started a bridge the usual kibitzers gathered on the banks to watch the construction. He soon had them at work heaving timbers and driving pegs. Burr reported after one job that his admiring gallery waded into icy water up to their armpits to help his crew. He added subtly that there was considerable drinking, but little intoxication.

In Burr's day engineers possessed no precision instruments to help them with their calculations. They built their bridges by guess and by gosh. The bad guesses, however, didn't remain long on the rural landscape to embarrass their builders. Unless a bridge was well built it fell apart in the first flood or wind-

storm that came along. The cautious engineer built his bridges with a wide margin of safety. The margin was so wide in many cases that decades later some of the bridges are carrying trucks weighing several times the original load limit. When a new bridge was finished the engineer checked it for sturdiness. The test was simple. The builder drove a herd of cattle across to test its vibrations and strength. Burr originated the arched truss which appeared in many bridges later, and which bears his name.

Not all early covered bridges were built by the towns. Often they were built by businessmen, who charged tolls for crossing. The location of a bridge determined its value as a commercial venture. Old records indicate that some of the most profitable ones were situated where there was a settlement on one bank of the river and a saloon on the other. Saturday night became the busiest of the week. The wise bridge tender soon learned which of his customers would be able to pay on the return trip and which should pay for the round trip on the way over.

The usual procedure for a person caught at the bridge with no money in his pocket, and with darkness in his favor, was to attempt to run the bridge or climb up and cross on the roof.

The toll rates for covered bridges were fairly standard, and were posted at the entrance near the tollhouse. The following is a typical list:

1. Each foot passenger — 1 cent
2. Each horse and rider — 4 cents
3. Carriage with horse — 10 cents
4. Sleigh and one horse — 5 cents
5. Passenger vehicle with more than one horse — 20 cents
6. Farm wagon with two beasts — 10 cents
7. A neat creature (cow) — 1 cent
8. Each sheep or swine — $\frac{1}{2}$ cent

Only one person is considered the driver of a team to pass free of toll.

In addition to his tolls the bridge owner was entitled to a part of the fine if he caught a traveler breaking the traffic laws on his bridge. A few old covered bridges still bear weather-worn signs which announce, "$2.00 fine for riding a horse over this bridge faster than a walk, or for driving more than 20 head of cattle over it at one time." One-half the fine went to the informer.

In many communities the covered bridge became a social center. It absorbed so much character from those who traveled it that it took on a character of its own. On rainy afternoons it became a meeting place for travelers and farmers who waited out rainstorms under its solid roof. On bright summer days it shaded the pool beneath it and gave the local boys a cool place to swim.

Country swains carved their initials on its timbers, coupling them with their sweethearts' in a bleeding heart frame. The rafters were a fine place for small boys to play. Their older brothers and sisters often called the structure "The Wishing Bridge" and as they gained courage changed the name to "The Kissin' Bridge." The toll was a kiss for every plank, and the slower the horse the more pleasant the crossing. The covered bridge also made a dry hard surface on which the local militia could drill. Every salesman that passed seemed to find room to add another poster to its walls.

The virtues of horse liniment and kidney pills were displayed on its walls. The bridge also became a refuge for mud-daubers and mourning doves that nested in the rafters and eaves.

There were many cases where the pride of community ownership prompted the citizens to name their new bridges. In southern Indiana is a bridge that earned its name. The broad side boards of the bridge disappeared with annoying regularity. Someone discovered that they were making their way into the neighborhood homes where they were used as tables for pasting wallpaper in the springtime. The covered bridge became known as the Papering Board Bridge.

Bridges were often named for local celebrities. One bridge in Monroe County, Indiana, was called the Nancy Jane Bridge, for Nancy Jane Chambers. Another bridge built at the same time was known as the Judah Bridge, until a few night travelers had their religion scared out of them by herds of hogs sleeping inside the structure. After that the bridge became known as "Judy's Damn Bridge."

Covered bridges, like English castles, were favorite hangouts for ghosts. Haunted bridges were usually debunked by the simple expedient of capturing the animal which had taken up residence. In one case in Missouri the spirits turned out to be an escaped pet raccoon wearing a collar and a short length of chain.

The covered bridge was not designed as a thing of beauty, and it seldom was. Taken out of its pleasant rural surroundings it was a drab structure, functional and weather-beaten. Generally the architecture varied little. Different engineers used different types of trusses and different designs for the portals, but outwardly the bridges looked much alike. Some had windows, some didn't. While some were single-lane tunnels, others were double-barreled to permit two-way traffic. Occasionally one was built with a sidewalk along one side for the convenience of pedestrians.

One covered bridge that varied from the usual pattern was the old Y Bridge at Zanesville, Ohio. There at the confluence of the Licking and Muskingum rivers the city fathers wanted a bridge that would connect three early settlements. The bridge they designed had three entrances, dividing in midstream.

The longest covered bridge in the world spanned the Susquehanna River between Columbia and

Wrightsville, Pennsylvania. It was 5,620 feet, a little more than a mile in length.

As roads are relocated and widened the old covered bridges are giving way to steel and concrete structures. Covered bridge enthusiasts have banded together to study the antique structures and to preserve a few typical ones for the benefit of coming generations. A periodical publication called *Covered Bridge Topics* keeps members informed.

The timbers built into covered bridges were generally high-grade lumber. When old bridges were torn down the lumber went into some other line of work. Many a barn has beams that once supported covered bridges. In Pennsylvania a match factory purchased and dismantled an old bridge, planning to turn it into match sticks. The timbers were so hard they couldn't be used.

Many covered bridges are still used by the towns that own them as storage places for city fire and maintenance equipment.

There is still occasional speculation about the reason for building a roof on a timber bridge. One theory was that they kept snow from the bridge, but there are still some bridges where local farmers are paid each year to haul snow for the floor to facilitate the passing of sleighs. The real reason is simple; the roof protects the wood from moisture and decay. One old Maine farmer summed up the question of why they covered bridges with, "It was for the same reason women wore petticoats—to protect their underpinning."

The future of the covered bridge is bleak. Although they grew up with the country, the country is now growing away from them. The covered bridge may successfully withstand the weather, but not the new highway engineers. They are perhaps not quite as permanent as Professor E. D. Sanborn of Dartmouth led his audience to believe in a public address which commemorated the completion of the Ledyard Bridge over the Connecticut River in 1859. "Let no vandal hand be raised to deface this noble structure," the Professor said, "or injure one fiber of its timbers. Palsied be the arm that shall aid in its demolition, and speechless be the tongue that would plead for its disfranchisement." The Ledyard Bridge stood for seventy-five years, and if the workers who finally tore it down in 1934 were visited by the professor's curse, the newspapers of the day failed to record it.

THE PATCHWORK QUILT

The patchwork quilt was the product of long winter nights on the farm in the days when bad roads bound the family to the confines of the homestead. Conceived in thrift, it became, in time, an artistic outlet, a means of self-expression. It was usually made for show and not for use. It was folded away in mothballs, to be given as a wedding present or passed on to a second generation. Sometimes it was displayed on the guest room bed or brought out for Sunday afternoon guests to admire.

Scraps of cloth left over from the material used in making aprons, dresses, and shirts were saved. The design was chosen and the pieces cut, matched, and stored away. They were sewed together by hand, a figure at a time. After the design was completed neighbor women were invited to a quilting bee. The backing of muslin or silk was placed on the quilting frame, the cotton or wool batting spread over it and quilted to the design. Care was taken that the stitches were uniform. The smaller the individual pieces of cloth, the more valuable the quilt. Sometimes the pieces were outlined by fancy crisscross stitches in silk thread. An all-silk quilt in intricate design set a woman high in a community.

When neighbors were invited to a quilting bee they went, come hell or high water. If they didn't they knew they would be torn apart. That is one reason for the inexhaustible number of quilts in the country.

A good quilter could recite the history and origin of every piece in her favorite quilt. Designs tended to become standardized within the family and within the community. From the South came designs such as "Dixie Rose," "Honeysuckle," "General Lee's Rose," and "Cannon Ball." From Revolutionary ancestors have come such titles as "The Pannier," or basket, which was supposed to have been brought over by Benjamin Franklin from the French Court, and the "Fleur-de-lis" or "Iris," which was of French origin. In the American highlands of Kentucky and Tennessee, where some of the best quilts were, and are now made, designs have been handed down for generations. Stained and yellowed, they are the only legacy these gaunt people have from their heroic past. Every substantial family has one or two.

THE HOME AND
THE FIELDS

The old-time farmstead was a tight little community, of necessity designed to be self-sufficient. Everywhere in America, except on the Great Plains where there was no timber, the first farmhouses were built of logs. The logs came from the first clearing, snaked to the site by ox or horse, notched and hoisted in place by human muscle. The logs were calked with clay and a fieldstone fireplace erected at one end of the single room. The roof was made of hand-split shingles. If a man had time he hewed the logs square and fitted them closely. ¶ As the farmer found the time from the eternal round of planting and harvesting he built needed outbuildings around the cabin. First came the barn, of logs also, with stalls for the family cow and the horses, a mow for hay, and perhaps a lean-to for the sheep. If, by good fortune, there was a spring on the homestead, the cabin was built near it, and a springhouse was one of the first outbuildings. Then came the outhouse, a smokehouse for curing meat, a root cellar, a woodshed, and an ash pit. Near the barn were the corncrib, the granary, pens for calves and hogs, a machine shed, and perhaps a shop. ¶ The buildings kept pace with the farmer's affluence; the cabin was enlarged and faced with clapboards, or replaced by brick or stone, and roofed with slate. The log barn was replaced by a sawed lumber structure, there were many stalls, and the mow was high. ¶ The timber, cleared to make new fields, was split into rails for fences and buildings. Following Johnny Appleseed came a host of fruit tree salesmen, and soon there were Pippin, Winesap, and Maiden Blush stored in the root cellar. The hive of bees brought from the East multiplied to a long row in the orchard, and berry bushes lined the kitchen garden fences. ¶ Wants and needs grew with progress. The affluent farm family was surrounded by hired hands and hired girls, indigent relatives who slept in attic bedrooms, in-laws who came to dinner. The community exerted its own social and economic pressures on the farm family, which found, as the twentieth century dawned, that their fields were no longer an island, and their way of life no longer in their own hands. Life became more complex, but in many ways much easier. The farmer willingly traded his hernia for electric power, his self-sufficiency for a community interdependence, and the toil and hardship of the frontier for the comforts of an ordered economy.

THE FINE ARTS

Time, space, bad roads, and a state of mind almost completely insulated the old-time farm from the world. In the days before the telephone and the daily mail the farm was truly an island, isolated in a sea with scarcely a sail from one year end to the next. Nations fell, kings were assassinated, tidal waves engulfed distant shores, but the seasons came and went and the old cow died, on the farm. The manners and morals of the Victorian age flourished on American farms long after the Queen was buried beside Albert near Windsor; William McKinley was dead a month before a drummer reported the tragedy to Cal Greene, who kept the general store at Sunrise in the Ozarks.

The county seat newspaper and the telephone brought the farmer somewhat into the stream of life —he knew what was going on in the great world before it became history. But culture, as we define it, was slower in coming, being more of an intangible thing, and meeting more resistance. The first direct exposure to a culture of sorts was made in the waning years of the nineteenth century when an institution known as the Chautauqua penetrated the heartland of America. The Chautauqua came in a tent; it was a curious compound of vaudeville, music, religion, oratory, and other of the fine arts. William Jennings Bryan delivered his "Cross of Gold" oration from a multitude of Chautauqua platforms at the turn of the century and set the pace of political oratory which has continued into the atomic age. The hard core of the Chautauqua troupe was a small group of second-rate opera singers, a concert pianist, perhaps a magician, the skeleton of an operetta troupe, and the inevitable Swiss Bell Ringers. The programs were pieced out by local talent. Small boys owe a dubious debt to Rubinstein, for it was his magic at the piano that inspired an epidemic of music lessons for youngsters throughout the Chautauqua belt.

The fine arts generally languished, partly because there was no time for them in the year-round struggle for the bare necessities of life. The rifle was more functional than a painter's brush, and the hand that guided the plow was not shaped for the pen of the poet. But there was a thirst for the finer things, and as life became easier and there was more leisure,

the culture of the Old World seeped into the lonely farmhouses through the pages of Shakespeare, the cheap chromos from the art galleries of the world, the occasional Ivy League teacher or preacher.

And our own budding American culture gathered followers in the rural districts. John Greenleaf Whittier's poems were printed in the schoolbooks, Currier and Ives prints hung on almost every parlor wall, and Stephen Foster's ballads were sung at country gatherings. Even the mail order catalogue pointed the way for rural fashions. Mandolin clubs were organized, spinsters painted china, and the yearning for the beautiful was expressed in the patchwork quilt, the sampler, the lilac bush beside the wall, and beautifully designed tools and toys. Here and there

the creative instinct became so strong that untrained hands turned out objects of art, wood carvings, oil paintings, and statuary, that have become treasured possessions of modern collectors. There has been a Grandma Moses in every generation.

The sensitive consideration for others, the true essence of culture, was never lacking in the American farmer. It came out in his hospitality, his neighborliness, and his integrity.

The hick farmer never existed except on the vaudeville stage. Unlettered, naïve, and innocent of the ways of the world he may have been, but he possessed the divine spark, deeply hidden sometimes because of geography and circumstances, but valid nevertheless. The yearning for beauty draws no line.

RABBIT HUNTING

The first snow of the season was the signal for a rabbit hunt. If the snow fell during the day preceding, so much the better. Not only does the cottontail feed at night but being a very sociable fellow he visits all his friends and is likely to indulge in a bit of horseplay as well. Toward morning, after a night of foraging for apples buried in the snow in the orchard and a visit to the kitchen garden for choice bits of leftovers, he "holes" up for the day. The new snow records all this for the hunter.

The rabbit knows he has left a map behind him and he has a special genius for making it difficult to read. He circles, backtracks, and jumps sidewise into the track of another rabbit. While he usually confines his night activities to a small area, he sometimes will strike out across hill and dale just for the hell of it. He usually returns to his accustomed bailiwick, where he makes a nest under a tuft of grass or weeds. A rail pile or shed floor will serve if he is caught out late and wants to avoid risk.

While dogs dearly love this sort of hunting they are really a handicap for they range too far afield and flush the game prematurely. The sport lies in the hunter's ability to solve the puzzle of the track pattern and to outguess the wily cottontail.

It was considered bad form to carry a scattergun on this type of hunt, for the rabbit is usually discovered crouching in his nest and the idea is to shoot him through the eye with a 22-caliber slug. If he is flushed he has won the game and is rewarded with an undisturbed escape.

Nature has camouflaged the rabbit perfectly by coloration and he is a master at supplementing this deception with some tricks of artful concealment of his own.

The game was dressed and hung on the clothesline out of reach of the cat to freeze. Fried rabbit with brown gravy and biscuits was by no means a minor factor in the enjoyment of a rabbit hunt, which whetted the appetite to a fine edge.

THE SMALL PEOPLE

The modern farmer, educated to the merits and advantages of thoroughbred animals, is likely to insist that his dog have something more than a patchwork ancestry. Our grandfathers, however, got along well enough with just a dog. Because of the influence of his English ancestry the traditional farm dog perhaps had more of the shepherd or collie in him than any other breed. He was bred for no particular purpose although if he could help with the stock, and most any breed of dog can do this, so much the better. He was expected to chase a rabbit out of a corn shock, catch a loose pig, bark at intruders, keep tramps moving down the highway, and grab a rat as it dashed from the corncrib to the rail pile. He was the companion of the farmer in the long, lonely hours in the fields and rode with him on the seat of his wagon when he delivered a load of corn to the village elevator. He slept on a pile of burlap sacks in the woodhouse in the summer and behind the cannon heater in the winter. He thrived on scraps from the table and the supplement of a young rabbit during the harvest season or an occasional field mouse.

Sometimes he had enough hound in him to track a coon on moonlight nights in the autumn and enough setter to flush a covey of quail. He often made friends with one of the horses, sometimes slept in the stall, and accompanied the team to the fields, sleeping in the shade of a fence row while the long furrows were plowed, near his master and his friend.

Sometimes he tolerated an attachment for the family cat. The family cat, the favorite which accompanied the farmer's wife to the milking, purring in anticipation of the saucer of warm milk, was fat and sleek, slept in the easy chair by the hearth, and was an expert at scrounging. She rarely disturbed her comfort to catch a mouse. Purely as policy she cultivated the dog and mourned but briefly for her kittens when they left her for the fascinating life under the barn.

The barn cat was another breed. She was judged solely on her ability as a ratter or mouser. Corncribs and feed bins were de luxe hotels for tribes of rats and mice and a farmer owed much to the lean cats which engaged them in eternal total war. These barn cats had one delightful tie with the indolent family cat: they shared the same pan of warm milk poured from the bucket at milking time.

Farm boys were great hands for pets, often to the consternation of their elders. The litter of skunks trapped in a hollow log, a young crow fallen out of the nest, a box turtle from under the hedge, were taken in and if they were not tamed, they at least forgot their fear of man. The animals and birds around a farm formed their own attachments, often without rhyme or reason—the rooster which ruled the barn slept in old Dobbin's stall, waited for him to come in from the field; the outlaw goose which attacked everything on two or four legs took up with the hired hand and followed him about like a dog; the cats liked anything which could contribute to their comfort. They bedded down on the motherless lamb brought in to warm by the stove, and suspended their ancient feud with the dog to share his warm spot in the sun.

The bleak statistical pages of the *International Yearbook* for 1910 will tell you that it was a year of strikes and lockouts. There were skulls cracked in Philadelphia and the shirtwaist workers in New York were milling in the streets. The work on the Panama Canal was progressing steadily and President Taft expressed himself as well pleased. A locomotive made headlines when it cut a red ribbon across the tracks into the new Pennsylvania Station in New York.

Halley's comet brightened the heavens with a hundred-degree shimmering arc in early May, providing more grist for conversation than anything since the

The great success of 1909. The SEARS is not an experiment . . . we guarantee that with proper care and careful attention the car will go from 1 to 150 miles daily and last as long as any other car. Piano box style body, detachable, with side lever steering. Two cylinder direct opposed, 4⅛ inch bore, air-cooled motor; the control is flexible as a steam throttle, with a range of 1 to 25 miles per hour. Two good oil lamps in front; oil tail lamp in rear. Acetylene attachments and generator furnished with oil lamps for $10.95 extra. The SEARS motor car is simple to operate; we have never found it necessary to teach a customer to operate it. $395 F.O.B. Chicago.

sinking of the Maine. Page 128 of the *Yearbook* divided the population of the country according to its stand on prohibition: 43,857,958 wet, 48,114,307 anti.

The farmer had his reference book for 1910 too, and if you want to see how he was living, what he was wearing, and the tools he worked with, refer to Sears & Roebuck's bulging 1910 catalogue. It reveals a life that seems very primitive to us. Means of getting about were limited. Fifty years ago the automobile was a fearful contraption. Few ventured beyond the pavements of the city with the temperamental gas buggy because dirt country roads were passable only by horse-drawn vehicles. Farmers rarely went to the city to shop, for the corner grocery held all the necessities of life. If they wanted to soar they sat down under a coal-oil lamp and opened up a Sears & Roebuck or Montgomery-Ward catalogue and there was a whole, great, new world in front of them. It was the only contact with the elegant life of the cities for millions of American farm dwellers a generation ago. It was definitely escape literature.

To convince the buyer that an order could be written and did not necessarily have to be given verbally and face to face with the merchant, Sears gave encouraging instructions in English, German, and Swedish. "Write us in your own way, in any language, and don't worry whether your writing is good or poor."

The blurbs for Sears were written by keen students of rural psychology. A riding plow with double shovels which saved many a weary mile in the fields was given the better part of a page while a single-shovel walking plow was relegated to an obscure corner. A housewife, immaculate in bustle and lace waist, is pictured beside a washing machine guaranteed not to raise a sweat nor ruffle a curl.

Let's take a look at some of the items in the 1910 edition of Sears. The first ten pages were the bargain counters. On page 1 fleece-lined bed slippers sell for 8 cents a pair; a pound of axle grease for 6 cents; and an all-iron steak beater for 4 cents. A ladies' four-strap hose supporter, however, was 12 cents. Bargain hunters were filled with a sense of wealth and power when their gaze fell upon page 2, which offered any article described there for only 2 cents. These included a roll of toilet paper, a set of six tin tart or patty pans, and one pair of steel pants guards for bicycle riders. The thrill of opening a box containing fifty articles was terrific, compensating somewhat for

the twelve hours of labor a farm hand had to put in to earn the dollar.

Entire farms were equipped from the Sears catalogue. Machinery, saddles, harness, fence, building material, and home furnishings occupied the bulk of the 1,183 pages. On page 1165 there is an assortment of "Chaparajos or Cowboy Riding Pants." A snazzy pair sold for $12.95 and were made of fine black angora fur. The Midwestern cowboy could outfit himself completely from the Sears catalogue, even to a six-shooter. A Colt frontier model was quoted at $25 with pearl handles. Every young blood wanted a genuine rawhide buggy whip. Sears' best value was a nickel-ferruled nifty for $1, one of the very few items in the book quoted at an even dollar price.

Windmills did much of the water pumping which wasn't done by hand on American farms. You could buy a twenty-foot tower and mill for $26.98 or a sixty-footer for $80.05.

There were, too, all kinds of card games, Old Maid, Palmistry Cards, Authors, and Flinch. There was an "improved Seroco reversible combination gameboard" mounted on three legs and selling for $1.98. A cosmic number of games could be played by means of the rings, shuttles, dice, ten pins, balls, and other trinkets which came with the board. Pyrog-

*Spring hat in beautiful rose and ribbon design.
A neat shape, not too extreme, that is flattering to all faces. Low bell crown trimmed with two clusters of half blown roses, shaded from pink to deep old rose. Twisted about the roses and around the crown, ending in loops on the left side, is No. 60 old rose taffeta ribbon. Comes also in burnt color with blue roses. Ribbon to harmonize. Price, $3.88.*

*Majestic Grand Organ appeals instantly to the artistic sense
of all who see it. The design is very rich and
very well balanced, and it will prove an ornament to
any mansion in the land in an unrivaled position
of preeminence. It is of a most beautifully sweet,
sublime, sympathetic quality.*

raphy, or the art of wood burning, could be mastered by the quick reading of a pamphlet which came along with a set of tools, costing in all $1.79.

The ills of the body were diagnosed, symptoms tabulated and prescribed for in pages listing salves, pills, emulsions, and rub-ons. There was a vast array of remedies for constipation, an affliction peculiarly common among rural folk who ate salt pork all winter. One of the most helpful nostrums was a wart-remover, "painless and harmless."

There was a complete line of mechanical aids to health ranging from steam bath cabinets to trusses and electric belts. For $2.95 you could buy a medical battery with an instruction book. A list of diseases, as long as your arm, which electric shock was said to cure, came with the machine. The medical battery was recommended for rheumatism, a catch-all term used by old-timers to describe any muscular pain. Grandpa and Grandma shocked the daylights out of themselves with these gadgets and imagined quick relief. It was a marvelous thing to use on the dog when he was asleep.

Sears was right up front with new ideas. They offered electric flashlights about the same time big city department stores put them on their counter.

They were among the very few articles costing more in 1910 than today. You can buy a good battery for 10 cents now, but the cheapest Sears had was 20 cents.

There was a full line of exciting games and amusement devices. In the larger cities "nickelodians" were still something of a curiosity, but Sears was right up on its toes and offered a motion picture machine which guaranteed wonderful, lifelike moving pictures. Sales resistance must have vanished in the face of this glowing description: "Imagine sitting quietly in your own home and seeing a great railroad train dash by on the screen at a tremendous rate of speed, pulling its long string of swaying Pullman cars as it flashes past."

Both women and men wore long underwear with drop seats, fleece lined. Since skirts reached to the ground there was no percentage in showing a shapely calf neatly done up in nylons, so stockings were incidental and strictly utilitarian. The fanciest pair offered by Sears cost 37 cents and was quoted as being made of imported lisle lace. Later, when Sears went to slick paper, and living models were used to display the more intimate articles of women's apparel, the boys on the farm got many a vicarious thrill from the pictures of voluptuous females in scanty underwear.

The most expensive item in the catalogue, next to the pneumatic-tired automobile, was a tombstone

*The Paragon Reducing Model Corset is guaranteed
to reduce the hips and correct protruding abdomens, when
worn tightly laced. The foundation for a perfect
fitting gown; the corsetieres' art is surely illustrated in
this elegant new model. Medium high bust, long supple
waist effect, slender sloping hips. And do not forget,
we furnish two strong full length lacers.
A $5.00 value for $3.45*

quoted at $385. Of course there were cheaper ones. One with a sleeping lamb in granite cost only $10.

Nor did Sears neglect to sow seeds of culture. They urged, "$9.95 for a perfect clarinet. Examine our other reed instrument values also." There was a galaxy of musical instruments with free instructions guaranteeing the buyer would astonish his friends. The "Famous Marx Piano Harp," with which "anyone can produce music without the aid of a teacher," moved many to cultural effort.

One could buy a brass drum for $8.85 and a triple-tone cornet for $26.35 in brass, $34.45 in silver plate with a gold-plated bell. There were magnificent organs with mirrors and multiple curlicues and ginger-bread trimmings. The best value cost $49.85, but if you really wanted to take top rank in society you could buy a combination piano and organ for $68. A stool was given free in both cases.

In all the 1,183 pages there wasn't a single mention of brassières. This modern necessity was a built-in feature of the corsets which every female wore. The corsets listed by Sears, which appeared to be designed for punishment rather than comfort, were ribbed with whalebone or steel stays and laced up the back. The purpose was to achieve a minimum waist and to make seduction easy the stays were made of whalebone. The cheapest sold for $1.40 with steel stays.

Nothing can beat our combination
Roman divan sofa, davenport and couch, upholstered in extra fine crushed plush, at $15.65. Also illustrated, in use, our elegant frosted hood aluminum stereoscope. Price each $0.49. And, think of it, for only 85 cents we supply 100 beautiful views.

It was bad form to show an ankle in those days, but a full bust was much admired and was freely displayed. Sears catered to this conceit by offering the "Famous H & H Pneumatic Air Retaining Bust form." This cheater was guaranteed against pin punctures and detection. It was said to be nature's only rival and strikingly lifelike.

The mail order catalogue is still with us, but it is no longer a magic carpet to waft us to an enchanted land. This is indeed a great loss to mankind.

1910 model with standard canopy top. This is our most popular surrey with genuine linen cord fringe on top,
priced F.O.B. our factory, Evansville, Indiana, at $65.95. Phaeton type green upholstered seats are close enough together
for easy conversation. Body painted black, mirror finish.

THE SPRING HOUSE

The pioneer looked for a spring and built his cabin near it, for he had no time nor equipment to dig a well. As he prospered he replaced his cabin with a better house, but the spring continued to quench his thirst and that of his animals, and supplied the only refrigeration known to generations. He built a stone trough and ran the cold, slow-flowing water through it. With stone from the fields he built a house over the spring and planted a tree near the door. The housewife placed her earthenware crocks of milk almost neck deep in the cold shallow stream, skimming off the cream for buttermaking. Dishes of food and leftovers of meat were set there for keeping.

It was always cool in the springhouse, even on the hottest summer day. A gourd dipper hung from the wall and the men, coming from the hot fields, stopped first in the springhouse for a draft of the cold water. The dog quenched his thirst from the overflow at the back of the springhouse and a flock of ducks noisily investigated the trickling stream for tidbits. Watercress grew in the shallows.

What a soul-and-belly satisfying experience to tip a crock of rich cold milk down one's parched throat after a morning in the fields. What an oasis at the end of the day when the body, dehydrated from long hours in the sun, called for huge gulps of water, cooled as it can only be cooled to human taste, by a journey through the dark and cold depths of the land.

76

THE ROOT CELLAR

Just before the first frost the men of the farm pulled the turnips and cabbage, dug the potatoes and other vegetables and carried them into the root cellar. The root cellar was built partly above, partly beneath ground. It was walled with brick or stone and earth was heaped around it. A solid roof, sometimes also made of earth, protected the contents from the frost. The proper humidity and temperature were maintained for the perfect preservation of roots until late in the spring. The mixed odors of apples, wet earth, potatoes, and the other fragrant roots were inviting and told an eloquent story of the fruitfulness of the rich earth. There were bins and shelves in the root cellar; the shelves usually held cans of fruits and vegetables and jars of preserves if these were not stored in the cellar beneath the house. Today root cellars are rare. Modern transportation brings an abundance of fresh fruits and vegetables to the crossroads grocery and much that was formerly stored as it came from the ground and tree is now processed for canning. Quick freeze units have also had a part in outmoding the root cellar, once indispensable on every farm.

WILD HONEY

My son and I and our accomplice, Charles "Chigger" Fortner, went out to rob the yellow ones on a warm summer day. We went only to rob, but there were black warriors who came both to rob and to kill.

Our objective was a big post oak tree with a hole in its trunk. Yellow bees streamed into the hole bearing the tiny nuggets from which they molded a fortune of golden honey. We were out to take that fortune, leaving them only enough to start anew. But when we had finished, the black ones came to slaughter and to take what we had left; and they were determined to leave the yellow ones without their queen.

It was the workers who had unwittingly led us to the tree. Some of them had come to a piece of honeycomb we had placed on a stump in an open field. We had watched as they gathered their loads and our eyes were upon them as they winged away bearing their burden of honey. After marking their course by a towering pine we had sprinkled flour on a single bee and measured the time between his departure and his returning. It had measured only seven minutes—seven minutes to go, deposit his load, and return. That

meant the tree probably was no more than a quarter of a mile away.

It was nearer than that, and we had found it after only twenty minutes of searching. We had chopped an X on the tree so no one else would claim it, and had set a day for the robbery. The day was in the early part of July, so the swarm would have sufficient time to find another home and lay in a store of honey for winter while there were still blossoms.

It was early morning when we robed ourselves for the robbery. With our screen wire hats, hip boots, heavy clothing and gloves, we looked like grotesque creatures from a bad dream.

The entrance of the yellow ones was no more than a dozen feet above the ground, so it was with great care that we started the teeth of the saw to gnawing away at the trunk of the tree. We did not wish to incite them to warfare too soon. The tree was a worthless one beset by age and decay, and its passing would leave room for the rapid growth of the young pines around it. The bees took no notice as the saw chewed into the tree, but streamed in and out of the

hole completely unaware that disaster was near. Soon the top of the tree tilted slightly and its leaves quivered. It tottered for a moment like a stricken giant, then crashed to the earth with a roar.

The falling of the tree filled the air around us with the sweet aroma of wild honey. There's no scent on earth quite like it. "I think it's a mixture of the wild fragrance of all the flowers, from which the bees have gathered their nectar," one veteran bee hunter said in trying to describe it. It's a sweet, aromatic, wild smell, which makes a man hungry for honey whether or not he ever liked it before. Experienced bee hunters with good noses are sometimes able to locate bee trees by the scent of the honey. Its fragrance is distinctly different from that of honey manufactured by tame bees. We sniffed it with pleasure as our tree fell and bounced and lay still.

Soon the air was full of bees. They were the ones who had arrived with their loads only to find their home gone. Other arrivals joined them, and they swept back and forth across the open space, puzzled by the thing which had come upon them. The tree had fallen with the entrance upward and scores of yellow warriors were streaming forth ready to do battle. They circled first around the trunk, their wings singing a war song and their little daggers ready for an instant thrust. Finding no enemy there, they gradually widened their circle until several were buzzing angrily around our heads.

Soon we moved in to take the honey. As we approached the log, the little warriors began to dive bomb us from every side and dotted our clothing with their white stingers. Nor did we entirely escape without feeling their wrath. They searched out every weak place in our garments and drove home their weapons. No soldiers could fight more bravely.

We sawed halfway through the log on each side of the hole, then split out the block, exposing an excellent supply of sealed honey and hundreds of bees. We fired some rags and used the smoke to drive the bees off the honey, then sliced it in blocks and filled our pails until they were heaped high. While we worked the bee army, which had been reinforced by many from the inside, continued its attack. However, there was one group of warriors which never joined the battle. They were tightly clustered around the queen at the upper end of the opening, ready to defend her with their lives.

We filled our pails, leaving sufficient honey in the log for a new start for the swarm. As we were gathering our tools, we noticed the arrival of the first of the enemy, the black ones. There were only two or three at first, but in less than five minutes there were scores of them. It was evident that they were raiders from another swarm who had been attracted by the smell of honey and were intent upon taking it by force.

The yellow ones rallied immediately to meet this new danger, a danger which they understood better than they understood our attack. Soon those which had been buzzing around our heads left us and joined the furious battle. Yellow ones and black ones fought on the log, on the ground, and in mid-air. The black intruders were big and tough-looking, but the yellow ones, who had already known disaster at our hands, seemed determined to sell their lives dearly.

But the warriors clustered around the queen had remained apart from the battle. Forming themselves into triple ranks they had encircled her and sat facing outward. Suddenly a band of the black ones formed a wedge and advanced toward the queen. The outer circle of the royal guard immediately fell upon them and there was a tangle of black and yellow bodies. They battled furiously for a few minutes; the yellow ones prevailed—the black ones were all dead. But several of the queen's soldiers had also died. The survivors reformed a circle around the queen, and then, to our astonishment, other yellow ones came to stand in the places of those who had died.

But there was no need to defend her again, for the black ones who had remained alive and able to travel, suddenly beat a retreat. The yellow ones were victorious, but it had been a costly victory. The battleground was strewn with the bodies of their dead and those of the black raiders. But the honey we had left was intact and most important of all, their queen was still on her throne.

We were silent and subdued as we walked away from that scene, carrying almost one hundred pounds of honey. Never before had we witnessed such raw courage as that displayed by the yellow ones. We had plenty of honey, but I was no longer proud of it. Maybe it was because I was feeling guilty—guilty of robbing such courageous creatures.

I went back to the tree the next afternoon. The honey we had left had been eaten and the yellow ones were knotted in a great ball around their queen. I was sure their departure was near at hand. There was no longer an angry buzzing. In its stead there was a steady hum—the contented song of a little people ready to forget the past and begin life all over again.

BROOK FISHING

If tired businessmen could turn back the clock the banks of all the little brooks of the world would be crowded with small boys and their dogs. Of all the days of our youth, the most delightful were those we spent with a dog, a fishhook, and a can of worms along the brook that skirted the farm.

Weekdays were taken up with school and chores, but Saturday was our own and from early spring until late fall we haunted its banks. There was a can of worms under the back porch, the by-product of a job of spading we had done in the kitchen garden.

Calling the dog, we climbed the gate to the pasture and walked down the cow path across the fields to the brook. It was quiet and restful there; dragonflies buzzed about the pools and a rare leaf floated down to the water from the overhanging trees. At a bend a weeping willow leaned far out over the water. Here a deep pool had been washed out and here the biggest shiners and sunfish lay. While the dog investigated the latest messages in the skunk and groundhog holes along the bank, we cut a willow pole, tied on the line, using a ketchup bottle cork for a bobber.

All the long afternoon, as the shadows lengthened across the pole, we sat and watched the bobber, hoping for the big one that we never caught. Chore time came too soon and we reluctantly crossed the meadow again, carrying a half-dozen small fry strung on a piece of packing string. That evening an indulgent mother served them, crisp and brown. We ate them, tails, fins and bones.

NOW IN AUTUMN

September

Now in late September the apple sweetens and swells upon the bough, the yellow pumpkins glow in the fields of ripening corn and in the fields and barn, animals begin to fill out with their first winter fat. The grains are in the stack and dry in the bins, and the hay is in the mow.

September is a strange and restless month, an in-between month. The crops are planted and cultivated, and man waits for the harvest. The time of great toil is over and there is only the gathering and storing before the winter comes. Yet there is a strange restlessness, too, for there is fear, rooted deep in the past when man and animal feared hunger and cold and the uncertainties that winter brought. Man watches and waits, and saves more than he needs. Animals are abroad day and night, pressing against time to store food or fat for the lean months. The skunk raids the garbage can, the porcupine leaves his accustomed haunts to stuff himself with the apples hidden beneath the orchard grass, and the squirrel fills his storehouse.

Pastures are brown and bare and the stock are given a few extra ears of corn each day. The cutters shock the rustling corn. Clouds of dust trail the drills across the fields after the corn is harvested, putting in the winter wheat. The farmer's wife searches her kitchen garden for a late tomato or a head of cabbage. Tender turnip greens appear on the supper table.

With the first cold rains of fall there is sound of hammer and saw as sagging doors are made secure and the siding on the sheep pen is made tight against the snows. The manure pile back of the barn is hauled to the field that will be in corn next spring and the Canadian thistles are grubbed out of the meadows. Rye and barley are planted for winter cover. Pastures are given a ration of lime and fertilizer to bring them up lush and green in the spring.

Just before the danger of the early frosts, turnips and carrots and late cabbage are taken up and carried to the root cellar, or buried under an insulation of corn stalk, straw, and two feet of earth in the garden. There are skimpy meals for most of two days while the women make sauerkraut. The cabbage is brought in from the garden in baskets, trimmed, and washed. Neighbor women help, taking turns at cutting and packing in ten-gallon earthen jars. The heavy jars are carried to the cellar where in course of time nature's chemistry will work the change that makes sweet, crisp cabbage leaves into the sour, malodorous delicacy.

Spring pullets start laying and some which show no promise are culled out and sent to market. To the joy of the menfolk there's an orgy of fried chicken, sometimes in the middle of the week. Late-bred sows throw litters and there's some trouble keeping the young pigs from chilling during the frosty nights. Horse traders call to pick up the aging animals that will be replaced in the spring by two-year-olds. Per-

haps these will be broken to harness this winter at the sleds, which is safer than an implement if one of them happens to be too spirited.

When the pastures get short the Jersey cow's spring bull calf will be hauled off to the butcher. It won't pay to put grain into it and what little fall grass there is should go to the milking cows.

School opens late in the month and the new teacher finds a room with a family near the schoolhouse. The kids grumble as they force their reluctant feet into unaccustomed shoes, but they are happy at the prospect of seeing old friends again. They trudge off, with their lunch boxes and new copybooks and slates, starched and stiff in their school clothes. Mothers welcome their absence after a summer of having them under their feet all day. A new schedule of after-school chores gets off to a bad start and it will take a deal of training before the woodbox is filled and the chickens fed and watered on time.

When the Rhode Island Reds and the Plymouth Rock roosters are beginning to crow and their legs are thick and long, there'll be chicken suppers at the church and the Ladies Aid Society will have a social to pay for a new aisle carpet. The women serve the chicken and potato salad, the cake and ice cream; some of the men stand in the darkness outside the church door, talking crops and perhaps doing a little surreptitious trading.

The first spelling bee of the season packs the community into the schoolhouse and little Lizzie Perkins, eighth-grade prodigy, spells down Miss Luella Jameson, spinster, who has been the perennial champion since she was in the eighth grade herself. The air becomes heavy with the fumes of the oil lanterns loaned for the occasion. Tired men and women, squeezed into the narrow seats, nod and doze, soothed by the monotones of the spellers around the walls.

October

Then comes October, the brightest and the saddest month of the year. There is a clear cold night and a sharp frost and the next day the trees along the creek in the valley sketch a line of color across the countryside. Mist appears over the far hills. The sere and yellow leaf scurries along in front of the cold winds and the cricket comes in from the field to his snug harbor on the hearth, and a family of mice moves into the attic.

Now is the time to dig the potatoes and pick the apples, for killing frosts are in the offing. The ground under the big walnut tree at the edge of the woods is covered with nuts and the first Saturday the kids will fill burlap sacks and bring them to the house to husk on the chopping block in the barnyard. The shellbark hickory nuts are falling out of their shells and there's a quart or more every morning for the picking. Grandpa brings in two baskets of wild grapes and mysteriously disappears in the cellar to make his own brand of tonic.

And now comes apple-butter making, an event of great importance to the women of the household and one of some complexity. Apple butter must come after the cider is made, for cider is a very necessary ingredient of good apple butter. Sometimes the peel-ing is done by hand with a paring knife, sometimes the family is fortunate to own a mechanical peeler. Great quantities of apples are peeled, quartered, and washed. Then the small boys in the family build a fire under the big copper kettle and the cooking starts. There is endless stirring and tasting. This is a two-day job and before the last of the butter is ladled into earthen jars for storage in the cellar, the whole family is happy that apple butter comes but once a year.

There is the canning, too, mostly the late fruits. A delicate spread, familiar to our grandmothers but almost unknown now, was made in late October from quinces and apples, diced and boiled in sugar in equal amounts of apples, quinces, and sugar. The choice ears of sweet corn, left on the stalk to dry, are tied in threes and fours and hung up in the shed to be out of the way of the rats and mice. There'll be parched corn with butter and salt on winter evenings. Pumpkins are carried to an unheated room under the eaves and will last for pies until well into the winter. The prolific Kiefer pear tree is stripped, the fruit wrapped in newspaper and spread out on the attic floor. These too, will last until after Christmas.

The men have not been idle. Harvest machinery is oiled and painted and stored snugly in the sheds; the hogs and cattle are brought in from the pastures and pens and feed bunks are repaired near the barn. A routine of feeding is started and grain carted off to the elevator to be ground and mixed. The floodgate on the branch is anchored against winter rains and a load of gravel dumped into the mudhole under the barnyard gate. The strawberry plants are covered with a mulch of straw and the windowpane in the kitchen door, broken last spring when the hired hand stuck a ladder through it, is replaced. The nights grow longer and the fire in the kitchen range is kept burning until bedtime.

Now comes Halloween, a season of dread and watching for those who have outside plumbing or gates which can be lifted from their hinges. Bands of small boys, with a sprinkling of tomboys in their midst, roam the countryside, waking the dog in his kennel and the rooster on his perch, and startling Grandpa out of his nap beside the stove. Goblin faces leer at the dark windows and the corn rattles off the window panes, for the kids make the most of their brief freedom from the rules of proper behavior. Halloween night itself is preceded by corn night and cabbage night and tick-tack night, and were it not for parental restraint, the season might stretch on into weeks of guerrilla warfare against the grownups.

There is a husking bee on the barn floor. Cider and baked beans and doughnuts are served and the most bashful swain of all finds the red ear, and blushes as he kisses the prettiest girl. There is a time of courting; buggy rides behind the old white mare with the harvest moon high in the heavens, the echo of a baying hound floating across the purple meadows, and the whippoorwill calling from the hedgerows.

November

October slides into November. A dead snag in the wood lot is felled and the sound of the ax rings out across the silent fields. An old rail pile is buzzed up for the kitchen stove and the woodshed is piled to the roof. The gutters are cleaned when the trees around the house shed their last leaves and the valves in the pumps are opened to forestall a solid freeze. A new grate is ordered for the base burner and the cat is penned in the corncrib overnight to discourage an invasion of field mice driven in by the cold. Straw and leaves are packed around cellar windows.

And now the trees are almost bare and the leaves are ankle deep in the wood lot and the angles of the rail fences are blown full. A haze falls over the sun and the hills are hidden in a smoky mist. The days are warm and nature and man bask in the false promise of Indian summer. Wild geese point their V's southward, high in the heavens, and the smoke rises straight from the chimneys in the frosty mornings. Then one day the clouds bank against the western horizon. The wind comes up and the sun winks out and the cattle, seeking the last grass shoot in the bare meadow, turn their rumps to windward. A cold driving rain, laced with sleet, comes out of the northeast. A mother hen, with a late brood of half-grown chicks, stands dripping under the eaves of the barn and scolds at the unkind ways of nature. Father winces as his bare feet strike the cold floor in the morning, and he tarries not, building the fire in the kitchen stove with great clatter and speed. The kids cover their heads with the extra quilt and dire threats are needed to spring them from their warm nests. Winter is making its first bid.

Then men scan the sky and carry the butchering tools out of the smokehouse. "After this blow it will turn crisp and cold," they say, "and meat will keep." Long before sunup the fires are cracking under the kettles of water and the big barrel is tilted back of the scraping platform. The first fat hog is dragged in from the pen and plunged into the barrel of boiling water. White and steaming, he is hung on the gambrels and the women are given the casings to clean for the sausage. The hams and bacon are carried into the smokehouse, where they are given a brisk rubbing with the mixture of salt and sugar and spices that only Grandfather knows how to mix. There will be fried tenderloin for supper and sausage and hot cakes for breakfast. The womenfolk will make headcheese and mincemeat and there'll be other delicacies of pork and corn meal and perhaps pickled pigs' feet for the Sunday evening cold table.

There will be a skift of snow on a morning, and the men will take their guns from the racks and the dogs will race out across the fields in front, the first to reach the thicket where the quail and the rabbits hide.

There's a red ring around a Thursday on the calendar in the kitchen, Thanksgiving, the farmer's own date for the end of autumn and the beginning of winter. After that come the heavy snows. Work is light. There are the chores for the men and the cooking and the churning and mending for the women.

Poets call the autumn the melancholy season, but to the farmer it is a fulfillment of the promise of the year, a reward for labor done.

THE OLD
OAKEN
BUCKET

HOW dear to this heart are the scenes of my child-
    hood,
When fond recollection presents them to view!
The orchard, the meadow, the deep tangled wild-
    wood,
And every loved spot which my infancy knew!
The wide-spreading pond, and the mill that stood by
    it,
The bridge, and the rock where the cataract fell,
The cot of my father, the dairy-house nigh it,
And e'en the rude bucket which hung in the well—
The old oaken bucket, the iron-bound bucket,
The moss-covered bucket which hung in the well.

That moss-covered vessel I hailed as a treasure,
For often at noon, when returned from the field,
I found it the source of an exquisite pleasure,
The purest and sweetest that nature can yield.
How ardent I seized it, with hands that were glowing,
And quick to the white-pebbled bottom it fell;
Then soon, with the emblem of truth overflowing,
And dripping with coolness, it rose from the well—
The old oaken bucket, the iron-bound bucket,
The moss-covered bucket arose from the well.

How sweet from the green mossy brim to receive it,
As poised on the curb it inclined to my lips!
Not a full blushing goblet would tempt me to leave it,
The brightest that beauty or revelry sips.
And now, far removed from the loved habitation,
The tear of regret will intrusively swell,
As fancy reverts to my father's plantation,
And sighs for the bucket that hangs in the well—
The old oaken bucket, the iron-bound bucket,
The moss-covered bucket that hangs in the well!

                  —Samuel Woodworth

PENNSYLVANIA BARNS

If there is any doubt about who wore the pants on early American farms, a look at the old-time barns will quiet the doubt. Into the barn went the bulk of the family savings and the profits from the cattle and grain. The house might be a box with partitions and the spring a weary trip with a bucket, but the barn had to be the newest, the biggest, and the handiest of all barns in the countryside. Anything was good enough for the women; the house, for the men, was only a place to eat and sleep. The barn was for the cattle and the crops, and only the best would do.

Barns have always been an avenue of self-expression for the farmer. They have satisfied his yearning for beauty and his desire to project himself into the material things around him. The best American barns combine a harmonious blending of beauty and utility found nowhere else in the world of rural building design. Like every form of art, barn architecture grew; it did not spring full-blown from the brain of some carpenter, but, little by little, evolved from simple beginnings to the masterpieces which still stand as monuments to the creative ability of unlettered country craftsmen.

The first barns were built of logs and were small because the farms were small. As more land was cleared, the barns grew in size, and as wealth accumulated, more money went into making the barn solid, enduring, and a thing of beauty. Craftsmen through the years perfected their skills and designs.

It was in the Pennsylvania Dutch area, in Lancaster, York, and surrounding counties, that barn building flowered, bursting into full bloom during the first half of the nineteenth century. Incidentally, this was one of the rare areas where the houses kept pace with the barns in design and sturdiness. The thrifty Dutch pioneers liked the creature comforts and they were sociable. They built homes to accommodate a host of relatives and friends for their famous Sunday dinners. The pioneer Pennsylvania farmer dug a cave out of a hillside and shored up the opening with logs. In the dark interior were stalls for his cow and his horse, and possibly a small storage bin for grain. His straw and hay he stacked outside. A split rail fence enclosed a small barnyard.

As he cleared more land and his livestock increased he used the logs from his clearing to build a larger and more pretentious structure. The roof was covered with hand-split shingles and the doors were planks sawed by an "up and down sawmill." The hinges for the doors were made of strap iron hammered out by the local smithy. If the farmer were a sensitive man he used hinges and latches of forged iron in decorative shapes. There was a mow overhead for hay and a central driveway where he stored his cart. The cows and horses had separate stalls on either side of the driveway.

On his third round of barn building, the Pennsylvania farmer bethought himself of a permanent structure, one of brick or stone and good, stout timbers that would last out his life and the lives of his grandchildren. He used the materials native to the district, limestone and kiln-dried brick, and oak, walnut, and chestnut. He hired experienced stone masons and carpenters, but when the timbers were joined, his neighbors came in for a barn raising. The frame of the barn went up in a day, and was followed with feasting.

About the middle of the nineteenth century a standard design had developed. Variations from then to the present were either elaborations or adornment. Size varied to fit the needs of the farm, and there were modifications to conform to the lay of the barn lot or the whims of the owner. Serving as they did the same type of general farming, housing the same kind of livestock, and storing the same kind of grain and feed, these modifications were minor.

The typical barn was set against a slope, which provided a natural ramp for entry into the driveway on the second level. This is the "bank" barn, common everywhere. The ground level accommodated the horses and livestock. There were from one to several rows of stalls, pens, a feed room, and perhaps a harness room. This level was entered only at one end, the other being against the ramp or hillside. There was an overhang from the second level to protect both man and beast from inclement weather. There were passageways among the stalls and pens; hay was dropped from the mow directly to the stables through a door or chute. Many of the later barns had root cellars which extended beyond the stalls into the hillside. The side driveway between the mows on the second floor was used as a threshing floor and to store machinery, which was taken out when the granaries and mows were being filled. The potato and turnip cellars were sometimes filled from a trap door in the floor of this level. Large doors, which extended from the ground to the eaves, could be opened to give free access to any part of the threshing floor.

Timbers, up to a foot square, were hand-hewn, mortised, and fastened together with stout pegs. The walls of the stables were of stone, rarely of brick, and extended above ground level on all sides. These masonry walls were sometimes carried upward on the ends on the famous stone and brick end barns. If there were a plentiful supply of stone on the farm, or if a man wanted to build for the ages, he constructed his barn entirely of stone, and labored to contrive timbering of the same durability. The original roofs were usually split shingles, but being the most perishable part of the structure, most of them have been replaced by metal, slate, or fabricated shingles.

Refinement and adornment reflected the personality of the owner or the builder. There were elegant cupolas, which served both as ventilators and as decoration; windows with scrollwork to match those on the dwelling; arched doorways, and fancy designs in brick and stone; paint, usually red, often with a white trim; and hex marks, to ward off bad luck to man and animal and keep away the ever-present threat of fire.

When the hex marks were first placed on barns, they were true symbols of the owner's belief in the supernatural, and a genuine effort to placate the forces of evil, especially witches. Later, they appeared on

many barns because the owner thought they added a pleasant touch. To many people, no Pennsylvania barn would be authentic without a hex mark.

The brick end barn is the rarest of all types of Pennsylvania barns and is generally regarded as the masterwork of the early barn builder. Virtually all of them are found in the rich farming region of southeastern Pennsylvania; there are a few across the line in Maryland. Most of them were built by the Amish and Mennonite descendants of German and Swiss emigrants.

They were notable for the geometric designs built into the brick work of the two ends and were usually larger than the average barn, and cost a small fortune for those days. Few have been built since the mid-nineteenth century.

The grilled designs built into the brick work served a double purpose—they are highly decorative, and they provide light and ventilation. The functional purpose of the designs are so well disguised by their good taste and proportion they seem to be there for their own sake and do not intrude their practical purpose upon the barn's appearance.

The designs were formed by laying the brick in such a way that openings the size of the end of a single brick formed the pattern. There is no evidence that the open work resulted in structural weakness. Some brick end barns 150 years old show no signs of sagging or weakness in or near the designs. A few rare builders incorporated designs in stone end barns, the designs being in brick set in the stone.

By the middle of the nineteenth century barn architecture and design had been brought to a high state of refinement. Farm magazines devoted pages to comment on barns, and there were barn designers and experts in every community. One of the best farm magazines of the period, the *Pennsylvania Cultivator*, published a complete description of what was known as the Switzer barn, a design which closely followed the typical layout of the period. The description of the barn is prefaced by a bit of boasting, easily forgiven when one understands the pride with which Pennsylvanians viewed their fine structures. Here are the *Cultivator*'s own words:

However much before us in Agricultural Improvements generally, the Farmers of the States North and East of us may perhaps be, we claim for Pennsylvania the distinction of being the only State in the Union in which the building of good, substantial, convenient and spacious BARNS is understood and practiced. Properly speaking, in other States, *they have no barns*—they don't know what a real good barn is—a stable or collection of stables, sheds and out-houses being their makeshift substitutes for them. This is a little singular, but it is nevertheless true. A journey through New York and New England, will confirm our remarks. There is hardly a real barn to be seen. Evidences of plenty there are, and of excellent farming. You see good houses, beautiful shubbery, admirable fences, clean and smooth fields, splendid cattle, plenty of *hay* and *grain stacks*—and lots of sheds and stables; but *no barns*. They will have to come into Pennsylvania, and take pattern from some of our mighty bank-barns, looming out in the horizon like double-decked men-of-war beside sloops, or like churches beside log huts. As in our war vessels, so in our barns also, we have both *single* and *double-deckers*, the latter being tremendous affairs, that would make our eastern brethren open their eyes in astonishment. Below

we present the floor plan of one of the *singledeckers*—a most superb new Bank Barn, called a "Switzer" barn, which was recently erected upon the farm of August O. Heister, Esq., on the Susquehanna, about three miles above Harrisburg. The engraving was made by Lowe, of Philadelphia, from a Daguerreotype by Barnitz, of Harrisburg.

Dimensions.—We expected to obtain from the architect of this barn, Mr. Isaac Updergrove, a specification of its dimensions, etc., but have not received it, so we must do for the present with a brief and less detailed description. It is one of the best and most convenient barns on the Switzer plan, in this vicinity. It is about one hundred feet in length, by about sixty feet in width, and proportionately high. It is built on a small hill side, so that the front or barn floor is on a level with the ground; while the hill is dug away and the stables placed beneath. The rear of this stabling is likewise on a level with the ground, though some ten feet below the front level. The cut presents this rear view only. As will be perceived, the barn has an *overshoot* of seven feet, the stone wall being brought out flush the entire width, which is an improvement. The walls are eighteen inches thick, and rise ten feet up to the front level.

The cost of this barn was about $1,500. It is weatherboarded on the outside—painted white—furnished with ventilators, lightning rods, and every improvement.

This, briefly, is the description of one of the best kind of Pennsylvania barns, and one of the best of the kind. We shall give other plans, from time to time.

91

THE BATH

Saturday night rolls 'round inevitably for the small fry, and with it the weekly ordeal of the bath in the washtub in front of the kitchen stove. The cold nips at the bare skin in the drafty kitchen, but once you are under the water you have a most wonderful feeling of animal comfort and you don't want to get out, dripping and twice as cold. The carrying and heating of water is a chore too, and sometimes if the kid is small and not very dirty, a grownup feels justified in using the same bath water. Any way you take it, the Saturday night bath in an unplumbered farmhouse is no joke and after it's over you have a special feeling of having accomplished something. It's a good thing this rugged old custom is dying out, thanks to hot and cold running water and a regular bathtub.

DANDELION GREENS

Along with sulphur and molasses, dandelion greens were thought to be a sovereign remedy for what ailed folks in the spring. They cleared up the phlegms left in the system by the long winter diet of salt pork and beans and compensated for the thickening of the blood which occurred during the cold months. Folks hungered for greens like the farm animals yearned for the first tender grass. The young plants which came up in sheltered spots in early April were regarded as the best. They were cooked with a piece of sowbelly or a ham hock and served with vinegar and butter. It was quite a job to gather and clean the greens. This usually fell to Grandma, who had the necessary patience.

93

THEY SET A GOOD TABLE

The other day I read an article telling how to get children to eat. It made me wonder. As I remember things back in Tennessee in the early teens of this century, the big worry was to keep the kids *from* eating. Was the food better? Was it the ingredients, or the cooking?

I can remember, for instance, when breakfast was a meal and not just a hurdle on the way to the 7:49. Fully dressed and ready to start the day, the whole family sat down together. Papa asked the blessing. It was short, because Papa said the Lord meant hot food to be eaten hot.

We had fruit to begin with. Not orange juice. Orange juice came with castor oil. We had black-berries or dewberries or strawberries. The berries were washed and sugared the night before and by morning there were tiny crusts of sugar crystals clinging around the edges of the top layer. With the fruit there was cream that flowed lazily out of the blue willow pitcher.

In full summer we had "mushmelons" and it was a long time before I heard they were called canta-loupes. Mama always had Mattie dust them with sugar but that was a secret from Papa. "Salt," he would say, waving the pink hand-painted shaker, "salt and pepper is all a melon needs when I pick it out." And Mama said, "Yes, dear, you always pick good melons." Mama explained to us girls, "What a man doesn't know won't hurt him."

In the winter we might have prunes. That sounds boarding-housey but Mattie stewed them way down with lemon juice and sugar. The yellow cream that curled through the amber juice like the stripes in an agate helped, too.

Then came oatmeal, cooked all night in the fireless cooker. And after that came the real breakfast. Pinky brown slices of cured ham that almost floated in red-eye gravy. And little crisp biscuits, made with sour milk and soda. Mama wouldn't put up with thick biscuit with a mattress in the middle, nor with baking-powder biscuit.

Of course we had grits with the ham, and the gravy from the platter was spooned onto them. The little kids were allowed to put open biscuits into the platter to pick up the last of the gravy, but you couldn't do that after you were six years old.

Sometimes there was bacon with a mound of soft scrambled eggs, and in winter there would be coun-try sausage made of lean meat and seasoned with sage and red pepper. That pepper never saw a can. It would have melted a can. It was the ground-up pods of long-nosed red peppers, home-grown and dried, and it made all other sausage taste sissy.

I guess that's about all we had for breakfast, but dinner was at 12 o'clock noon. Everybody ate at home, and there was a noonday hush over the whole town. Probably over all middle Tennessee.

For just an ordinary day we might have round

steak. It was cut thin and had flour beaten into it with the edge of a cracked saucer. Mattie got the grease sizzling hot in the heavy iron skillets and then trailed the limp floury slabs into it. When the meat was brown on both sides she put tops on the skillets and let it cook ten minutes or so. Next she made the gravy. All the fried crackling bits that stuck to the bottom of the skillet floated up into the rich milk and flour, and the whole thing got an extra dousing of salt and pepper. It was cooked till it made a sulky "plop, plop" sound.

There would be mashed potatoes as background for the gravy. In summer there would be black-eyed peas cooked with salt pork and a pod of red pepper. Okra, of course. And I mean just okra. Not some gosh-awful combination concocted to shame a noble vegetable. Little pods of okra cooked quickly in boiling salted water, served with butter, need nothing but an open mind and an open mouth. There was always a platter of sliced tomatoes in the summer. Big red slices, the color of Christmas. And fried corn: corn cut from the cob and fried in bacon drippings till a brown crust formed over the bottom of the pan. Cream and lots of salt and pepper were added, too.

We had all kinds of desserts. But the thing I remember best was a kind of calendar of cobblers. First came the dewberries, then the blackberries; then there was a triumphant pause for strawberry shortcake. Then came the peach cobblers.

You could smell a peach cobbler all through dinner, and when Mattie opened the oven door to take it out you had to swallow quick because that aroma would make the taste buds of a mummy burst into bloom. Cobblers came to the table in long black pans and were put in front of Mama on two asbestos mats, while the juice bubbled and oozed through the fancy gashes cut like fern fronds in the brown crust.

Well, that was dinner. After that we tore back to school. Maybe we worked off the excess calories that way. Surely none of us was ever fat.

And after school we were starved. We could always have tea cakes, big thin cookies that spilled sugar off the top. Mattie made them by the thousands. Then there was a little barrel of gingersnaps. They were good if you dunked them in milk and ate them quickly with the crispness going but not quite gone.

Supper came about half past five. It was mostly dinner over again. Warmed up, I mean. There would be one new dish added. It might be baked macaroni and cheese. Sharp, crumbly rattrap cheese covered the top of the big black pan and ran down through the delicate custard. It came to the table hissing and bubbling and just right.

Hash, too, was a supper dish. Pure hash, undefiled, has nothing in it but beef, potatoes, onions and gravy. Hash is an accomplishment, not a catchall.

Another supper dish was chicken pie. It had no discernible relationship with the individual casserole, one biscuit, one teaspoon of chicken and a cup of tired green peas, that is served under that name in Tea Shoppes. Our chicken pie was made from two hens cut up and cooked till the meat was falling from the bones. Then it was covered with gravy and chopped hard-boiled eggs. In the middle of the pan went a teacup upside down. Over all this went a short, thin, biscuit-dough crust. The cup, by some mysterious process, gathered the gravy under it so that the crust was never soggy. When Papa cut through the crust he would lift the edge of the cup and a great gush of rich gravy was released just at the right moment.

Of course we always had ham—boiled ham, never baked. Our hams came from the country. A good one was at least three years old and weighed around 17 pounds.

You first soaked it overnight in warm water. Then you put it in a washboiler surrounded by sweet-smelling hay (don't ask me why) and covered it with water, tossing in a handful of mixed spices, three or four little red-pepper pods, some brown sugar and molasses. Then you let it boil on the back of the stove till you could stick a fork to the bone. It was cooled in its own juice. When the ham was cold, it was sliced with a knife as sharp as a razor. It was supposed to last for a long time but it never did.

No, it wasn't any trouble to get us to eat. And what we had was just regular fare. I know, because I grew up in the golden age of "spend the night." Breakfast was the same at all my friends' homes.

I think the food was better then. And it wasn't the ingredients. It seems to me that Mama and Mattie had a skill, accumulated by generations of good cooks, that lots of people lack now, and a great pride in "setting a good table."

APPLE CIDER

Just before the first frost, we picked the choice apples and stored them in barrels in the cellar; then we gathered the windfalls and loaded them into the box bed of our farm wagon for the annual trip to the cider mill. My brother and I needed no prodding on this job. The Winesaps, Pippins, Northern Spies, Jonathans, Russets, and Rambos, and even the lowly Ben Davis, a good keeper but without sweetness, were thrown together into the wagon. Each added its delicate flavor to the blend. If an extra tang was wanted, a couple of bushels of crab apples were included. It was thought that late apples made the best cider; and they should be fully ripe, juicy and not "mealy." As we loaded the apples, we threw out the mushy ones.

As we jolted along the dusty road in the warm autumn sun the smell of apples lifted around us. If your nose was sharp you could pick out the peculiar perfume-like odor of the Delicious and the musky tang of the Russet. The apple smell clung to our clothes and bodies.

At the cider mill the wagon pulled up at the end of the waiting line of loaded wagons, the horses stomping and switching flies. There, the smell of fresh apples was enhanced by the fermenting pomace heap behind the mill. We climbed down and joined the other small boys around the free barrel, which sat in the shade near the press. There was a tin cup there, but we shunned this, for we had brought along our own supply of rye straws. Inserted in the bunghole, a straw was our preferred method of bringing cider to lip. It came up in just the right volume so that each sip could be rolled around the tongue and the full flavor enjoyed. When our bellies got tight we had to stop, but cider tasted good even after you were full. Of course, we had what grandfather called the "backhouse two-step" that evening, but it was worth it.

It was a long wait through the summer until the fall apples ripened, and one year my brother and I jumped the gun. We had a tree of early Yellow Transparent and another of a variety of small red apple we called the Strawberry. We gathered up the windfalls under the two trees, quartered the apples, and ground them in the sausage grinder. After we had two or three tubs of pulp we pressed out the juice in the sausage press. The press lacked the necessary high pressure, and we sprung the handle, but working most of the afternoon we turned out five gallons of what we regarded as excellent juice. Grandpa smacked his lips over it too, but he took a dim view of the sprung handle and he showed us that we had squeezed only about half the juice out of the apples. "We'll get a regular cider press for you next year," he said.

The purpose of making cider in the old days was not primarily to supply a delightful beverage; cider was made then to supply the farm vinegar. Farmers have always found it difficult to keep sweet cider for any great length of time—it's just too darned good to drink. So those who wanted both vinegar and a drink made two barrels. The drinking cider was rolled into the cellar, a spigot hammered into one end, and a tin cup was hung on a convenient nail. Then the family went on an apple juice spree.

The barrel reserved for vinegar was rolled to the sunny side of the kitchen and there it remained until nature had taken her course with it. Then it was spigoted, set up on a platform, and referred to daily.

As soon as cider is in the barrel, a subtle change begins—it gradually loses its delicate flavor, some of the sugar changing to starch, and it starts to ferment or "work." By the next morning, in warm weather, there will be a thin layer of bubbles on the top—the bacteria have started to multiply and fermentation will progress rapidly. The head increases and the taste takes on a snap and zing which pleasantly tickles the tongue. After a week, the alcoholic content will go to 6 per cent; sweetened apple cider will go to 11 per cent alcohol.

Then one must take care, for this is "hard" cider. Small boys should be forbidden its comforts when it reaches the hard stage. The temperance societies warn that here we have an alcoholic beverage.

A hard cider jag is as authentic as one achieved on champagne or corn squeezin's. Hard cider stimulated many a country brawl in the old days, and was the inspiration which prompted many a tall tale. One Pennsylvania citizen, whose equipment on a fishing excursion included a jug of his best, swore to the end of his days that he had caught a mermaid in the Allegheny River. He reported giving her a swig from his jug, and throwing her back into the river.

As the alcoholic content reaches its maximum, another change sets in. The hard cider starts to sour, and it gets sourer and sourer. A stringy mass forms, composed of vinegar yeast, which is known as the "mother." Cider vinegar can be kept for a year or so if tightly stoppered; otherwise it loses its strength.

Cider is a profitable by-product for the fruit grower, for it uses culls and windfalls, which, like the cow's hide to the meat packer, is often the margin of profit. The fruit juice vitamin fad boosted cider sales, for cider is the cheapest of all commercial juices, and stands up favorably with citrus, berry, and grape.

Cider is made today in much the same way as it has always been made—apples are reduced to a pulp and the juice squeezed out. In the old days farmers with small orchards had hand presses of their own, but the community mill got the bulk of the crop.

The hand presses were simple—a grinder to chew up the apples and a press operated by a screw, both mounted on a wooden stand. The large presses had greater capacity, for water or steam power were substituted for hand power. The chief drawback of the small hand press is that it will not exhaust the pulp of all its juices. The first juice from a run is the free juice released as the apples are ground. This has no "body." As the pressure increases the juice gets heavier and more flavorful.

Cider made from a mixture of apples is better than that made from a single variety. For example, the juice from the Grimes Golden is almost colorless, and bland; from the Delicious very sweet.

At a power cider mill the apples are scooped into a hopper and from there are carried by a chain or belt conveyor to the grinder or chopper. The result: mass of juice and pulp is about the consistency of thick applesauce. It includes skins, cores, seeds, and an occasional worm. A decayed spot in an apple discolors the cider and damages the flavor. The same can be said of a worm. Though spots can be cut out and the good part of the apple used, it is not always possible to detect a hidden worm. Shakespeare knew that, for he speaks of "a goodly apple, rotten at the core." In the old days, before we became germ conscious, the apples were not washed. Today the apples are thoroughly cleaned under high-pressure water, which also eliminates most of the danger from residual sprays.

From the chopper the pulp falls into a bin directly above the press to await the pressing operation. A slatted wooden board is placed on the platform of the press, and a frame, with sides several inches high, set on the board. Then a cloth, made of burlap or similar material, is laid over the frame and the pulp is allowed to run out until the frame is heaping full. The cloth is folded over the pulp, corner-wise. Then the frame is lifted off, another slat board is placed over the first layer of pulp, followed by the frame and another cloth. The capacity of a hand press is 6 to 8 layers; that of a power press, 8 to 20 layers. This stack of prepared pulp is called a "cheese." The press is then set in operation, squeezing the juice out between the slatted boards and through the cloth. The juice runs into a trough at the base and thence into a barrel or tank. It may pass first through a filter or clarifier.

A large hydraulic press will turn out 300 gallons at a pressing. A hand press, using a cheese from 6 to 8 layers, will turn out about 12 gallons at a pressing of from 4 to 5 bushels of apples. A hydraulic press will get 16 gallons of juice from the same apples.

On the larger presses the pressure may go as high as 22 tons, applied from the bottom. About 8 tons pressure, applied from the top, is the limit of a hand press. A heavy press will get up to 75 per cent of the juice out of an apple, which is 86 per cent water.

After the cheese is devoid of its juices, the pomace, or "pummies" as the old-timers called them, are shaken out of the cloth. Today pomace is used as cow or hog feed, but formerly it was dumped behind the mill and was the source of a pungent, distinguished odor which covered the neighborhood. It is a legend that in one of these heaps of pomace, a "sport" seedling, later to produce the first Delicious apple, grew up.

SWEETS

Next to bread and salt there was no item of food more sought for in the old days than sweets, and too often harder to come by. Cane sugar from Cuba and the South was plentiful in the East, but in the wilderness, cut off from a trading post, the settler had but one source, the wild bee. The location of a bee tree was a carefully guarded secret, guarded until fall when it was ripe and full of honey for the Thanksgiving cake and the Christmas pudding.

New England farmers soon learned to make sugar and syrup from the maple trees and this industry became a major colonial enterprise. The "boughten" sugar of the early Midwest was the golden brown product of New England farms.

In the South first, and later spreading to the North, the settlers learned about sorghum from the Indians. Sorghum is not as sweet as cane or maple, or even honey, and it has a twang not relished by all. However, it is a popular syrup for corn bread and flapjacks in the South to this day.

The sorghum press, in the early days, was often the only mechanical gadget in the community. Almost every farm grew a patch of sorghum and no family felt secure about the year ahead unless the sorghum jugs were full.

Maple, sorghum, and cane syrups are easy to make —boil the juice in a flat pan until syrupy. If you want sugar, boil longer. However, don't try to make sorghum sugar. It's so black and bitter and unsweet that even a bear, who is a sucker for sweets, won't eat it.

99

OF HORSES AND HARNESS

When the rubber-tired tractor replaced the horse something wonderful went out of farming. The relationship between a farmer and his horse cannot be understood except by those who have worked with the noble animal, day after day, year after year, and observed his single-minded devotion to his master, his untiring willingness to work and sweat at his master's bidding. He asked nothing in return but feed and water, the better to do the day's work asked of him.

Neither the master nor the animal was demonstrative. The man gave the horse a slap on his rump as he took off the harness and fed him after a day's work. The horse nuzzled his master as they rested in the shade at the end of a long corn row.

The farm horse was a different creature from the fine-boned, high-mettled animal of today's race tracks, the only equine which the vast majority of modern Americans know about. Many farmers kept a fast trotter for show or for the journey to town or church on Sunday; and every Kentucky tobacco grower had a mare or two that boasted bloodlines capable of "nicking" well with Domino or Ben Brush, whose produce might someday turn up in the winner's circle at Churchill Downs or Saratoga. But these were not farm horses.

Most of the animals which furnished the motive power for wagon and plow were grades. That is, they were not purebred. Still they were far from the swaybacked, spavined critters the term plow horse calls to mind today. The teammates of the big hitches were huge, statuesque animals whose powerful hearts pumped blood descended from the armor-clad chargers of the medieval knights. Weighing often a ton or more, they were sired by big gray or black Percheron stallions brought here originally from the provinces of France. Some came from the loins of the powerfully muscled sorrel Belgians, some from the chunky English Suffolks, a few from the towering black Shires with their white-feathered pasterns; still others from the flashy, blazed-faced Clydesdales, the breed which is today the sole remaining symbol of the draft horse in America. These are the big-footed, high-stepping horses we still see on a rare day on our city streets in the chrome-studded harness of an Anheuser-Busch wagon.

Harness? Harness was almost as important as the horse. To harness a horse was an everyday chore; yet it represented a skill which is now lost. The modern tractor jockey who tried to switch to horses would have a sweat-lathered, sore-shouldered team before his plow had turned a half-acre.

A set of harness was a thing of many parts. There were the hames, the collar, the traces, the crupper, and the tongue chains; there were breeching, the collar pads, the bellyband, the reins, and the bit; there were the blinders and the neck strap and the tugs. These are the parts of a harness once familiar to every farmer, but now represented by unknown words, for the art of harness making and even the art of harnessing a horse are passing into history.

A set of harness was wonderfully designed to enable the horse to pull a plow or a wagon or a carriage with the least effort and the maximum efficiency. The harness was made of stout cowhide, riveted and sewn together, and of great durability and strength. The harnessmaker was a respected artisan who often tanned his own leather and fashioned the metal parts on his own forge. The village blacksmith was also a harnessmaker of sorts, and was called upon to do most of the repairing and replacement.

The harness for a work horse was heavy and cumbersome, and to get it on the horse, and off, and hung in the proper order on a peg back of his stall, was no small trick.

To keep a horse in top shape required personal attention, almost as much attention as the farmer gave his children. To work a horse with a pebble in his hoof was to risk laying him up for days, if not permanently. To put him away with a full ration of grain before cooling him out properly was to ship him to slaughter with a case of founder. And the lack of a horse could bring disaster, even the loss of a kingdom.

Undoubtedly this interdependence of horse and man was one of the factors that contributed to making farming a unique activity. And it added to our vocabulary the term "horsesense," a term still used to describe the intellectual capacity of a man well able to take care of himself, his affairs, and his family.

WINTER PAUSE

Some farmers would have you believe that farming is unremitted toil from one year end to the next. Be not taken in by this gentle conceit, for after the sweat and heat of harvest comes winter, a time of ease and sleep for the farmer. He does his morning and evening chores, and an odd job now and then, but when the bad days come and the wind howls in the chimney, he snoozes with his feet in the oven, and the newest kitten purring in his lap.

And well he might take his ease, and well might his conscience be untroubled if he has been a wise farmer and prepared against the season. His stock will be safe and snug, the granary full, and the hams hung in rows in the smokehouse. But if he is not prepared, like the foolish virgin he will pay for his carelessness and his indolence. As he nods by the fire the dumb little field mice will be burrowing beneath the snow to girdle his young apple trees and the disc and the planter he left in the field will be deep with red rust when the snow goes off in the spring.

His good wife may prod him out of his warm corner to buzz up a pile of old fence rails for the kitchen stove, or he may join hands with a neighbor to cull the wood lot for good trees to sled to the mill.

A mild day may prompt him to repair the floodgate where the branch leaves his farm, preparing against the time when the spring freshets will swell the gentle stream to a roaring torrent.

When the country roads glaze over with hard-packed snow he may be tempted to repair the broken runner on the sleigh his grandfather was so proud of when he bought it in the city more than fifty years ago. He will make the easy drive to his neighbor, the sound of the bells bringing the womenfolk to the windows. But when the frost nips his nose and his ears he grows impatient with the old mare, and makes a mental note that the new coupe in the shed may not be as quaint as a sleigh with a hand-painted sunset in oil, but it comes with a heater.

He eats big meals and his wife indulges him with the vittles he likes best. He loiters at the table, remembering how in planting and harvest he ate and ran. He may become a problem to her, underfeet the better part of the day, and by the time the back of winter is broken, along about Washington's Birthday, he will be happy to start the spring plowing.

But if you are not farm born, don't be taken in by him. Farming is a snap in winter.

THE DAY'S WORK

When Adam was banished from the Garden of Eden, God put him to work on a farm, condemning him to a life of toil for his daily bread. Like all farmers, Adam became horny-handed and stooped, and no doubt was troubled with rheumatics and an aching back. In time, some men escaped to the trades and the crafts, and some even found devious ways of making a living by not working at all. But farmers have always toiled, made little money, and their lot was not envied. ¶ Farming was once an endless round of endless tasks, and, until mechanized power took over less then a generation ago, the farmer worked from sunup to sundown, and often during the planting and harvesting he worked into the night. ¶ There were two kinds of labor on a farm—work and chores. Chores were work too, but more time-consuming than tiring. They came at dawn and they rounded out the day. Work was planting and plowing and harvesting and making hay. It took sweat and muscle and a constitution durable enough to keep it up day after day. Most chores were easy; boys and women could do them, the boys until they were old enough to handle a team, and the women always when the men were busy. Chores and work ran into each other and overlapped. Some, like mending fence, were as hard as work, and for men only. ¶ The women might help the men, but few men helped the women. Preparing meals, housekeeping, washing, cooking, and canning were work tasks for the women. They had chores too, mending, making soap, gathering the eggs, weeding the garden. They too were endless. ¶ But the rewards were there, and ample—ample enough to keep the farm family happy, mainly because there was no time to be unhappy. Each day something was attempted, something accomplished. A great reward was rest after toil. How sweet was this rest after a day in the fields, a bounteous supper, and the deep featherbed in the room under the eaves.

APPLE BUTTER

The good farm housewife spurns boughten apple butter as an inferior product and prefers to make her own. Apple butter making is an event on the farm, approached with elaborate preparations, something like a family reunion or a wedding.

There's a great deal more to making apple butter than the cookbooks will tell you. Theirs is a dry mathematical formula, and while butter of a sort can be made by following the recipes, the superior product takes a know-how which cannot be bound into the pages of a book.

Here's the way that Nora Weaver, of Belle Hollow, Tennessee, goes about making her famous apple butter. Mrs. Weaver, called Aunt Nora by all the

the barrel and Aunt Nora draws off a bucketful of the fragrant juice. She has already set up the copper kettle in the yard and has a brisk fire going under it. The kettle must be copper. This is very important. An iron kettle will not do, for the apples will dissolve off the iron and the butter will taste of it. The copper kettle should be first washed with salt and vinegar.

The kettle is filled with cider and the boiling begins. The cider is boiled down to about half its volume, or until it is about the consistency of thin molasses. This is set aside in a cool place until the next day. No experienced apple butter maker would think of telescoping the delicate operations of butter making into one day.

While the cider is boiling, being stirred constantly by Aunt Nora's youngest son, Andrew Jackson Weaver, Aunt Nora and some of the neighbor women are peeling and quartering the apples. Tart or sour apples, or what are known as "cooking" apples, are best because a sweet apple will not cook up. The cores are taken out cleanly. Fallen apples are just as good for butter as choice fruit provided all the damaged parts are cut away.

After the required amount of apples are prepared (a bushel of apples will make about two gallons of butter) and the cider and spices are on hand, the cooking begins. This is usually started the next morning, early.

The apples are dumped into the kettle with just enough water to start the cooking. Soon after they start to bubble and steam a small boy is set on a stool within range of the kettle, a long wooden paddle is placed in his hands, and stirring never stops until the butter is finished. A moment's hesitation may result in a scorched taste to the butter.

The quartered apples will cook down considerably. To keep the kettle full, Aunt Nora has a reserve of big pots (enamelware and copper, that is) of apples on the kitchen stove, cooking to the applesauce stage. These are added to keep the kettle full.

After the apples are cooked to the appearance and consistency of ordinary applesauce the boiled-down cider is added, and then the sugar. A little less than half as much cider as apples is added. If you have four gallons of apples you add two gallons of cider. The amount of sugar (granulated of course) depends on how sweet you want the butter. For ordinary tastes four cups of sugar is added to every gallon of butter, but if you have a sweet tooth you add more.

children in the community, begins on her husband, Ben. On a fall morning, just before the first frost, Ben hitches the team to a bed wagon and with all the kids he can gather up in the neighborhood, drives to the orchard, stopping under each tree. The fallen apples are loaded into the wagon and the kids and Mr. Weaver ride over to the Belle Hollow cider press. The apples are crushed and pressed, and after Mr. Adams, the cider press man, has taken out his toll, the barrel of cider is hauled back to the farm. All the kids, of course, are so full of cider you could crack a tick on their tight bellies.

The barrel is rolled up to the kitchen door and set up on a couple of sawhorses. A spigot is driven into

At the same time the sugar is added the spices go in. Here personal preference is the guide. Most people like cinnamon, so ground cinnamon is added to taste. Aunt Nora's family likes about a teaspoonful to the gallon. Cloves, nutmeg, and ginger can be added also if you like those things. The best way to find out how much sugar and spices to add is to dip out a spoonful, spread it around on a saucer to cool, and then taste it. Aunt Nora spends a lot of time tasting, for as the butter cooks down it changes in taste when the moisture evaporates. When it suits her taste (or perhaps when Andrew says, "Gee, that's good") it is time to stop adding sugar and spice.

After the desired flavor has been achieved, keep on boiling it. It will by this time have reached the color of good strong coffee without cream. From here on it is a matter of getting it to the preferred thickness. will be when it is placed on the table. Some like it stiff, so that when it is dropped from the spoon it remains in a little pointed mound; some like it "runny," so that it can be poured. This is how it's preferred for hot biscuits. It makes no difference, it's all apple butter.

After it has reached the point where everybody is satisfied, the kettle is set off the fire for canning.

Standing on a bench near the kettle is a platoon of boiled-out jars made ready to receive the butter. If you are a dyed-in-the-wool apple butter maker you will be satisfied with nothing less than "crock" jars, each holding a quart, half-gallon, or even a gallon. These jars are hard to find nowadays, but are thought to be just the thing for apple butter, keeping the light from the contents and having some mysterious virtue of adding a supreme touch of flavor. The hot butter is ladeled into the jars and a tin cap placed over the top and sealing wax poured around the edge. Don't let the butter cool in the kettle for it may taste of copper.

Fortunately you never come out even and there'll be a part of a crock left over. This is intentional, for the kids would have been reluctant to help at all if they hadn't been sure of this reward. The odd butter goes into a dish and at suppertime is flanked by a plate of golden brown biscuits and a slab of cow butter.

Some years Aunt Nora has made as high as twenty-five gallons of apple butter, although the average yearly consumption of the Weaver family is about twelve gallons. The extra jars are just in case the apple crop fails the next year.

GOOSE DOWN

In the spring, a few more feathers than usual blowing about the barnyard indicated that it was time to pick the ducks and geese. They were penned up for the night so that the feathers would be dry for the picking. Sometimes a round robin was organized, neighbors helping each other. The picking was done in the shelter of an outbuilding where the air was quiet. The feathers were stuffed into an old bed tick and stored. When the plucked bird was released it honked loudly, wiggled its tail, and retreated to the shade of a barnyard tree where it spent the day muttering profane comments on the strange ways of humans. Sometimes, for baby pillows and pillows for the best bed, the down was separated from the coarser feathers. In two or three years the flock produced enough feathers for a feather bed and bolster.

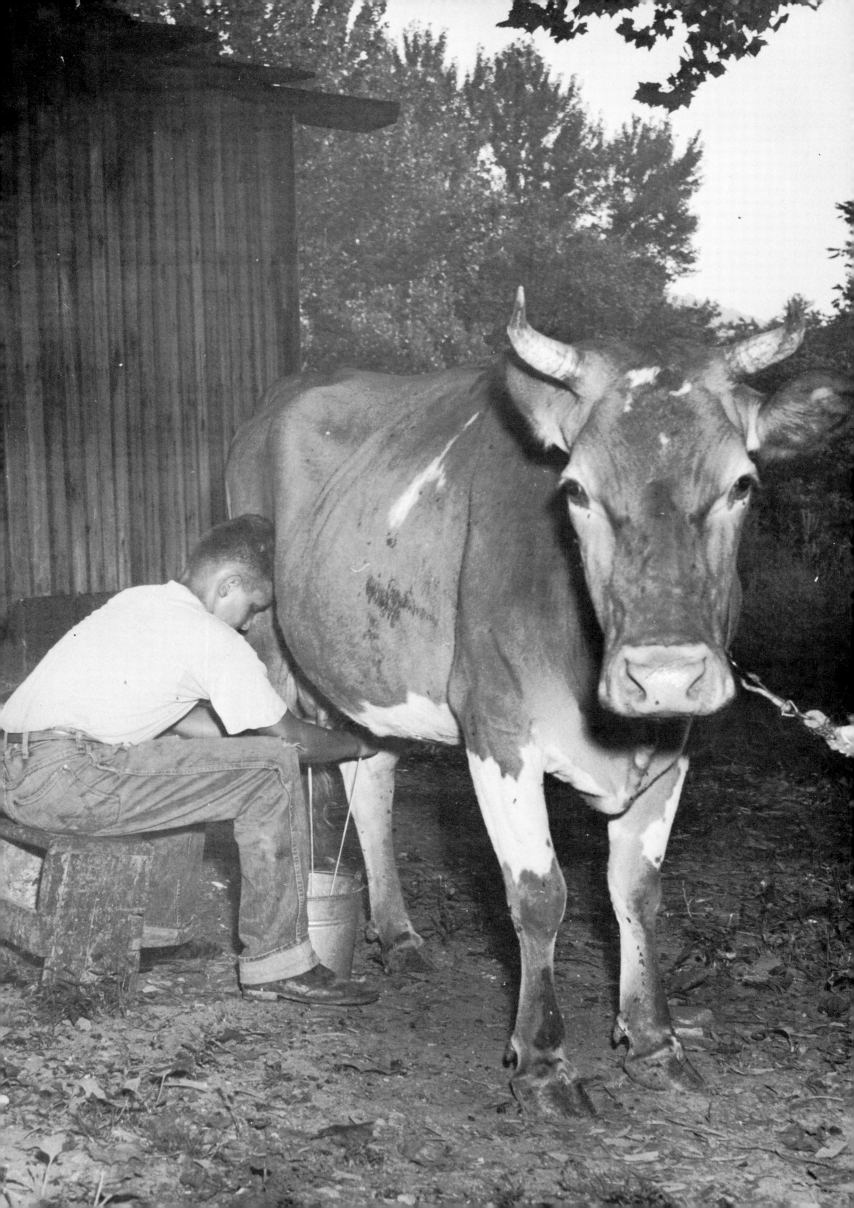

THE FAMILY COW

The family cow, that foster mother of America, where has she gone? Countless farm and small-town youth were disciplined and trained for the tasks of the world by the family cow, and the nation is the poorer for her passing. Like the old soldier, she did not die, but passed slowly into limbo to emerge as a sleek animal with a herd number and a long and distinguished pedigree. Today she is attended by technicians in spotless white coats and has become a milk factory with no personality and no function except to produce milk high in fat and large in quantity.

The family cow, as she was known down through the years, was a symbol of family life, the hub around which the little world of the small town and the farm revolved. Those of us who cared for her, and subjected ourselves to the iron discipline of milking and feeding her and bedding her twice a day, 365 days a year, know that we got something from her besides the milk and butter and curds that came from her free-flowing udder. The family cow made men out of small boys.

We undoubtedly have a better milk supply as a result of the family cow's demise, and we have a sounder and more efficient dairy economy. But there was something about the family cow that made up for her lack of high production.

When Bossy went, she went quickly. I milked a family cow and I'm not an old man, but it appears I may well have milked a family cow about as recently as any family cow milker, because between the time I sold my herd and went away to school and the day I returned from War II the family cow faded away.

When my family moved to a small town south of Des Moines in the early thirties our family cow provided a family of five with all the milk we could drink, and we drank a great deal. We had a little bench-type separator and Mother made cottage cheese and creamed it and we ate this by the ton, mixed with grape jelly.

From the cream we made butter, and we used plenty of that. Father had all the buttermilk he wanted, and he loved the stuff. When my herd was at full strength—three milkers, three resters, and a calf, I sold raw milk in gallon buckets on a nice little route. I delivered every day on a bicycle, hanging the little covered buckets on my handlebars. It was legal, it was profitable, and some of the time it was fun.

But Bossy's contribution in dollars and cents is not what I miss, although she made a very real contribution, at two bits a gallon, to my high school and college expenses. It is the friendship of the cows themselves, the management practices (some strange, indeed) through which farm animals were adapted to small-town living, and the way in which daily chores contributed to the growing up of boys, that come to my mind when I think of Molly, Polly, and Sue.

All of our cows were characters. I've talked to other ex-family cow people and all of their cows were characters, too.

We probably had a dozen cows from the time we bought Molly for eighteen dollars at a community sale until I sold the noble Frieda to pay my first year's college tuition. Yet, I can remember every cow by name, what we fed to each one, how much milk they gave, how many calves they had and when, and the sex of each of these and their names. Everything around our place had a name, even the turtle that lived in a hole under the kitchen.

I can remember winging home from school after Mother called the principal to report that Susie had broken down the fence around our little lot and eaten Mrs. McClellan's grapes. Not just once—often. That was why we finally sold her at the community sale.

Then we got Dolly. Dolly calved a month early and I found her bull calf lying in the cold mud. He was worth $1.50 for veal and nothing whatsoever for any other purpose. Still, it was a victory when he revived under the stove in the kitchen.

But Molly, perhaps because she was my first venture, was always my first love in spite of her wanderings. She was a rangy beast, covered all over with red hair, and she had a great voice, clarion-clear, full-throated, with fine tone and character. She bellowed at the slightest provocation. She was big-teated and easy to milk and to a growing boy that was important. It was only at the pail that she fell short of perfection. She gave about a quart a day with great difficulty.

I thought the world of Molly but Father thought differently. We traded her for a smaller, more settled type, with less voice and smaller teats and greater power of production.

Bessie cost twenty-four dollars. She was a true brindle. There are a good many man-and-boy farmers today who have never seen a truly brindle cow. Bessie was one of these, striped like a tabby cat.

We bought Bessie at the same sale where we sold Susie down the river. I left Susie in a cold, muddy alley at the sale barns. As I left, leading Bessie, Susie's lonely honking near broke my heart.

Bessie and I became great friends, but she didn't last more than a year. She had stomach trouble and an itchy skin and a high molar and had to go the way of all cows with such deficiencies.

I was fifteen when I took Bessie to the sale—alone this time. When we came into view, a scalper promptly struck up a conversation. Seeing Bess at the end of the rope, he offered me thirty dollars as she stood.

This seemed a fair price, but I knew that scalpers made a good living matching their optimism against other people's pessimism by buying for a price ahead of an auction and consigning the animal themselves.

I turned him down. That afternoon Bess brought thirty-three dollars. When the sales commission was deducted there was thirty dollars and eighty-four cents left. Father gave me the eighty-four cents.

Our next animal was Polly. Like Molly, she broke out all the time. We sold her for beef and got Frieda.

Frieda's acquisition marked a new peak in our cow business. All through the Susie-Polly-Bessie-Molly era, we'd dreamed of some day having a really good cow. Near town was a dairyman with an excellent herd. We'd visited there often. He announced a dispersal of his herd and I wasted no time in getting out to his place. Frieda was a standout—four-year-old, well built, of good mixed blood, and fresh.

The dairyman wouldn't sell her ahead of the sale— she'd been advertised and he said it wouldn't be honest. But he did do one thing—he promised me he'd sell her first, and at that kind of sale big buyers frequently didn't get warmed up until well after the sale had started.

I had $85 in the bank and drew a cashier's check for all of it. When the bidding opened I started boldly.

Bidding went to $80 all too quickly. This was to have been my limit, for trucking her home would cost $4 and I wanted some lunch. But we soon passed the $80 mark—in 50-cent and finally 25-cent bids—and I kept going. Unbelievably she was struck off to me at $84.25. We walked home—four miles, in the dark, with rebellious Frieda on the end of a rope.

Later on, there was Alice, whom I raised from a calf, and Alice's second calf, and Cynthia, the one who wouldn't eat alfalfa. And later still, I bought Frieda's daughter, Flossie, from the man who had bought her at the dispersal sale when she was a calf. They made a great family.

Roughage, not grain, was the biggest feeding problem in the handling of a town cow. Each fall I cut sweet corn fodder from every garden in our end of town and carted it home on a coaster wagon. You can get a whole shock of sweet corn fodder on a wagon if you tie it on right.

It was a big treat for the cows, but it was a back-breaking job to clean up. Stalks stick to your fork and get soggy and you can't scoop 'em or pitch 'em or do anything but pick 'em up one by one and throw them out on the pile.

Saturdays I worked all day for a load of hay. It mattered little how much a day's work was worth or what hay was bringing—you pitched hay for a farmer and then brought the last load home. I'd take the horses back on Sunday morning.

To house the cow, I spent hours insulating the old carriage shed with cardboard cartons, and rigging plumbing from old gutters. This contraption led from the pump near the house to the barnyard, where it emptied into a sawed-off barrel.

You hear tales about milking in the dark by the light of an old kerosene lantern, morning and night every day all winter, and milking outdoors morning and night all summer. I did all those things.

For pasture, we either staked out the cows in the wide ditches along the highway or rented pasture from elderly ladies who lived on the edge of town.

There were two lovely ladies—one a widow and the other a spinster—who had pasture for rent. They, too, had cows. Cows are gregarious and thrive on company. Town cows get lonely. They wear themselves out bawling and patrolling the fence, leaning methodically on every post, and making very little milk.

I used to walk to pasture and milk there rather than drive the cows back and forth. Feed was served in a dishpan. It was up to the milker to finish milking before the cow finished eating and walked away.

We practiced some feeding tricks that would be impossible on a big dairy farm, but they were effective. One was hot mash. In winter we'd put feed in a

dishpan and run steaming hot water into the ration before taking it out to the cow. She liked that fine. We poured hot molasses over poor hay, and she liked that, too.

Our cows were always thirsty. No growing boy will take the time to clear the ice out of a washtub and lug enough buckets of water to keep a cow giving all the milk she should, and no cow will drink all she needs when she has water in front of her only three times a day.

Modern dairymen would scoff at a cow eating melon rinds, leftover salads, potato peelings, overripe fruit, pea pods, corn shucks, spaghetti, etc. We fed garbage. One of our cows, Susie, liked meat.

This mixed diet didn't seem to offset the flavor of the milk much. We used our milk raw, but we used it very quickly. Milk was also kept scrupulously clean, not by modern standards, but by my mother's. Mother said she could see germs with the naked eye. When she poured the warm milk through a cheesecloth strainer about all she got out were the frogs and the flies. But it looked clean and tasted fine.

We did have trouble with wild onions. In a big dairy, one cow with off-flavor milk probably doesn't affect the whole bulk milk tank. When the herd is just one cow, and that cow is filled with wild onions, the milk is fit only for onion soup.

Management in those days meant getting the cow bred on time. We usually walked her over to the nearest dairy farm to be bred and then walked her home. We tried to plan things so the cow would come fresh when school started in the fall.

Leading a cow that far is not easy, even when she's calm. But when she is in heat, it's a real experience. When we took off on these adventures we used a rope halter, tied as tightly as possible, and twenty-five feet of one-inch rope. Sometimes the cow was in front, sometimes we were in front, and sometimes we bolted along abreast. The idea was to keep the rope taut. We'd snub the rope around a hip and dig in our heels. Much of the time we'd be on the ground. An occasional petunia bed suffered en route.

When a cow became mournful, we turned to Bailey's for the needs. Bailey's Cyclopedia of Agricul-

ture isn't well known today, but we couldn't have done without it. It consisted of four giant tomes and covered just about everything that was known about husbandry. Many of Bailey's theories have since been disproved, but I suppose even a modern cow would respond to a good dose of salts, and Bailey prescribed salts for almost everything.

All our cows got enormous doses of warm Epsom salts dissolved in quart bottles and forced down despite protests. Bailey's had a chapter on "How to Drench."

We gave salts to cure constipation; we also gave them for diarrhea.

Another favorite remedy was nux vomica. To this day I haven't the faintest idea what the physiological function of nux vomica could possibly be. But we gave it to ailing cows. Seemed to pep 'em up.

For a really sad cow, with dry nose and glazed eye, we threw in a tablespoon of ground ginger.

Bailey's also spoke of what to do with a high molar. One of our first cows, Bessie, had such an infliction. It pained her and she wouldn't eat—not even molasses. I got her mouth propped open with a short broomstick and filed the tooth down with a wood rasp. It never bothered her again, thanks to Bailey's.

Another medical episode involved Susie's eyeball. She was eating soybean hay and in reaching for a bean punctured her eyeball with a weed stem. A cow, blind even in one eye, is a problem because she is difficult to drive. So I had good reason to bathe her eyeball in hot boric acid, morning, noon and night, for weeks. Finally, it healed. It left a big scar, but she could see.

We were bothered occasionally with impaction. I understand this condition better now than I did then, but I still don't know quite what causes it. Impaction usually resulted when we fed swept feed, which we sometimes could buy for a bargain. My recollection is that the powdered feed formed a cake and stayed more or less dry all the way through the cow. When it got to her rectum it packed tight at a sharp turn, which, according to Bailey, lies just under her backbone. Impaction was something we dreaded since it meant reaching into the cow a full arm's length and removing the obstacle manually.

I wonder now why we never had leptospirosis, or brucellosis, or acetonemia, or hemorrhagic septicemia, or for that matter, aftosa. In later years we tested for TB, but we had few major health problems which we didn't cause ourselves with poor feed, poor hay, or irregular hours.

Warbles were always a nuisance, especially on the heifers I used to pasture in the timber for seventy-five cents a month. We used to pop warbles out of our animals all winter.

We had a "slick" way of disposing of manure. We had an old trailer and made a tin bottom for it out of some galvanized roofing. We would sprinkle this with salt. Then we'd fill it with raw manure as it accumulated. A week would collect a full load. On Saturdays, we'd hitch a Model A Ford to that trailer and haul it into somebody's garden and tip it backward. The whole load of manure would slide out in one tightly frozen block, slippery only where the salt had kept it moist. Soon most of the gardens around had their blocks of manure, ready for the gardener come spring.

The manure business was seasonal, but milking and tending the cow were 'round the clock, 'round the year. Up every morning before dawn all winter, to feed and milk, home for milking, feeding, and bedding every night. Strangely enough, it wasn't unpleasant. There was always a half-hour of peace and quiet, morning and evening, to plan a day's work and to go over what had been done or learned or missed. I used my chore time to think, to conjure up football plays, to memorize parts in the school plays, and to practice debate. Cows liked to hear me sing; at least they never complained. How often have I wished, since I have grown up, that I had a half-hour in the morning and a half-hour every night when I could depend on being alone and unbothered.

Sitting there milking, I once coaxed a rat to come out of his hole and finally got the thing to sit up and lap milk out of the end of the stream. That took three weeks. In all those years, my dog, Bud, never missed a milking.

Chores seize on a boy and won't let go. I have little sentimentality about the good old days nor do I set great store in the adage about giving a boy a cow to keep him from crime's door.

Undoubtedly, modern town kids, just like farm kids, have their own way of solving the problems the family cow once solved for me. A lot of things the cow did for us the wood-burning cookstove did for others, and no one bewails the passing of the cookstove any more than they do the demise of the frozen pump, or the carriage horse, or the garden gate, or the whitewashed picket fence.

Twenty years from now, today's young people will reminisce about whatever it is they have now that their teen-agers won't have by that time, and some will say that the kids of 1980 are surely going straight to perdition for the lack of those things.

I won't say that the youngsters today are headed straight for hell because they haven't got a family cow. She came from whence no one knows; she played her little part; and now she's gone. Bless her memory.

Forbear, my friends, to weep.
Since death has lost its sting;
Those christians, that in Jesus sleep.
Our God will with him bring.

Margaret Wells.
March th ss
1809.

SAMPLERS

Humorists insist that when that fabulous ship, the Mayflower, landed on the American shores it must have carried a record-breaking cargo of unidentified stowaways to account for the millions who now claim direct descent from its passengers. Nothing, of course, is said of the baggage of these fictitious ancestors, but it seems certain that the twenty-four women on the official passenger list carried with them their sewing samplers and may even have passed the time on that dreary voyage improving their stitches.

The sampler of the colonial period, a narrow linen strip usually about seven inches wide and two or three feet long, was used by the owner to record her techniques in the cross-stitch, the drawn-work, faggot stitch, petit point, darn, and the other fancy stitches which she might later want to study before attempting their use in the decoration of linens and wearing apparel. The sampler, literally "a sample of stitches," was no new thing even at that time, its origin dating back to the time of Chaucer, when they were known as ensemplers. One of the earliest historical mentions of a sampler appears in the account book of Elizabeth of York, which shows that on July 10, 1502, the following transaction was made, "for an elne of lynnyn cloth for a sampler for the Queen viii d. To Thomas Fische." Other early documents record royal inventories listing samplers as prized possessions.

The earliest existing sampler produced in America was made by Loara Standish, the daughter of the bold but bashful Captain Myles Standish, military leader of the new colony at Plymouth. On her long linen strip Loara sewed wide bands of geometrical and floral designs with home-dyed thread using eyelet, satin, buttonhole, chain, outline, and cross-stitches. At the bottom of her sampler she inscribed, with yellow and blue thread, "Loara Standish is my name" and below this, being a pious Pilgrim girl, she further stitched:

Lord Guide my heart that I may do Thy will
And fill my heart with such convenient skill
As will conduce to Virtue void of Shame
And I will give the Glory to Thy Name.

The first American sampler is typical of the period, being the product of a mature needlewoman, and its inscriptions and devices were to be models for many more to follow.

Samplers grew out of the need each woman felt for a reference work for the multitude of fancy stitches which she might wish to use in her sewing. There were few, if any, books available to these women though there is an obscure reference to a sewing book printed by Peter Quentel in 1527 and later there appeared "The Needles Excellency. A New Booke wherein are Divers admirable workes wrought with the needle newly invented and cut in Copper for the pleasure and profit of the industrious. Printed for James Boler and are to be sold at the Syne of the Marigold in Paules Churchyard. 1632." The women created their own compendia of stitches by using them in decorative bands sewn onto the narrow-loomed cloth of their day. Later when they wished to embroider their linens or some bit of finery they could find the desired stitch on the sampler and recall how it was made.

With the beginning of the eighteenth century came changes in the production of samplers. The improved looms of the time turned out a much wider cloth and the samplers changed from long narrow strips to wider, more nearly square, pieces. The change in shape brought with it a change in design element. Borders took the place of the bands and greater unity was achieved in the decorative effect. Another change of this period was the change in age of the makers of the pieces. Before this time mature women had produced the sampler, but now they became the work of young girls, the show piece which the girl produced to demonstrate her proficiency with the needle.

The young girls in school learned their needlework along with their alphabet. The girls ranged in age from little Polly Fuller, who, at four years old, produced a sampler with two alphabets, her name, and the date, to girls in their teens doing much more elaborate work. Mary Smith, who was just five, turned out a very workmanlike job with the usual two alphabets and the inscription, "Mary Smith is my name and with my nedel I wroght the same." She became a bit confused, however, when she came to the date for she has carefully stitched it as being 17014. The older girls showed greater proficiency with their needles and usually embellished their work more elaborately with needlework pictures and verse. Occasionally the school influence became overwhelmingly apparent when a sampler with the usual alphabets is decorated by stitching on the multiplication tables. Another pedantic theme that was occasionally used was the map of the state in which the sampler was made. One such map-sampler, made by Elizabeth Ann Goldin in 1829, gives, in addition to the map of the State of New York, the population of the state, the length and breadth of Long Island, and a brief reference to two victories of the Americans over the British.

These great-great-grandmothers of our bobby-soxers left little record of any of the giddiness that we generally associate with their descendants. It is impossible to imagine the lass of the Revolutionary period swooning over a recording but we do know that they sighed for love. Their sighs are sometimes recorded on their samplers in the form of love verse. One little girl worked onto her sampler, in language that the bobby-soxer would never use but with a sentiment she would understand,

> Oh let my name engraven stand
> Both on thy heart and on thy hand
> Seat me upon thine arm and wear
> That pledge of love forever there.

The needlework pictures, used to adorn the samplers, covered every conceivable subject from portraits, contemporary buildings, and pastoral scenes to Adam and Eve. The latter were usually modestly hidden behind enormous fig leaves and one prudish little girl even clothed this shame-free couple in Quaker costumes with Cain and Abel neatly stitched into knee breeches.

The verse that the girls chose ran heavily to piety and goodness in praise of parents, praise of beauty and nature, and verse mourning the loss of kinfolk. One lugubrious girl, Betsy Cook, dwelling on her own death, wrote, "This work in hand my friends may have, when I am dead and laid in grave." And, under a willow tree, depicted a tomb marked "Miss B. C." In all this welter of goodness and piety one inscription stands out for its vigor and honesty. It reads,

"Patty Polk did this and she hated every stitch she did in it. She loves to read much more."

During the last part of the eighteenth century and the first of the nineteenth the sampler makers began to include genealogical data on their work. Usually the names of the parents with their birth dates were recorded followed by the names and dates of all their children. The date of the death of any member of the family was stitched in later. Some samplers carry back to include the grandparents. Genealogists have found these samplers to be almost as useful as the old family Bible for tracing the family tree.

There are almost as many samplers associated with George Washington as there are beds in which he is alleged to have slept. Some of these were owned by families who entertained Washington and are said to have been admired by him. And what is more natural than that the great man visiting his friends should compliment the family on the excellence of the wife's needlework? Other Washington samplers carry verse celebrating his leadership and there are many that mourn his death, such as the one produced in 1804:

> Mourn Hapless Brethren Deeply Mourn
> The Source Of Every Joy Is Fled
> Our Father Dear The Friend Of Man
> The Godlike Washington Is Dead.

Since the Civil War the making of samplers has gradually died out though a few still appear now and then in the needlework section at the county fairs. Collectors, decorators, and museums have taken up the sampler and there is a fairly brisk trade in them. Some of these collectors specialize in particular kinds of samplers, such as the all-white samplers or those of a particular period. The prices paid for samplers are not, however, in the same class with rare books, old violins, or grand champion bulls, so if you should find an authentic old sampler in your attic do not expect it to pay off the mortgage; you will probably find that its greatest value is in your own home as a decoration.

In the sewing classes of our schools the modern girl studying Home Economics has available books, illustrations, and patterns as sewing aids. Usually she makes her own loose-leaf scrapbook in which she pastes cloth with trial stitches along with descriptions and drawings of her new stitches. She would probably not call this a sampler but it serves the same purpose as the early ensemplers of Chaucer's time, a place to record stitches for future reference.

EXOD

God spake these words and said. i am The
Lord Thy God

I

Thou shalt have None other Gods but me

II

Thou shalt not make To Thy self any Graven image Nor The Likeness of any

III

Thou shalt nor Take The Name of The Lord
Thy God in vain for The Lord will nor hold
him Guiltless That Taketh his Name in vain

IV

remember That Thou keep holy The Sabbath day Six days shalt Thou Labour and do
all That Thou hast To do but The Seventh
day is The Sabbath of The Lord Thy God in

Chap XX

V

honour Thy father and Thy mother
That Thy days may be long in The land
which The Lord thy God giveth thee

VI

Thou shalt do no murder

VII

Thou shalt Not Commit adultery

VIII

Thou shalt not steal

IX

Thou shalt not bear false witness against
Thy neighbour X

Thou shalt not Covet Thy neighbours
house Thou shalt not covet Thy neighbours wife nor his servant nor his maid nor
his ox nor his ass nor any thing that is his

Elizabeth Taylor mark This Sampler in The 11 year of her age

ICE HARVEST

Icehouses, once common enough on the better farms of America, have, with few exceptions, long ago been made over into extra chicken houses or split up into kindling wood. The decline set in about fifty years ago when mechanical refrigeration and power lines began to go to the country. There are a few survivors, some in isolated parts of New England where the high lines have not yet penetrated, some at the less fancy summer resorts.

To put up ice one must have good water—a pond or lake, a river or stream with a sizable pool of deep water. Many of the first farm ponds were built, not to supply water, but to supply ice.

The ice harvest usually came toward the end of January or early in February, when the ice was about ten inches thick. The best temperature for cutting was a few degrees below freezing, so the water would freeze quickly on the cakes after they were taken out of the pond. But it seemed that it never was a pleasant twenty-five degrees; frequently it was zero or below. Men did not dare to wait, for too often a zero spell in the Northern states is followed by a thaw which would spoil the ice.

After the snow was scraped from an area the ice was "plowed out." The ice plow was a weighted, horse-drawn contrivance with a row of sharp teeth which cut a narrow furrow six or seven inches deep. A marker scratched a line for the next cut. The plow was run one way over an area, then over the other at right angles, plowing out a checkerboard pattern of cakes of a more or less standard size, twenty-two inches by twelve inches, weighing about a hundred pounds. Sometimes the cakes were broken apart with a bar, but particular people liked to have the edges smooth, so the last two or three inches were sawed by hand. The ice saw was straight-bladed and four or five feet in length with a handle like a lawn mower.

After the cakes were cut, they were poled through the dark water to the shore. Here a long plank sloped into the water; the trick was to give the cake of ice enough momentum so that its weight would carry it up where someone with a pair of tongs could snag it. Every year, it seemed, someone fell in; he either lost his footing or his pole skidded. The lad was fished out, rushed to the nearest house, and hustled into the kitchen to warm by a crackling fire in the big range. He was peeled to his birthday suit, rubbed down, and then got into dry clothes. This was followed by two or three cups of strong coffee and a few doughnuts, a treatment pleasant enough to make a lad consider falling in purposely.

Half a century ago the ice was hauled to the icehouse on two-horse bobsleds. Layer by layer the old weathered icehouse was filled. A sprinkling of dry sawdust was scattered between each layer of cakes. This made them easier to separate when they were taken out. A two-foot-wide layer of sawdust was tamped lightly between the ice and the sides of the building. After the last layer was pushed up the long, oak plank, the whole heap was covered a yard deep with sawdust.

Some farmers not only cut ice for their own needs, but supplied it for neighbors. The going price was five cents a cake. But the thrifty farmers owned their own ice-cutting equipment. It took an average of three hundred cakes to last a family through the summer; at five cents a cake this was fifteen dollars, one-third the price of a good cow.

Time was when ice harvesting was a major industry in the northern half of the United States. No one knows when a farsighted colonial farmer first conceived the idea of storing ice to use in hot weather. Old records reveal that many icehouses were built in New England after the Revolution. An entry in George Washington's diary shows that he stored ice in winter. The diary, dated 1785, says, "Having put the heavy frame into my Ice House, I began this day to seal it with Boards."

As towns grew into cities in the first half of the nineteenth century, the demand for ice grew rapidly. Within a few miles of the major population centers gigantic rough-board icehouses were built on the shores of ponds, lakes, and rivers. Ice for New York City was cut and stored 150 miles up the Hudson; every day the loaded ice barges went to the city.

Ice became a spectacular item of international commerce. In 1805, Frederick Tudor of Boston conceived the idea of sending ice by ships to the West Indies where ice had never been seen. In the next thirty years, Tudor made a fortune shipping the cold luxury to the West and the East Indies, to South America, China, and England. In 1853, A. J. Downing, one of America's famous pioneer landscape architects, wrote, "American ice has sent into positive ecstasies all those of the great metropolis [London] who depend upon their throats for sensations."

One of the most important centers of ice cutting was the Kennebec River in Maine. Thousands of men and youths gathered to work for the big companies; farmers came down from upper Maine, up from Massachusetts, and east from New Hampshire. The companies built stove-heated barracks to house the workers—barracks as barren as the giant storage houses for the ice. Some of the icehouses were six hundred feet long with double-boarded walls, insulated with sawdust between the walls.

As the cakes shot up the chutes, powered by gasoline engines, they were forced through planers which cut all cakes to uniform depth and width. And when spring came and the river ice went out, a fleet of schooners came and loaded the ice cakes. Then the ships scattered for the places of earth with their valuable cargoes. A very few of these commercial ice-cutting plants are still in operation.

Ice harvest today is a rush affair, just as it was a century ago. Cold spells frequently last only two or three days. Today, mechanical equipment does most of the sawing, but human muscle power is still used to push the cakes to shore. Beside many a northland pond is a large unpainted icehouse where thousands of the cold cakes are stored each winter. A gasoline engine or electric-motor-driven chain pulls the cakes into the building. Next summer, vacationers and villagers will buy the ice by the pound.

Solid Yankee farmers still want plenty of ice for cooling milk in the milkhouse and for the big wooden refrigerator in the back kitchen. On a hot afternoon, someone will propose a six-quart freezer of ice cream for supper.

But each year the ice harvest grows smaller. The metal strands that carry magic power stretch farther into the hills and along the back roads. A farmer no longer has to freeze himself in winter to keep cool in summer.

LILLIE COOKS FOR THRESHERS

When the longest days came and the fields of shocked grain danced under the July sun, the threshing teams started around the rings. The old-timer will tell you it was a hot, dirty job, but it had its compensations— threshing dinners made harvesttime for the thresher-men like a summer of picnics. Every housewife in the ring tried to outdo the ones before her in the table she set.

The old horse-drawn engines, and the steam tractors that followed them, are gone now, and with them the threshing dinners, the all-time peak of American cook-ing. "Back yonder when I was a girl in Kentucky," Mrs. Lillie Bainum says, "how we looked forward to threshing. What a grand time it was!" For a moment

this lively sprig of a woman, who has seen fifty years of farming in Ohio, is silent. She folds her hands in her lap and her quick blue eyes are softened by remem-bering—but for a minute only, because Lillie Bainum loves to tell a story, and this is one of her favorites.

"It was generally in late July or early August that Mama would call, 'Run fetch me a basket of apples, Lillie. The threshers have sent word that they'll be here tomorrow and there's pies to be baked.' Then she was on her way to catch half a dozen or so fryers to dress and put in salt water for the next day."

Mama, Mrs. Bainum says, was a real pusher. She had to be. Papa died when Lillie was just a little girl and Mama had to carry on alone and make a go of the farm

123

and the family. There were seven boys to be taught how to handle the crops and three girls to teach how to sew a fine seam, or patch a shirt, or turn out a batch of biscuits. If the boys were ever undecided about things, they went to Mama. Maybe, at tobacco setting time, they came in and asked her to help pull plants. They were raised, the ten of them, to heed what she told them.

At threshing time, while the engineer got his fires going and the men were standing around waiting until the dew was off the sheaves, Mama and the girls were in the big kitchen seeing that their stove was fired up just right, getting the dinner under way, and setting the dining table, which had to be lengthened to a full twelve feet.

Neighbor women came over with their men, who were trading work. They knew that Mama, with three girls, didn't need any help, but they liked to be with them, especially on threshing day. "They were all just anxious to eat at Mama's table," Lillie says.

There were often as many as twenty hands. The first note of the dinner bell had hardly sounded before the threshing crew and the men who worked around the separator came in for the first setting. After they were through and the dirty dishes had been readied up and the empty bowls filled, the others came, those who were pitching sheaves in the field, and those who had teams.

"We always knew where the engineer sat because the cloth at his place was a sight when he finished," Mrs. Bainum says. "He went with his sleeves rolled up and was grease all over. Mama gave him good lye soap to wash up with before dinner, but he didn't scrub all the grease off. We were used to it, though, and never thought much about it—though Mama would never use her best cloths on threshing day."

The table groaned under the weight of food when the men came in. There was a platter of fried chicken at each end of the table and platters of baked ham beside them. The dishpan full of potatoes which had been peeled earlier in the morning were mashed or creamed so that the men could have their choice. There were boiled cabbage, cole slaw, applesauce, garden peas, green beans, and noodles. And great bowls of chicken gravy and ham gravy to go along with the mashed potatoes and hot biscuits. Hot biscuits, if you please, with butter and grape and apple and blackberry jelly and preserves, too. Good cool milk was brought up from the springhouse and coffee and ice tea were there for those who liked them.

"Mama most generally made apple pies and chocolate cake for dessert," Mrs. Bainum says, "and, as a rule, there were chipped-up peaches, too. The cake and pie were passed around on a big tray. You'd never get Mama to cut a pie in any more than four pieces, either. 'Law!' she'd say with a laugh to poke fun at you if you started to cut one in anything but quarters, 'Give a *working* man a little bitty piece of pie?'

"She always made the biscuit dough herself—with her left hand, too, which I could never do. She used a great big wooden tray for mixing and had two pans the size of the oven ready before she called the men in to dinner. The biscuit dough was made with sour milk—or buttermilk or clabber—and those biscuits would raise so high when Mama made them. She allowed eight biscuits to a man.

"We had a big wood-burning range, of course, and always baked in it. The gas stove I use now in hot weather does make good biscuits, but it doesn't bake like our old wood range did; no indeed."

When she knew the threshers were coming, Mama would scour and scrub the wash kettle, and then scrub and trim a big country-cured ham to boil for the next day. Mama's fried chicken, Mrs. Bainum says, was famous all over the country. She had mostly Plymouth Rocks and raised them herself. Even without a brooder, she would put down five hundred or more at a time with setting hens.

After dressing, she soaked the chickens in weak salt water overnight. When she was ready to fry them she cut them up. She put a large pan on top of the range and heated the lard and butter, about half and half, enough to about cover the chicken. Every piece of chicken was rolled in flour, put in the hot grease, then pepper was sprinkled over it, and the pan was then placed in the hot oven.

"With those old wood ranges you could do this and the chicken would come out as brown and pretty as it could be. She'd drain off a part of the grease, pour in a little water, and cover the pan to steam the chicken so it wouldn't be so hard. She made the gravy in the same pan, too. A little flour was stirred in with the grease until it was brown—Mama never wanted any white gravy—and then whole milk was added. For a bunch of hands at threshing time you had to make aplenty because there aren't many men but like gravy."

Threshing had its social side, too, but Mrs. Bainum denies that she cut a bigger piece of pie—when Mama wasn't watching—for the best-looking bachelor. But she blushes as she denies it!

"In those days we wore just a common calico dress to work in—not our best calico, law no!—and a gingham apron, the tie-around kind. When we went outside we all wore our old slat sunbonnets. After we finished in the kitchen after dinner, Mama would say, 'Well now, let's put on our clean aprons and go out to the threshing machine. I want to see how the crop's turning out.'

"Back when I was a girl the engine was pulled by horses. After a few years, though, steam engines came in and we always had to have coal on hand when we knew the thresher was coming. The most important men in the outfit, I guess, were the separator boss and the engineer. They saw that the separator was set just so and that all the belts stayed together, and that the old engine always kept a head of steam. Every boy in the county wanted to haul water for the engine. The water boy drove the tank wagon and filled it at the creek by a hand pump. What with one threshing dinner after another, he usually got fat and lazy before the season was over.

"We always had our team and wagon there at the thresher and as the sacks were filled we hauled them away to the granary. We didn't take the grain to market until the price got right, later," Mrs. Bainum says. "I used to help hold the sacks at the thresher. I've done nearly everything on a farm a man can do,

I guess, except cradling the wheat. Working in the wheat I never minded because most of us raised the kind that didn't have beards, but how I hated working in that old beardy rye!"

There was only one accident during threshing time that Lillie Bainum can remember. "I guess you could call it an accident," she says. "The horses ran away with one of the wagons. When you set the engines back then, you know, you dug holes to put the wheels in. Then, when the engineer went to pull the engine out, it would give a big *Chug!* Well, that's what happened and the horses went lickety-split with no one ahold of 'em. Down the hill they ran, across the creek, and into a rock fence. The fence is what stopped them. And the wagon wasn't damaged as much as you'd think.

"Yes, threshing certainly has changed since I was a girl," Mrs. Bainum says sadly, "Now a combine does everything—only takes two or three men and mostly the women don't want to feed them. If there was anything we liked, it was to get off a big dinner for men working. We didn't want anyone to sit down to the table and act like the food wasn't there. We liked to see men really eat. Wonder why it is women in this day and time don't seem to take the interest that we did in cooking a big meal? Maybe it's because they don't have a wood stove that will bake a pan of biscuits like Mama used to make."

125

THE HOTBED

Early in March when the crocuses have bloomed and are beginning to dry up and blow away, there comes the first good hotbed day. The skies look as though they never heard tell of rain or storm. The wind rustles the swelling buds on the old cherry tree, and the forsythia bushes are dormant save for an errant yellow blossom that hopped out too soon and looks as newly born as spring itself.

It's still too early to take down the storm windows around the house. Along the fence row, in back of the kitchen garden, the bleeding hearts, tulips, and hyacinths raise slender green blades above the ground. In the hayfield, the clover sown in February has taken root, and the ground is flecked with pale green. For the last week there hasn't been a freeze at night and today the sun has warmed things up so that a man can go around with a good flannel shirt and no coat.

Grandpop had been waiting out the weather, getting everything ready for his hotbed.

The frame is made of white cedar and has withstood the freezing and thawing of ten winters. The plants in Grandpop's frame used to grow tall and leggy, but recently he has been experimenting with a new commercial glass that lets in more ultraviolet light. A friend of his in the greenhouse business recommended it saying it licked the problem of leggy plants, except in cases of a week-long overcast sky. Grandpop has just finished puttying in the new glass.

No one can mix a "hotbed batter" like Grandpop. About ten days before he thinks the weather will be ripe, he collects a pile of fresh stable manure around four feet each way. He mixes this with one-third leaves, usually oak, beech, or birch. "Equalizers," he calls them. After mixing in the leaves he wets them down with a couple of buckets of water. In two days, fermentation takes place, and the batch steams. Grandpop remixes it and about the seventh day begins to worry about the sky. He wants a clear day; today he has it. Plain manure will keep a hotbed warm for two months, and by adding leaves, another three weeks is added, taking care of tricky little freezes that come up in May.

Grandpop digs two feet into the hotbed and puts the rich earth from there around his roses. Into the first eighteen inches of the frame he packs manure, spreading it evenly and firmly. Into the last six inches goes some of the earth he has just removed. Grandpop is fussy about his hotbed and when a thermometer shows the temperature falling away from ninety degrees he starts to plant. He waters early every bright day, and always keeps the frame open a notch, closing it before the sun loses its afternoon power. When the evening weather looks frosty he covers the frame with a couple of feed sacks.

This morning Grandpop is laying pepper seeds in. He made straight rows by pressing the edge of a long board into the smooth, fine earth. He has a lard can full of earth and a sieve by his side ready to use when the seeds are put in. He will sieve earth over the seeds and then press the ground down with the flat side of his board.

Grandpop has a dozen hotbeds that he takes care of during early spring. People from the city drive out to buy his green peppers, cabbages, tomatoes, eggplants, and squash. He sticks in a few zinnias in the corners for Grandma but still she never forgives him for putting that good medicine cabinet thermometer into his hotbed batch.

"You'd think he'd have more sense," she says.

All that Grandpop asks is that when the redbud and dogwood begin to color up the hillsides, and the Herefords start to take down the new growth of grass, he can be out there, breathing in the same air and feeling his feet sink just a bit into the earth.

MOON'S PHASES, ETC.

March

New Moon the 1st, 11 o'clock 12 minutes in the morning; stormy.

First Quarter the 9th, at 6 o'clock 50 minutes in the morning; unsettled.

Full Moon the 15th, at 9 o'clock 22 minutes in the evening; warmer.

Last Quarter the 23rd, at 12 o'clock 4 minutes in the morning; stormy.

New Moon the 31st, at 4 o'clock 19 minutes in the morning; colder.

THE
RAG
CARPET

On long winter evenings and on rainy days when a few minutes could be snatched from the work-full day, the women of the household sewed strips of fabric end to end for weaving into rag carpet. No old clothing, wool, cotton, or linen, was ever thrown away. It was stuffed into the handy rag bag and later torn or cut into long strips, which were sewed together, and rolled into balls. It was taken to a carpet maker whose loom wove a simple crisscross pattern. The strips, as they came from the loom, were about three feet wide and as long as the quantity of rags permitted. The strips were laid on the floor and tacked down. Choice, brightly colored rags from Sunday dresses were often made into throw rugs, which were very special and were placed in the center of the parlor floor, chiefly for show. A half-dozen large balls of rags made a yard of carpet. When the carpet wore out it was thrown on the back porch as a foot wiper, or was used as a bed for the dog or the orphan lamb in the spring.

THE WINTER WOODPILE

Elmer and I are a couple of die-hards when it comes to sawing wood. Not that we have anything against the chain saw, which can mess up enough wood in a day to last you a year. We both admit the chain saw is a great invention, and a boon to loggers, but we like sawing wood by hand, the way people like to fish or hunt, and we have plenty of time, both of us. No one is pushing us, and we like to talk while we saw wood. With a chain saw you can't hear your own voice, let alone the other fellow's.

Shuttling rhythmically between us, our saw hums a drowsy, rocking lullaby. The clearers rake away the sawdust and winnow it out into neat little piles. The whole of nature murmurs with our saw. All about us the air teems with myriad insects, mesmerized by the warm, yellow sunlight. And the foliage is at its height, with the stands of dark-green spruces among the riotous maple colors, suggesting the presence within of dreamlike palaces.

"Best time o' year to saw your wood." Elmer's nasal twang blends with the thrumming of the saw. "Fell your trees and limb 'em while the sap's still in the leaves. Then the logs saw better and your wood dries faster." Little capsules of folk knowledge transmitted by Green Mountain kin survive in Elmer.

If it hadn't been for sawing wood by hand, I would never have come to know Elmer as well as I do. For years now Elmer has been helping me saw my winter wood. I say help, but it really is the other way around. Though I pay Elmer and board him (Elmer will not work for you unless you board and lodge him), he is the boss, the officiating high priest of these autumnal rites. Out of the maple, beech, yellow-birch, black-cherry logs snaked in the yard in front of the wood-shed Elmer and I make music, with a crosscut saw as our only instrument, aided by a few saw-wedges, a couple of axes, a light sledge, and two flat files.

The yellow-birch log we're now bucking shivers and causes the saw to shiver with it. For some reason the two smaller logs resting against it do not seem to hold it in place. We cannot maintain the needed co-ordination between muscle and metal which is the essence of enjoyable sawing.

"Restless, she is," Elmer mutters churlishly. Without straightening his body he reaches for the ax and slivers off a small wedge from a nearby log. This he "shims" in between the log and the skid nearest the thick end.

"That'll make her stay to home," says Elmer vindictively, as if the log were an ornery woman who must be held steady for her own and everybody else's good.

The saw takes up its happy song again. Yellow birch saws easier than maple and the unimpeded saw takes greedy bites out of the less resisting wood. There's an easy, effortless swing to the arm, but the sawing lacks the finer-grained, cleaner cut of maple. Still the sawyer's enjoyment is not diminished, for yellow birch is not gushy like balsam, which stifles the saw with pulpy, excelsior-like sawdust and waxes it with its gummy bark.

Sawing wood hasn't hurt Elmer any. On the shady side of seventy, he is ageless. Somewhere between fifty and sixty he got cast into a mold that still retains its form and hardness. He lives alone, raising potatoes, beans, pumpkins, sugaring a little, berrying in season, water-witching for summer folk, linin' bees in the fall, and sawing wood, not so much now as he used to, but still preferring that to any other chore.

"You still pestered by hedgehogs?" This was a sly allusion to my city naïveness when I first came up to Vermont. I had thought then that the hedgehogs nested under the sills of the old fallen barn, and that they came out at night to keep us awake with their noisy carpentering. I had killed at least a score of them, and still there were more. Then Elmer enlightened me. They didn't live under the barn, they came from the woods.

"Then what's the sense in killing them? No matter how many I kill there'll be more to come."

"Certain, certain, but them as you kill won't come back."

That was when Elmer began to take on dimension. I knew him slightly then. To me he was much like a piece of the Vermont scenery, a pokeweed on the Green Mountain landscape. But as we sawed wood season after season Elmer took on stature. Grain by grain his character sifted out, until there it was, a meaningful little pile, like the sawdust from a knot in the wood.

Again the easy rhythm of the saw is suddenly lost to us. The saw's teeth grate, the blade itself trembles. The sawdust no longer flows out but spits out in separate motes. Elmer inserts a wedge in the crack. Still the saw drags on the arm, whines like a pup. It's not the labor we mind, it's the knot's insinuation into the rhythm of the muscles, into the saw's respiration. But we keep at it, and in a minute or two we cut through the knot; and the saw again breezes hungrily, its teeth grinding out the hardness of the wood and spilling it in foamy cataracts. We, too, breathe easily again, and listen, in our subconscious, to the saw's restored droning, to its hum.

With his country-wise counsel Elmer has saved me no end of trouble. But I always ask for his advice. Unless you ask, he will let you make a fool of yourself and say nothing. He will let you dig a springline up a rocky hillside to a spring he knows will run out the first dry spell. And when you ask him why he didn't warn you, he'll say, "You didn't ast me."

Even when you ask, Elmer presumes not to instruct you. "If it were mine, I'd do thus and so." Or he will direct your attention to the ways of nature, or to Providence, or to the Lord Himself, as when I asked him whether I should seed my lawn in the fall or in the spring. Elmer thought a moment and then replied, "Well, now, when does the good Lord do His seedin'?"

"In the fall, isn't it?"

"Well, He ain't no fool."

We roll another log on the skids. This one's a giant. I feel as though we've laid the ghosts of six generations of Green Mountaineers, men who knew this great

131

tree, knew whether it was "thrifty" with its sap, knew the color its leaves turned in the fall. It has fallen to my lot to cremate this giant of the sugar lot. Its ashes will go into the garden, back into the soil.

Elmer squats down to examine the trunk. The age of the tree can be read in the concentric rings, but what interests Elmer is a dark configuration resembling a cogwheel ingrained in the heart of the tree.

"Been tapped too hard," says Elmer.

"You mean too deep?"

"No, too close, too often."

The flesh of the trunk is gnarled and twisted, and the saw complains. Its teeth grind slowly; the sawdust comes out sparingly, mere snow-spitting in the air. Elmer inserts three wedges as soon as the cut will take them. They are like a crown on the log. He taps the wedges gently with the sledge, alternating the strokes because the wedges have a tendency to bounce up. Only by skillful strokes does he manage to sink them deeper into the crack. And then the saw begins to breeze more freely.

"The wood's too nervy," says Elmer to describe the seams, sinews, and tendons through which we are sawing. His speech breathes of the days when these forested hillsides were mowings and pastures and dotted with farm dwellings which are now mere cellar holes overgrown with birches.

Every minute or so Elmer drives the wedges a wee bit deeper. They are not the regulation saw-wedges loggers use. They are homemade, smithed out of old worn-out saw-blades. All of Elmer's tools—saw-wedges, saw-sets, gauges, ax-helves, snaths, the wooden clamp on which he mounts the saw to file it —are of ancient vintage, heired from his grandfather. "Do just as well," says Elmer, "no usen spendin' money for boughten ones."

Elmer is a living link of life as it was lived up here a hundred years ago. Tractors roar up and down the countryside; bulldozers uproot trees and level off mounds, changing the contour of the old familiar landscape; monstrous balers clatter over mowings and scoop up windrows with incredible speed, flicking the hay out in concentrated packages. Chain saws drone in the woods with the noise of airplane propellers; red oil trucks pull up into backyards and in a matter of minutes pump a month's heat into a drum buried in the earth.

In the midst of it all, with calm imperviousness, and enviable serenity, Elmer lives the old life, a life of absolute self-reliance and self-dependence. His chores, his heating and cooking arrangements, his water supply, the entire pattern of his life, or any part of it, cannot be disrupted by a dead spark plug, a dead battery, by blown-out fuses or transformers or condensers, by frozen pipes, by the tyranny of dripping faucets or the erraticism of flush toilets, or the whims of plumbers, mechanics, electricians. Elmer has never surrendered, even partially, reliance on his own ingenuity and ability to handle matters in his own individualistic way. He has never given up the humanly possible for the mechanically and electrodynamically uncertain.

Frugality is ingrained in Elmer. He wastes nothing, least of all the movements of his body. He is sparing with his gestures, sparing with the twitching of his face muscles. When he laughs only his throat laughs. His face and eyes never smile. The strokes of his ax are clean and precise, the bit striking where it's meant to. He draws the saw in his direction just so much and no more, and then releases it to me.

Each succeeding morning, as we near the end of our wood sawing, the air gets chillier. The frosty grass crackles underfoot, and the insect world is benumbed. But as the sun swims out from behind the spruce-crested ridge and throws its diaphanous mantle about us, we can hear the rustle of the earth as it stirs from its shallow lethargy. Bees and wasps begin to drone in the air, and to dart toward the house, where they hover and drum against the windowpanes, searching for cracks to crawl into winter quarters. The drumming sound of a partridge comes from the sugar lot; the sharp, reedy call of a blue jay flying abovehead has the sound of winter in it, as have the querulous, witch-like imprecations of a flock of crows chasing a hen hawk above the pasture.

Let it come. The huge pile of bucked-up hardwood drying in the sun is a comforting sight. There's reassurance in every block. I can feel the hardness and substance of the wood, the concentration of heat in it, the warmth against the stubbornness of a Vermont winter. When you saw wood year after year, the way Elmer and I do, and burn it to cook with and to warm your house, you become familiar with the temperaments, characteristics, and qualities of different woods. You come to know them by grain and bark, by their degree of hardness, by the way they burn and saw and split, and the scents they give forth as they burn. You come to feel about woods as you do about people, and you treat them accordingly. You do not have the respect for the hard-splitting, quick-burning yellow birch that you have for the clean-splitting, longer-lasting maple. Still you are indulgent with yellow birch because it is a generous, friendly wood; it will burn for you green when you are all out of dry wood. As for beech, it is good, clean wood, saws well, splits neatly, and burns brightly when dry. But there's something prosaic, plebeian about beech. It lacks the high nobility of maple and oak, or the impulsiveness of yellow birch.

"Well," says Elmer as the last block topples off, "You've got wood enough to burn." He takes a long, slow pull on his old pipe and blows a cloud of smoke into the brisk autumn air. The smoke smells more like sawdust than tobacco—that would be Elmer.

133

ASH PIT SOAP

Hardly anyone can remember when you couldn't buy a bar of soap at the grocery. Yet not so many years ago, as time goes, soap making was one of the important chores of the farm woman. The process was simple, but it took time. The crude product was functional, but rugged.

The first step in making soap was to build an ash pit, preferably of stout oak planks. The pit was made in the form of a triangular box, five or six feet long and some four feet high, with a trough at the bottom. The trough channeled the liquor from the pit into a receptacle. Into the pit went the ashes from the kitchen stove and the fireplace—wood ashes; coal ashes wouldn't do at all. Once or twice a week a bucket of water was thrown on the ashes, but a good rain would do as well. The idea was to keep a constant drip of lye-laden water out of the pit. The lye (the chemist would call it potassium hydroxide) was collected in a stone jar and saved for the big event of soap making.

While the lye was being collected, all the leftover fat, grease, oil, and rancid lard from the kitchen were likewise being collected in a well-covered can stored beyond nose range of the house.

When the day came, the grease and lye were dumped into a big iron kettle in the yard and the small boys of the household kept a brisk fire burning all day under the brew. Finally, the lye and the grease made one, which was soap. It was allowed to cool, and was then cut into hand-sized squares. Time hardened it, and before a batch was used, it had to be chipped into the wash water.

Homemade soap had authority. If used on the hands it took everything off but the bones; the stains and grime came out of clothes in a jiffy. It was hard on the fiber, but everything it touched was sterile.

Certain gifted housewives had the knack of making a passable hand soap. Only clean, sweet-smelling grease was used, a minimum of lye, and a dash of scent. This was saved to impress guests and for the tender skin of the younger children. Soft soap was ordinary homemade soap taken off the fire early. It was kept in stone jars and used on especially stubborn laundry. It was good for poison ivy too; no germ or bug could live in its presence.

When commercial soap came along, old-fashioned housewives deplored its lack of potency, and longed for the homemade article. This gave them permanent dishpan hands, but less scrubbing; and dishpan hands were no disgrace in those days.

GO
FETCH
THE
COWS

The cow path did not come down from the hills as the crow flies. It meandered down the fragrant lane between the orchard and clover field, circled the maple grove and zigzagged with the stake and rider fence. It was as though in some faraway forgotten time, old, unhurried Jerseys had been allowed to pick their own path, and had in their leisurely, bovine way stopped here and there to nibble grass, their feet following their eyes from clump to clump, always seeking the greener and sweeter.

So it was that a little more time than was needed was spent bringing in the cows from the hill pasture; but this time was never counted as lost by anyone in the family, from the youngest, who raced barefoot in the summer dust, to the oldest, tottering on a cane, glad for the chance of solitude and meditation.

The cow path was a quiet lesson in peace and beauty. "Go fetch the cows" was a command Mother gave her quarreling children most any time during the day, be it eleven o'clock in the morning or two in the afternoon. Of course, we knew she didn't want the cows, but we were expected to walk up the path to the pasture, and returning, report on something we had seen along the way. It was a magic distance, for by the time we got back, the blue sky, the summer breeze, and the noisy quietude of insect hum and bird-song had absorbed our ill humor and restored our gaiety. And as we grew older we found that these things renewed our faith in the permanence and reality of good things. It was difficult to nourish a grudge when you were hastening home with the news that the quail eggs were hatching, or to doubt a Master Plan when the good green grass came to heal the hoof-scarred earth.

Every season had its special charm. In the winter there was the delicate featherstitching of the chickadees that bordered the snow-drifted path. Crisscrossing rabbit tracks led off into the glistening plum thicket and old black crows sat quarreling noisily in the dead sycamore.

In the summer the elderberry spilled its heady perfume on the gray rick-rack of the rail fence and birds flitted in and out the hedgerows like bright shuttles weaving a colorful pattern in wild rose and lazy daisy.

In autumn shocks of yellow grain stood like sentinels in the bordering stubble-field, guarding the newly disturbed homes of the bobwhites and meadow mice and offering shifting patches of shade for the crickets and tired old summer grasshoppers.

Yes, there was peace along the cow path, peace and beauty and a quiet dignity that found its way to our hearts and has never yet let go. How wise my mother was to make us open our eyes and see!

CHORE TIME

Noah Webster, who wrote his dictionary in an age when chores were genuine and important, defines the word as "a small or odd job, the regular or daily light work of a household or farm." This definition leaves much to the imagination, since it does not list what the daily or regular work might have been. Ask an oldtime farmer for a list of his chores and he would likely come up with a list as long as your arm. And no two farmers could agree on some of the borderline cases.

The most important chore was feeding the animals. A variety of livestock, of different ages and types, multiplied the chores. Horses were fed, when working, three times a day; hogs, cows, sheep and poultry, twice a day. Calves usually were fed by hand for a spell after they were taken from the cow. In addition to grain, hogs usually were fed the slops from the house or a slop made of bran, ground grain, and warm water. The chickens gathered around the corncrib at feeding time and were thrown a scoopful of shelled corn from the floor.

The horses and cows had to be bedded and the stables cleaned, the water trough filled, often by a hand pump, the sick animal treated, the farrowing sow bedded and fed, the orphan lamb taken to the kitchen on cold nights, a gate hinge repaired, the garden weeded, the fruit gathered, the eggs collected from manger and strawstack, the mother hen penned away from varmints for the night, the woodbox filled. And there was always the milking, morning and evening. Some of these chores were for the women, some for the growing boy, some for the hired man. There was no strict division, everybody taking a hand as needed. Chores kept the farmer and his wife on the farm 365 days a year, brought them home early from picnics and the fair. There was no thought of a vacation; the oldtimers worked from sun to sun.

Certain tasks, while regular, were not daily, and were not regarded as chores. These included mowing the weeds around the fence rows, a rainy day task; repairing the floodgates and the fences, a slack season job. Machinery repair, except in emergencies, was seasonal also, usually done in winter. Hauling out the manure from the feed lot, the plowing and planting of the kitchen garden, butchering, clipping the pastures, drainage ditching, new fencing, were not regular work and they weren't chores either. Work was harvesting and planting—all else a chore or an odd job, depending on how you looked at it, Noah Webster notwithstanding.

When the first tender green of new grass appeared in the spring the farm animals were turned out to pasture. To the boy on the farm fell the chore of bringing the cows from the fields, and from early spring to late fall the misty mornings and dusky evenings saw him trudging slowly along the long lane.

In the mornings, to his eyes still heavy with sleep and his senses not yet tuned to the realities of the day, the long lane became a highway into the unknown and his simple chore a journey full of danger and adventure. The mists distorted even the most familiar landmarks into strange and spectral shapes. Indians and robbers lurked behind the hedges, and beyond the hill, faintly outlined in the morning light, was a city and a harbor with ships. The experiences one might have were sometimes dreadful, sometimes ex-

citing, but never dull. Often as a relief, from somewhere behind the curtain of fog came a familiar sound, the tinkle of old Nellie's bell, clear and distinct in the stillness. Nellie was bell cow of the herd and not far from her, browsing among the dew-laden clover, were the members of her entourage. It took a deal of shouting, supplemented occasionally by a clod or pebble, to get the herd moving. With Nellie in the lead, the cows and the calves and the team of horses in single file started for the barn, where with the aid of the farm hand they were given a supplemental ration of oats and corn. There was no lagging at this job, for smoke was rising straight upward from the kitchen chimney proclaiming that breakfast was on the table. That, to the boy on the farm, was another adventure.

WHEN THE DAY'S WORK WAS DONE

On summer evenings when the day's work was done and the supper dishes washed, my father and mother sat on the back porch. Sometimes they read the paper; sometimes they just sat and rested. They had always worked hard, and being tired was a natural and good thing to them.

They didn't talk much; each seemed to know what was in the other's mind, for they had lived together for almost half a century. When my mother had a hard day, my father knew it. "I'll dry the dishes for you tonight," he used to say. But my mother knew that he was tired, too. "No, you won't," she'd tell him. "You'll break them faster than I can wash them."

When their children left home and old age came along and slowed them down, they said they would stay on the home place and keep it going rather than live in the city with one of us. They didn't have much, but their lack was more of thrift than of poverty. Sometimes my mother admired a fur coat in the catalogue, or my father said a baler would make his work a lot easier, but they were never really unhappy about the things they knew were out of their reach. They got a lot of satisfaction out of the first lamb in the spring and the first greens out of the garden.

Their greatest pleasure was to have their children come home, with their grandchildren. They stuffed them with food and spoiled them. My mother liked to show off her grandchildren to the neighbors. They were the fruits of her life, the rewards of sacrifices, and doing what she thought was right and proper.

They never set money value on their time. They'd doctor a sick pig, worth maybe ten dollars, for weeks. If it died anyway, they were sorry for it, but not because it was worth ten dollars. They spent what they had and after that they did without, always saving a little against a rainy day. When we went home we always took a present—something we thought they wanted. My mother always said, "You shouldn't have spent all that on me." My father said, "Better save your money, son."

They never wanted anything for free; and they were proud. When my mother saw this picture she scolded me. She was embarrassed because her shoe, which she had cut to ease a corn on her little toe, showed so plainly.

144

In 1902 this machine thrashed all the wheat in five counties. And I and one other thrashed all wheat in seven counties in 1904. Mr. J. C. Wamble owner on machine

7814

THE OLD RED BULL

Up on the hill stands an old red bull.
He eats and eats but he never gets full.
OLD RIDDLE

Our Great Uncle Judson Wamble was a farmer and thresherman. When he died, at the age of ninety-two, a bucolic champion of the good old days was lost to mankind, for he had lived through several eras and remembered them all. He had a tongue like a buggy whip, a memory like an elephant, and a windy and cantankerous opinion about everything.

He passed away one afternoon sitting in his rocking chair under the willow in the back yard after he had put away two-thirds of an apple pie and most of a leftover ham hock. He had been sitting there, pulling on his sour old pipe and cussing a noisy tractor in a neighboring field. When he suddenly became silent his daughter, our Aunt Nancy, knew something was wrong.

In his later years he spent a lot of time airing his opinions about tractors and new ways of farming. When he was running the farm he wouldn't have a tractor on the place. Even now, his last team of horses roamed the hill pasture in idleness, a souvenir of what he was pleased to call "the good years." Both horses were nearing thirty and were lean and gaunt in spite of the vast amount of feed which Uncle Jud stuffed into them. Summer evenings his slow footsteps would turn to the hill pasture, where he would commune with his friends in a silent language they all knew.

146

"When I was doin' the farmin' here with horses I didn't spend a dime on anything but harness," he told his nephew who had taken over the farm. "Your gasoline bill was twenty-four dollars last month and the whole place is smelled up with stinkin' grease and fumes. There's nothing like the good clean smell of a horse and his manure. It fits right in with farmin'."

He refused to look at the figures when his nephew tried to show him the economies of tractor farming. "All you want," he said, "is to get your work done early so you can run downtown to a movie. When I was doin' the farmin' here with horses I put in an honest day's work, sunup to sundown. No time for gaddin' around. I got my fun at the county fair, once a year. Every time you get a little cash ahead it burns a hole in your jeans and you won't rest 'till you get something that runs with a gasoline engine. That old mare out there dropped twelve colts in her lifetime. I'd like to see a tractor do that."

"That's right," Jake admitted, "but how about a horse eatin' his head off when he ain't workin'?"

"Hell's fire," Jud shouted, "that shows what kind of farmer you are. Don't a horse make manure when he ain't workin' as well as when he is?"

When Uncle Jud was in his prime he owned and operated a threshing rig. He often said the best years of his life were those when he took his rig around the threshing rings in the county. He could spin yarns by the yard about the fights he won, the brobding-nagian meals he ate, and the lusty flirtations among the farmers' daughters.

He had seen threshing progress from the flail, which his own grandfather had used, to the combine. When he was a kid he was given a buggy whip to keep the horses moving around on the threshing floor, tramping out the grain. A little later the first threshers came out, crude affairs with a revolving cylinder driven by a team of horses on a treadmill, and still later, when he was a young man, he had worked one summer firing an upright steam boiler on a portable outfit.

"I can smell that old teakettle right now," said Uncle Jud. "Live steam and wood smoke and sizzlin' oil. Went right along with the smell of sweat and horses and dust around the separator. Today you can't take a breath without gettin' a whiff of gasoline!

"Me and a neighbor, Joe Pults, put in one thousand dollars apiece and got a brand-new outfit, a J. I. Case separator, painted bright red, a traction engine, a straw stacker and a water wagon and pump. That was in '75. We lined up about a dozen jobs that first year. Joe run the engine and I took the separator and we got a half-wit boy to haul water. Don't know why, but every kid we got to haul water was a half-wit. Must have taken that kind of a feller to haul water all day, sleep in the mow at night, and always eat at the second table."

The fourth man on the crew was the feeder, who stood on a platform in front of the maw of the separator and fed the sheaves into the cylinder.

Uncle Jud said neither he nor his partner knew anything about operating a rig when they started but they learned as they went along. "I caught on first," he said, "but Joe never could get on to that engine. He'd run her too fast or too slow and he was always losing a head of steam. He blamed everything on the water boy or the wood he used. I remember, though, the worst accident we had was really the water boy's fault. The so-and-so went down to the creek for a tank of water and he musta gone fishin', for pretty soon Joe gave two or three short toots on the whistle, indicatin' he needed water. The boy didn't come and Joe saw he would have to pull his fire. He wasn't fast enough though, and the boiler let go with a helluva bang. Blew out six tubes and we had to work all night and part of the next morning puttin' in new ones. That boy got fired but the one we got in his place was a half-wit too."

After that first season Uncle Jud bought his partner out and hired a professional engineer. He said Joe wanted to sell because he was having trouble at home.

"Joe got so greasy around that engine his wife wouldn't sleep with him. Spite of his bath night the grease kept accumulatin' on Joe and it was Christmas before he was anywhere back to normal clean." Things went better the second year; he made a profit and he got used to bathing.

According to Uncle Jud anybody could run the engine, but setting the separator was an art. For one thing you had to know something about meteorology; gauge the wind for a whole day in advance. The separator was set so that the wind would blow directly away from the machine, carrying the dust and straw toward the stack and not into the faces of the men working around. Sometimes when it changed the dust got so bad a new set had to be made. The separator had to be level too. If it wasn't, bearings would get hot on the low side and the wheat would settle over the screens and part of it would go out with the straw. It was leveled by digging a hole under a high wheel or jacking up a low side.

Those old separators were a maze of belts. The main job of the separator man was to see that everything movable was kept well oiled and to keep the belts at the right tension. "The first few weeks I run that machine I couldn't shut my eyes without seeing belts," Uncle Jud declared. "There musta been miles of them. When the dew happened to be heavy or we got caught in a shower they would stretch and fly off. Then along about noon they'd dry out and start bustin'. The first ones were made of leather and we laced them up with rawhide. A little later they started to make them of rubber and fabric and they held good and we'd patch them with clips."

Lining up the engine with the separator was the engineer's job. After setting the separator just right he'd make a turn and face the separator, lining up the drive wheel of the engine with the master pulley on the separator. Then the long heavy belt was stretched out, lifted over the drive wheel and the pulley, and the engine was backed up a little to tighten it. Uncle Jud remembers that he got a thrill every time a set was made and the wheels started to turn for a day's threshing. The big belt would slap a couple of times, there'd be a chorus of screeches as all the belts, little and big, slipped on the start. Then the tempo of the engine would increase and the cylinder would begin to roar and from the inside of the machine would come the deep-throated rumble of its bowels. At a sign from the separator man the first sheaf was thrown on the cutting table and the day's work began.

About the first of June Uncle Jud's engineman came to live with him and the two of them spent several weeks making repairs and getting the rig in shape. The season opened soon after the Fourth of July, and continued on into September. If it happened to be a wet summer the wheat might start to sprout in the shock, so the farmers on the tail-end of the ring often ricked their crop. The ricks were put up near the feed lots so that the straw stack would go down into manure. When the wheat was threshed out of the field the straw stack went up in the wheat field for convenience of a short haul.

Sometime during the late winter or early spring there would be a meeting of the ring. One of the important items was the choice of a thresher. The size and condition of the various rigs, the honesty of the thresher, the behavior of the crew, and the efficiency with which the thresher went about making a set and cleaning up a field, were all discussed. A schedule for the trading of help was made up and a policy decided on for the feeding of the crew. Since each farmer had a set place in the threshing schedule, this was adjusted automatically by dropping the first man the year before to last place and stepping up the other members. There were from a dozen to fourteen farmers in a ring. Uncle Jud threshed three rings and never had any trouble. Once in a while a disgruntled member would pull out because he thought he was unfairly treated, but there was always somebody to take his place. There were no contracts, either among members of the ring nor between the ring and the thresher. The thresher set the price per bushel for the threshing. In early July the thresher notified the first farmer in the ring when he would be at his place.

Ordinarily it took from eight to ten teams and four to six pitchers in the field to keep the wheat moving to the separator. When it was dry and the rig was good it might take more. If the haul from the separator to the granary was short, two or three teams could take away the grain. If it was hauled to the elevator, which might be on a siding several miles away, it took more, depending on the distance. Sometimes the wheat was sacked, two bushels to the sack. It took a good man at the sacker, one who could toss 120-pound bags around all day. Sometimes it was run loose into a tight-bottomed wagon.

Work started in the morning as soon as the sheaves were dry. The engineman got up before daylight to get his fires going and a little later, if there hadn't been much dew, the separator man and the farmer walked out to the field and after twisting a handful of straw, got into a two-man conference about when to start loading. If the straw broke when it was twisted it was time to start. The teams from the neighboring farms were standing by near the separator, summoned earlier by a long whistle blast, and the pitchers and the drivers were sitting on the edge of the wagon frames, chewing tobacco and talking.

Smoking was not allowed because of the ever-present danger of fire in the separator or the stack. Almost everybody chewed tobacco. Those who worked around the separator said it "cut the dust."

Uncle Jud kept a barrel of water handy near the separator for chance fires. When a farmer wouldn't furnish coal for the engine and a load of old posts and fence rails were piled up near the set he was alert for

a spark that might set off a fire in the stack or around the separator. A dust explosion in the separator was also a possibility.

"Only had one bad fire in my rig," Uncle Jud boasted. "That was at Dan Collins' place. All we had to burn was some old rotten rails and they went through the engine like castor oil through a kid. A hunk of burning fence rail as big as my hand flew into the machine and the straw caught. The separator exploded and blew one side and most of the top off. Fire belched out on the feeder and scorched him pretty bad. He lost his eyebrows and most of his hair. Took us two days to get her goin' again. After that we wouldn't make a set unless we had coal."

The first outfit Uncle Jud owned lacked most of the automatic features that came in later. The straw spewed out of the separator and fell onto the elevator

of the stacker which carried it to the stack. Several men took it away and built up the stack, tramping it down and laying it so that it would turn water. A good stacker was much in demand and was paid a premium over the usual $1.00 or $1.50 a day the other hands got. It was hard, hot work in loose straw, and it was always dusty. When the "Farmer's Friend," the automatic blower and stacker came in, and the stack was built up by shifting the blower, farmers didn't like it at first because they said it pulverized the straw and the stack would take water. They also couldn't see why its great jet of air wouldn't "suck wheat out of the screens."

In the early days another important man on the separator was the "weigher." He held a peck measure under the grain spout and tallied off each bushel. Uncle Jud said the tally man was often a bone of contention. If the rig owner hired him, the farmer was likely to accuse him of faulty mathematics; if the farmer hired him or did the work himself, the rig owner accused him of going to sleep, or poor eyesight. When the automatic weigher and counter was perfected those arguments ceased, but cynical farmers always insisted that a sample hopperful be weighed before starting a job. In Uncle Jud's case this ceremony was usually performed with considerable heat because he felt his honesty was being questioned. He admitted that he knew several tricks for cheating the weigher (allowing dust to collect to be weighed every time it tripped) but he said he never resorted to such "low tactics to make a few cents."

The feeder was one of the permanent crew. On each side of him on the platform in front of the cylinder stood a band cutter who cut the bands on the sheaves as they were pitched from the wagons. The feeder reached over, pulled the sheaf in front of him and with one sweep fanned it out and fed it into the whirling cylinder. The cutters used Barlow pocket knives honed to a razor's edge. The work of the band cutters and the feeder had to be nicely synchronized to keep the sheaves flowing steadily and evenly into the cylinder. If the cutter had to make an extra pass at the twine band, or he was out of timing, the feeder's hand or arm was likely to be in the way and a nasty wound resulted. Band cutters usually worked all the way around a ring, gaining skill at each job. Some of them boasted that they "never drew blood all season." An extra thrifty farmer might want the twine bands saved to tie the grain sacks. This added an extra operation for the cutter. An inventive engineer thought of the simple expedient of adding a row of knives to the cylinder and the feeder and the two cutters became unemployed victims of progress.

Breakdowns were frequent and sometimes costly, especially in time. The season was short and the schedule was tight, and plans were made weeks in advance. Pies were baked, meat purchased, and help engaged. A delay caused no end of confusion. But the machinery was far from foolproof; in fact, in the early days it was rather primitive. The causes of breakdowns were cosmic in number.

"Every time a belt broke I'd swear to quit the business," Uncle Jud said. "A belt no longer than your arm could hold you up for an hour." Sometimes when everybody was anxious to get started the sheaves might be "tough" and then there was a series of stops while the separator man crawled into the belly of the machine to cut out the straw jam. The separator was not the only offender. A steam engine could be a cranky hulk of hell-born metal. A blown gasket or a leaky steam tube, or just plain perverseness, caused frequent delays.

"The thing that scared me most was something getting into the cylinder," Uncle Jud said. "Sometimes there'd be a stone caught in the butt of a sheaf and this almost always knocked some teeth out of the cylinder. We always watched out for such things when we done a job for someone who was on the outs with his neighbors. He might slip a harrow tooth or a horseshoe into a sheaf, just to be ornery." Sometimes a pitchfork got away from a careless pitcher and caused a noisy and costly diversion.

The band cutter usually intercepted these foreign articles, but when the automatic feeder came in the discovery was announced by a terrific clatter and the zing of teeth flying from the cylinder.

Since threshing came at the hottest season of the year and was a dusty job, the men drank vast quantities of water, usually supplied by a "water boy." If a farmer didn't have a small boy in his family there were plenty of applicants for the job. Although the standard wage was only twenty-five cents a day, the fascination of working around the threshing outfit and of being an important man among men made the job one of adventure rather than labor. Uncle Jud had a nephew, Kenny Dean, who lived in the city and liked to visit the farm during the threshing season. Uncle Jud generally got him on as water boy at nearby jobs. Kenny's hero was the engineer.

"He got mighty sick one day on a chew of Star plug the engineer give him." Uncle Jud related. "He was always trying to throw the jug over his arm and drink with one hand, like the men did. Lost two teeth that way one summer."

The water boy circulated around the separator and made periodic trips to the field to supply the pitchers. He carried the water in either a jug or wooden keg and everybody drank out of the same vessel, scorning a tin cup. Some of the more fastidious made a concession to sanitation by pouring out a dribble before taking a drink.

"One feller in the ring had a sulphur well and nobody liked the water," said Uncle Jud. "Thought it would physic them. So this feller hauled up a load of early apples and had a barrel of cider for us. Every-

body drunk too much. There wasn't much done the next day. Too weak. It was worse than the water.

"One other time Dan Collins promised us a keg of beer if we made a thousand bushels the first day we was at his place. You should've seen the sheaves fly. Made it before sundown. Then the next year everybody tried it, but the women didn't like it, and the preacher either, and so we was done out of our beer."

According to Uncle Jud there was a good deal of harmless chicanery connected with threshing. There was a hot rivalry in the ring for the highest yield per acre. This led to some curious exaggerations. When the fields were planted the acreage was likely to be stretched, but when it came threshing time it had mysteriously shrunk. Forty acres at planting became thirty-five at threshing.

It was the custom for a farmer with a half-day job to furnish one team and one extra man. He usually sent his best man and team and took pride in the beauty of his load of sheaves and the number of loads to the separator. Sometimes a slack loader would put up a dummy load, sheaves laid loosely and hollow in the center. Social pressure and ridicule generally cured such characters. There was a kind of prestige connected with getting the first load up to the separator at the beginning of the day, but the man with the last load at sundown felt imposed upon.

Uncle Jud was a great trencherman and his fondest memories dwelt on the bounteous meals which went with threshing. Each housewife tried to outdo the other in variety and excellence. The men were not unwilling victims of this rivalry. There was no question of feeding or not feeding the whole crew, sometimes thirty or forty men, both the noon and evening meal. The pace was set by the first dinner of the season and thereafter every farm wife in the ring tried to outshine every table that was spread before. There was usually three or four kinds of meat, relishes and preserves, two kinds of potatoes, mashed and sweet, dishes of beans, cabbage and other vegetables, and gallons of gravy. Both pie and cakes were served and everybody ate both because they didn't want "to offend the missus." Chicken was not one of the favorites. There was a belief that a farmer who served chicken saved up all his tough old roosters just for the threshers. Beef, preferably steak, was the favorite, with roast pork a close second.

The men were expected to remember every detail of the meal to report to their wives so that they could add an original touch to brag about when it came their turn. The quality of threshing dinners went up, ad infinitum, in the Midwest. They are still regarded as the acme of American cookery.

A half-pound of meat was considered about right for each man if there were plenty of side dishes. Sometimes a stingy housewife would skimp on the beef or pork and slip in some wieners, which were held in low repute. She got a bad name if she tried it too often. Sometimes a generous farmer would have a tubful of cold pop and some even passed out cigars when the job was finished. For anyone who was unduly affected by the "dust in his lungs" there might be a snort of whiskey to fend off pneumonia. This was administered surreptitiously as a medicine, for the country was a W.C.T.U. citadel in those days.

There was some exchange of help in the kitchen, especially among those who had no grown daughters. There were generally two tables, the threshing crew and the men who worked around the separator sitting at the first table. They came up first, while the teamsters were feeding their horses.

To men who had pitched heavy sheaves or wrestled sacks of grain all morning the sweetest sound in the world, sweeter than the song of the sirens, was the sound of the dinner bell. At its first note the engine gave a tired chug, the elevator man climbed down from his post above the cylinder, and the feeder untied the bandanna that had protected his mouth from the dust. They climbed into an empty grain wagon and rode to the house, jumped out in haste, gave their sweaty faces a brisk treatment from a tub of cold water, and trooped into the dining room.

The smells that greeted them were almost as good as the meal itself; the fruity sweetness from a row of apple pies cooling on a bench on the back porch; the sweet-sour tang of relishes and homemade pickled cucumbers; the masculine and substantial steam from a hot beef roast. All these mingled into a composite aroma that flowed from the open kitchen door and tickled the nostrils and set the gastric juices in action. When the women leaned over to serve, the men caught the scent of food about their starched bosoms, a scent not unlike that of hot fresh bread.

The first table ate in a hurry, and got back to the set. The second table was the favorite because the meal could be eaten more leisurely. Woe to the housewife who ran out of a favorite dish. It was a matter of pride to have the men say that the second table was as good as the first. The evening meal was always eaten in haste because the men had chores to do at home and since sundown was the accepted quitting time, these jobs had to be done in darkness.

Uncle Jud liked his drink now and then and since he had a legitimate claim of a dusty job, he rarely failed to get a homemade remedy. He got to know the rare farmer who kept a bottle of blackberry wine for sickness and where he kept it hidden. Sometimes he would not wait to be invited, helping himself to a long swig to carry him through the afternoon.

The thresher crew was always in a hurry to get one job finished and go on to another. They knew that wherever they were they would be fed. But when a particular job was finished in the middle of the morning or afternoon a delicate question arose as to whose duty it was to feed the men. Should the hungry men move on to the next farm and work an hour or two, or loaf around and eat on the job they had just finished? It was tacitly understood that if the rig pulled away before ten-thirty or before three-thirty, the meal was on the next farmer. If one of the good "tables" was in prospect at the next farm, there was a rush to finish; this worked in reverse also.

A natural parallel to this delicate question involved breakdowns and stoppages due to rain; should the men go home to eat or sit out in the barn and tell tall stories until mealtime? The farmer risked acquiring a reputation for smallness if he refused to feed the men and yet it was an expensive concession to a reputation. The decision was not an easy one.

"Most farmers had the idea that threshermen made

a lot of money," Uncle Jud said. "What with repairs and bad debts and wages a feller didn't make a lot, even in good years. I could figure up a fortune on paper but at the end of the season I didn't have much.

"We got three cents a bushel the first year I had a rig. A thousand bushels a day was a big day for us. Later on when the blower and self-feed outfits came in we could make up to fifteen hundred bushels a day when the wheat was filled good and it was dry and we had no breakdowns. Later the price went up to four cents, but by that time wages went up too. I had to pay the engineer and feeder high wages and then there was the boy on the water wagon. A good engineer got $5.00 a day and a feeder $2.50 when ordinary wages was $1.50 for harvest. If the wheat was poor like it is some years, all straw and no grain, then we'd blow half the country through the blower and get only a piddling of wheat. We lost money on that kind of a job. We always got a half-cent less when we threshed out of the rick."

Farmers weren't using much fertilizer then. The soil in most places was still good and although there was no improved seed, the yield was about the same as today. A good field would make 30 to 35 bushels to the acre but the average wasn't much more than 20. Uncle Jud was skeptical about stories of high yields. "A thresher from the West once told me he knew of 18 acres in Washington that made 127 bushels to the acre. Had a newspaper piece about it. I didn't and I don't believe him. That's more than corn will make."

Uncle Jud sold his rig in 1914. He said he knew the gasoline tractor would spoil farming. Some farmers were already buying small separators because they had the power right on their farms in their tractors. There was also talk of combines in the wind, and he didn't like that either.

"People got so they didn't want to feed the crews and that was bad. I found out the real reason I liked threshing was the meals we got. It was like three months of Sundays."

AUNT PHOEBE BANKS

Aunt Phoebe Banks, aged eighty-six, tough as raw-hide and gentle as a saint, came out to Arkansas from Connecticut when she was a girl. She helped her father and brothers clear a section of land, married, and raised a family. When her husband died twenty years ago she wore out her grief in the fields, bringing in the unfinished harvest.

She lives on her little farm, cares for her kitchen garden, keeps a cow, a pig, and a dozen red hens, and puts up vast quantities of food which she stuffs into her grandchildren when they come to visit her.

She rises at five-thirty, has her small breakfast, and does the chores. In summer she weeds her cabbages and turnips, milks her cow, churns the cream, does her preserving and canning. In winter she quilts and mends. She totes buttermilk and pumpkin pies to old friends and exchanges small talk.

She heats her water for her washing in a black pot in her yard, scrubs her Mother Hubbard dresses on a tin washboard. She makes her own lye soap.

In 1935 she had an attack of flu and didn't winter well. That has been her only illness, although she has a touch of rheumatism now and then. She believes in poultices and rub-ons and hot herb tea for sick folks. She reads her Bible daily and goes on Sunday to the little oak church near her home.

When she was younger she made regular trips to town to sell her produce, driving a lazy mule named George. She makes these trips rarely now, what with the rheumatism and George's advanced age.

Aunt Phoebe can't be pushed around. She boils with righteous anger and lets fly with ancient rural epithets, but all her vices are gentle ones. A cherry appears on the end of her nose in winter, the result of a frostbite in '84.

Aunt Phoebe is as independent as a hog on ice. She disdains help for herself, gives it freely to others. The dinner bell in the yard which once called her husband from the fields at noontime is her telephone, rung in case of fire or emergency.

She likes people; she likes to have her photograph taken, but sits as stiff as a ramrod and is self-conscious in front of a camera. She talks to herself, to her pig and her cow and the rooster. She hates Republicans, spurns sympathy, wears no man's collar. You'll accept Aunt Phoebe on her own terms.

LORE & MYTH

On Thanksgiving Eve, 1873, a nameless tramp was found hanging from the rafters of the covered bridge over Salt Creek near the little village of Adelphia in southern Ohio. He was cut down and buried in potter's field, but thereafter he haunted the bridge and was seen by numerous reliable people, from time to time, until the bridge was carried away in a flood fifty years later. ¶ The specter of the bridge was not unusual. It was a poor community indeed which could not boast of a haunted house or bridge or tree. There were few in early rural America who questioned the existence of ghosts and extracurricular activities of the departed; they doubted only the claims of unreliable persons who had seen them. ¶ Of the same piece of cloth as the haunted bridge was the belief in spells, planting by the moon, astrology, and·the presence of devils in bad people. Witchcraft died a slow death and the wonders of the universe were explained by the lore and superstition which lay hidden in the dark recesses of the mind, remnants of pagan beliefs going back to a dim past on European farms. ¶ Settlers in the New World brought with them, too, the myths, legends, and folkways of their European ancestors. Bundling, the shivaree, and courtship, marriage and burial customs had their roots in the rural lanes and villages of medieval Europe. ¶ New World heroes took on some of the aspects of pagan gods and ancient heroes. Johnny Appleseed, Davy Crockett, even Jesse James, were soon endowed with the lusty virtues of Robin Hood, Siegfried, and Ulysses. ¶ The sprouting of a seed was only one of a multitude of mysteries the farmer had to explain. At every turn, in his work and his off hours, he encountered a major or minor mystery of nature. He was both curious and perplexed, and in his curiosity and perplexity he turned to the Bible or to the lore and myth relayed to him by his grandmother. The Bible he took at its face value, and its sacred myths became a part of his everyday life. The profane myths of his race he accepted too, for they were blessed by time and experience and the word of his elders. ¶ But as science lighted up the dark corners of the universe, and one by one the mysteries dissolved in fact, the farmer ceased to wonder. He no longer saw a spectral body hanging from the rafters of a bridge, nor did he plant his crops by the moon. Rather, he turned on his radio for the morning weather report, and became a modern man. He accepted the challenge of the age.

THE MOON AND ANDY

When Andy Neufarth came to work for us, we knew we were getting a good man, but we didn't know we were getting the moon, too. From that day until he retired, almost everything here on the farm from planting to repairing the roofs was done according to the phases of the moon and the signs of the zodiac.

Andy offered no sympathy when jobs we'd hurried him into doing at the wrong time—like the fence posts the frost heaved out of the ground—didn't work out.

"Done it in the wrong sign," he'd say. "Set 'em right and they'd of stayed down."

Besides the moon, Andy believes in good soil, good tiles, gates that swing freely, good fences, and tight buildings. He shows his German descent in his thoroughness and the way he holds on to his belief that a farmer should keep one eye always on the moon.

Andy is past seventy but his stocky legs are still good and he eats three square meals a day. When he grins, his tanned face puckers up around the bulge made by his cud of tobacco. His working uniform is a battered felt hat, a denim shirt and jeans held up by police and fireman suspenders. Rust marks measure the moves the buckles have made as the elastic stretched.

Andy's attitude toward planting by the moon is as unchanging as the trade-marks on his suspenders. Here on the farm we always went along with it, because somehow he and the moon turned out good crops and the posts he set under the right sign stayed in the ground.

Andy was not just another moon planter. He often disagreed with the cult, and for very good reasons too. Most moon farmers plant corn and other above-ground crops when the moon is waxing, but not Andy.

"That's fine," he said, "but I'm raising corn, not silage. Corn planted when the moon is filling will ear out two joints higher than corn planted when the moon is waning." He planted in a waning moon, and the picker did a better job with the ears lower down.

"Stuff like melons and cucumbers are different," he explained. "You plant them in the wrong of the moon and they just bloom, bloom, bloom, and you get nary a pickle."

Potatoes and other crops which bear below the ground should be planted in the dark of the moon.

Aquarius, the water-bearer. January.

Pisces, the fishes. February.

Aries, the ram. March.

Taurus, the bull. April.

159

Gemini, the twins. May.

Cancer, the crab. June.

Leo, the lion. July.

Virgo, the virgin. August.

"Otherwise," Andy says, "the crop will work to the surface and turn green from sunburn.

"Some fellows have it figured to the day," he says. "When I was living near Brecon, Dan Denman used to work his ground up and then let it lie. But some morning you'd look out and the whole family would be planting potatoes. The sign was just right."

Claiming that farming by the moon will work and proving it are two different things. Andy's prize exhibit is a fence along the lane behind the barn.

He and his son-in-law set those fence posts, steel posts at that, in the light, the waxing of the moon. Each frost has lifted them a little higher until the bottom wire is now a good eight inches off the ground.

Shingles are the same. When Andy sees a roof where the shingles have buckled he'll tell you: "They should have put on those shingles in the dark of the moon. If they had they'd lay flat forever."

While the moon is the big wheel in Andy's farming operations, the twelve signs of the zodiac govern certain minor activities, like castrating livestock. "When I was a boy on my father's farm," he says, "my uncle who had the next farm came over one day to help with a male hog we had to cut. Four hours after we'd finished with him, he was dead and stiff. We had cut him when the sign was in the heart.

"This sort of surgery should be done when the sign of the zodiac is between the thighs and the feet," Andy says. "Otherwise, you stand to lose your stock."

Our veterinarian once stopped by to castrate a colt. Andy knew the sign was wrong, and protested. The vet said he "didn't give a damn about the moon." The colt almost died, but Andy loves horses too much to enjoy this sort of victory.

Andy puts up a tough argument because he has half a century of experience to draw on. Take the plank test.

"You take a board," he says, "and lay it on the lawn when the grass is growing. If that plank is put down in the light of the moon, in three days that grass will turn yellow, but it won't die. Do it in the dark of the moon and all the grass will be dead in three days."

We found out, down through the years, that it was just as well, and a lot more peaceful, to let Andy have his way. Our skepticism bounced off his head like hail off a tin roof, although we made gallant efforts to counter his beliefs with the sober facts of science.

We found that belief in planting by the moon is as old as the pyramids and as new as the cornpicker.

The stronghold for the belief has always been on the farm, among people who actually do the planting. Scientists, on the whole, have given moon planting the brush-off as a piece of superstitious hocus-pocus. Flammarion, the great French astronomer, was one of the few to give the theory a fair test. He concluded, "There is no material difference to be attributed to the moon."

A German woman, who was more a swami than a scientist, spent ten years in pseudo-scientific experiments in planting by the moon. She tried a variety of plants and vegetables. In testing wheat, she planted thirty selected grains in each of eight dishes. These were watered every two days for fourteen days. At the end of two weeks the plants were pulled up and the root, stalk, and total growth was measured. Similar experiments were carried out with corn, lettuce, and cabbage, and such exotic plants as pimpernel, lovage, thyme, wormwood, and rue.

After ten years of experiments, cautious Frau Kolisko announced that she was unable to make up her mind whether or not there was anything to moon planting. She made a slight exception of wheat. In this case, the maximum desirable effect came from new moon to full moon in August (these were indoor plantings) with the same period in September being somewhat less favorable.

All this scientific palaver, however, doesn't bother Andy. He goes right on, firm in his beliefs and sure of his crops. He does have a sort of reminder in the form of an old bank calendar which hangs in his kitchen. Under the legend, "Explanation of Signs of Zodiac Shown on Weather Chart and Almanac Calendar," we find the following advice:

Grain for future use or seed should be harvested at the increase of the moon.

Avoid the first day of the New Moon for planting, also the days on which it changes quarters.

Harvest all crops when the moon is growing old—they keep better and longer.

Have your hair cut in the waning moon.

Shear sheep in a waning moon.

Don't butcher hogs when the moon is waning. If you do, the pork will shrink in the skillet.

Graft and prune trees in the increase of the moon.

Timber sawed in the full of the moon will be sappy and will soon rot.

Make sauerkraut and cut weeds during waning moon.

Libra, the scales. September.

Scorpio, the scorpion. October.

Sagittarius, the archer. November.

Capricornus, the goat. December.

THE GENTLE ART OF BUNDLING

In the interests of propriety they had to draw the line somewhere, so they drew it down the center of the bed. The swain lay on one side of the line, the damsel on the other. This was called bundling. Usually the line was imaginary, as in Holland, Ireland, and Wales, where the custom originated, but in America the line was sometimes accentuated by a dividing board laid cross the covers and securely anchored at head and foot.

The custom was born of necessity; the simple dwellings of medieval Europe had but one heated room— the living room with its fireplace. When a suitor for the hand of the farmer's daughter came a-courting the presence of the family understandably cooled his ardor. Instead of the sweet nothings he yearned to whisper, his conversation was limited to the weather, his family, and the crops. Since parents (and don't ask why this has always been true) desired above everything else to marry off their daughters, they encouraged what might stimulate a proposal.

So, they guided the lad and the lassie to the cold and cheerless bedroom, tucked them under the warm covers, fully clothed, and hoped for the best.

Travelers and the chance guest in these homes, like the suitors, shared whatever beds were available. The Dutch apparently were the first to establish the custom as a convenient method of conducting a courtship. They called it *questing* and it was under this name that it came to America with the first Dutch settlers. The Welsh, Scotch, and Irish settlers brought along their own version, and practiced it under conditions which duplicated those of Europe of an earlier day.

There have always been two varieties of bundling: bundling to accommodate the chance guest or the traveler, a matter of expediency or necessity; and bundling as an established part of the courtship ceremony. These two are not to be confused.

Those who believed in bundling as a part of courtship asserted that it was downright cruel to send a suitor abroad into the bitter, dark night of a New England winter. Usually he faced miles of cold walking. The kind thing was to invite him to stay out the night. Half a bed was better than no bed, so he was asked to share with the daughter, and to conform to all propriety, the two of them bundled, fully dressed. Some rare ones used a dividing board in the bed, securely anchored at each end and pressed down over the covers. Other safeguards were bundling sacks, and nightdresses tied at neck and hem. Skeptics have said, however, that the knots were more often than not slipknots. One ingenious parent attached a string of sleigh bells to the bedpost. The clothing was usually regarded as sufficient.

As bundling flowered and its possibilities were explored, it became a rather common custom for a maid to place a lighted candle in the window, just as the Amish used to paint the front gate blue when they had a daughter of marriageable age.

It was in America, then, that bundling came into full bloom. Better living conditions and public sentiment had sent it into decline in Europe, but the climate under which it existed in the Old Country was duplicated at later date in the colonies. In its heyday, from 1750 to 1780, its was prevalent throughout New England, extending south to bordering states. It was strong in Pennsylvania, where the Dutch made much of it.

It became common enough to excite the reformers, and, as a social problem, it occupied about the same place in the public mind as integration and juvenile delinquency do today. Washington Irving, chief chronicler of colonial America, says that bundling was chiefly responsible for the rapid increase in the population, and as such, was a darn good thing. He adds that but for bundling the incidence of spinsters and roaming bachelors would have been much greater in colonial times and that love certainly would have died of exposure in the bitter New England winter. Many an unwary bachelor was trapped in a bundling bed.

Jonathan Edwards led the anti-bundlers. Edwards roared out a sermon against bundling and his example was followed on down the line by lesser clergymen.

Strangely enough, colonial wives and mothers were the chief defenders of bundling. They quoted both sacred and profane history to back up their contention that bundling was entirely proper and acceptable. The sleeping arrangements of Boaz and Naomi were

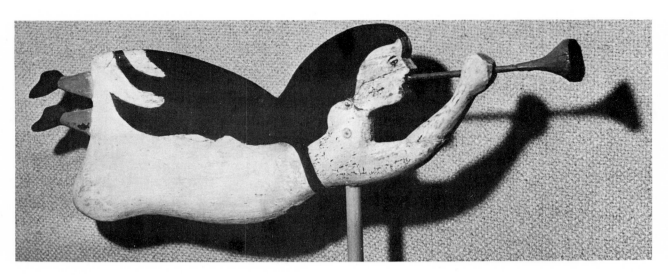

cited as divine sanction for the practice. Poets endorsed the custom. Israel Perkins, a learned Connecticut clergyman, penned a long poetic defense in 1786. The gist of his thought is contained in the opening stanzas:

> Since in a bed a man and maid
> May bundle and be chaste
> It does no good to burn out wood
> It is a needless waste.
>
> Man don't pretend to trust a friend
> To choose him sheep and cows
> Much less a wife which all his life
> He doth expect to house.

While Perkins, one lone clergyman, versified in defense of bundling, the men of Puritan cloth were quite unanimous in branding it a major social evil. There is a well-documented report on a Rev. Seth Pethwick who carried on a most vigorous crusade against bundling. In spite of female hecklers in his audience, he promised fire and brimstone for bundlers. But he met an untimely end. Late one winter night he pulled his horse into a farmer's barnyard and asked for shelter. The farmer cordially invited him in and sat him down to a big supper. Soon after, begging fatigue, he asked to be shown to bed. The farmer told him he was to bundle with his daughter in the only available bed. Rev. Pethwick's reputation had not seeped into the Vermont hills, and the farmer was not prepared for the explosion of unbuttoned wrath. "I would rather sleep outside in the cold than become a party to this sinful, this evil practice," shouted the parson.

"You shall have your wish," said the farmer. "No foreigner is going to come into my house and tell me I'm a sinful man." The parson was marched outside,

shoved into a small outhouse and locked in. In the morning, it is said, he was found standing, frozen as stiff as a board.

It was not the clergy, however, which gave bundling its death blow. It was ridicule, and the weapon was a ballad published in an almanac in 1785.

The balladier described bundling with frank and unblushing realism. The title was mild with no indication of the dynamite to follow: "A New Bundling Song, or a reproof to those Young Country Women, who follow that reproachful practice and their mothers for upholding them therein."

Everybody knew that everybody else knew the poem, and hesitated to have its lines directed slyly at them. As a consequence, bundling went into a swift decline and by the turn of the century, 1800, had died out as a common custom. In some places it died hard, partly because the backwoodsmen didn't give a damn, and public pressure was not felt in isolated communities. Partly, of course, bundling hung on here because they had too few beds in their chilly houses. The practice was reported as late as 1804 in New York, and in 1827 on Cape Cod. In Pennsylvania, among the Dutch, it persisted until mid-century.

A curious twist of bundling turned up recently in the Pennsylvania law courts. A Pennsylvania matron sued for divorce on the grounds that her husband had used a centerboard in the bed for fourteen years. This she endured, but when he compounded the insult by driving a row of spikes into the centerboard, she yanked him into court.

This must be one of the few centerboard beds extant today, for the line our ancestors drew was usually imaginary. This, of course, made of bundling an art for, as G. K. Chesterton said, "Art consists in drawing the line somewhere."

JOHNNY APPLESEED

It worked, at any rate, for Yankee Peddler John Chapman. There weren't many other fruit tree growers or anybody else during the half-century between the 1790's and the 1840's who were footloose enough—even among the restless people who followed the frontier across America—to have accomplished such a feat.

For Johnny Appleseed's famous chain of apple nurseries ultimately reached all the way from the upper branches of the Allegheny River in Pennsylvania, down through the west foothills of the Appalachians to the Ohio River, westward across the bounds of the Northwest Territory into the heart of the new state of Ohio, up the long forks of the Muskingum River and along the land divided under the Great Lakes, until it finally reached northwestern Indiana.

It was a four-hundred-mile stretch as the crows flew. John Chapman, however, followed not the crows, but winding streams and Indian paths through untouched wilderness, or at best the rough-hewn "traces" that the vanguard of pioneers cut through, just ahead of the first rush of settlers. So, the dozens of little appleseed plantings that eventually made his name a symbol of the taming that turned wild America into a fruitful land really followed an intricately meandering route that extended more like a thousand miles before the pioneer horticulturist lay down to his well-earned rest in 1845. Even if John Chapman had not sown, in addition to his appleseeds, the magic folk-talk that would flower into one of America's favorite hero legends, he would still hold a special place in the history of American horticulture merely by the simple facts of his remarkable nursery projects.

The story of these plantings begins in northwestern Pennsylvania, late in the 1790's; the most reliable tradition says 1797. In December of that year, the story goes, John Chapman, who had come from Massachusetts and who would have been just twenty-three at the time, showed up along Big Brokenstraw Creek in the wilderness of what is now Warren County, and there planted the first of his long series of little appleseed plots now so famous in the lore of the Middlewest.

The young Yankee had somehow gotten into this far-removed corner of the Allegheny Valley ahead of the main tide of settlers. Land had just gone on sale there, but his immediate objective seems to have been to get a quantity of appleseeds growing as quickly as possible in some spot where a crop of young seedlings would be ready to sell to settlers when they arrived to establish their claims. Here in the Brokenstraw country, people would be coming in a steady stream all through the next ten years. The story is that Chapman's seedlings started all of their first orchards.

The next year, he turned up fifty miles down the Allegheny in the neighborhood of Franklin. Local stories there say that he not only planted seeds but tried to establish a land claim. He failed in the latter effort partly because his main interest was in nurserying, and partly, perhaps mainly, because there was something in John Chapman that could never be tied to any particular plot of ground.

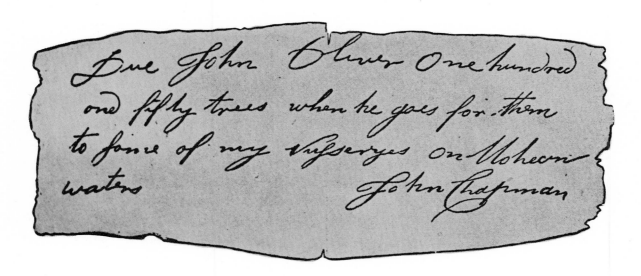

By 1800, he had been a hundred miles farther southwest over the Ohio River inside the Northwest Territory. It was Indian border country, only five years removed from the Treaty of Greenville following General "Mad Anthony" Wayne's victory over the Indians at Fallen Timbers, and still much too trigger-touchy for comfortable pioneering. But Chapman must have been there early, for first comers to Carroll County, Ohio, about 1800, found a plot of young apple trees waiting for them along Indian Run.

By the next year, he was down the Ohio River in what would become Jefferson County, and the same year seventy-five miles on west along the general line of Zane's famous trace into the very heart of the new country on the Licking branch of the Muskingum.

Then three years later he was planting twenty-five miles farther north along Owl Creek, where the city of Mount Vernon stands today.

In 1804, there is evidence to suggest that within the same twelve months, the far-roving nurseryman actually made visits both to the banks of Owl Creek in north-central Ohio and to those of the Allegheny 175 miles away. This span of travels, probably traversed twice, with various nursery plantings scattered in varying stages of growth along the way, sets the pattern for the extraordinary business that had been developing. And it really characterizes all the rest of John Chapman's career, except for the fact that the terminals of the annual itinerary would gradually shift westward so that forty years later, the east end would be resting in central Ohio, and the West in Indiana.

People have thought it queer that Chapman should have been building a business out of *seedling* apple trees. Nobody plants orchards of seedling trees today. Appleseeds, most people know, never feel any obligation to produce fruit that is true to type. So complicated has been the business of cross-pollination through countless generations of ancestral apple blossoms that the laws of genetic chance make any faithful reproduction of a parent apple well-nigh a miracle. In fact, as any schoolboy knows who has nibbled the wild apples along country fence rows, such native fruit is almost always a long throwback toward primitiveness. The seeds from a delicious McIntosh or Baldwin may bring nothing but insipid, greenish fruit with leathery texture and inferior size. Our name varieties today must be multiplied for the nursery markets, not by seeds, but by grafts or buds set carefully into growing root-stock, before a nurseryman can sell them under guarantee.

Apple offspring were no whit less wild in 1800. Consequently, it has seemed strange indeed that John Chapman should have gone roaming into the trans-Appalachian wilderness planting appleseeds for anybody's use, let alone to put money into his pocketbook. Yet it is a fact that the great part of the pioneer orchards across much of the Middle West were planted with seedling trees. The reason? Simple. There was rarely any other nursery stock available and the settlers had to have apples of some kind just as soon as possible.

That urgent need of the pioneer for apples is something else another century can easily overlook. Apples have been relegated in normal diets today chiefly to side dishes and casual eating, and the family orchard has wholly disappeared from many a farm. It is hard

to realize that in the history of most communities the first apple crop once marked something of a first stage of permanency.

Apples meant not just fruit in season; they were one of the few crops that remained basic through the year. They could be dried and butters or jellies made from them that could be kept through long periods of time in an age when the simplest of modern canning techniques were not only still unavailable but undreamed-of. Even more vital was the cider production. Cider each fall meant not merely a pleasant beverage of increasing strength but those two invaluable by-products fundamental to every housewife's food program—boiled cider and vinegar. Without them her whole preserving, pickling, cooking, and baking routine remained not merely primitive, but almost impossible.

Cider had a further important role in the economic development of the West. Apple brandy, the ultimate distillation of the fermenting juice, would in time flow in sufficient quantities from the first presses and stills of the Ohio Valley that it would be among the first exports of considerable bulk to reach New Orleans after the Mississippi became American in 1803.

Almost any apple would squeeze out juice for cider, or cook down into apple butter, or feed livestock. Grafted trees with guaranteed names were unavailable anyhow to most newcomers over the mountains. The average migrant to the West had neither the packing space to bring such bulky treasures over the many-weeks-long trails, nor the ready cash to have them imported once he had chopped out a place for himself in the wilderness.

Here is where John Chapman stepped into frontier logic with his apple seedlings. As soon as the hundreds of little trees he sold to the men making the first clearings had started growing, they would be grafted with slips from the nearest available good trees, often with scions sent from the East. The important thing was to get the trees established. Many of them would never produce anything but coarse, wild fruit, but even that would have some use, and once in a while among the native seedlings there might even appear by the chance of variation and heredity, some new superior fruit, perhaps a Stark or a Grimes Golden that would prove even better adapted to the south slopes of this new country than any of the importations from the seaboard.

John Chapman's market was ready-made, there-fore, by a peculiar combination of geography and history, and he was by no means the only nurseryman from the East who rushed in to profit from it. Even while Chapman was making some of his first trips down the Ohio in 1801, for instance, there were already commercial nurseries growing at Wheeling, at Marietta, and at other early settlements down the Ohio River.

It was not John Chapman's business of sowing appleseeds, then, that was queer, as storytellers sometimes suggest, but the peculiar quirk of management he gave it. Most men, whatever their trade, prefer to settle down ultimately in a stable home in some particular neighborhood. Nurserying, however, could not settle down in 1800. It was too specialized a business. Its local market in the first wave of development was soon exhausted, except in a few thickly populated centers. Anyone expecting to make a living by selling cheap apple seedlings to first settlers, therefore, had to keep up with the settlers or else stay behind and be absorbed into other business and the next stage of community economy. Most of the appleseed planters were soon absorbed. Not John Chapman, and the fact immediately set him apart as out of the ordinary. People wondered.

They still do, although we know a great deal more now of his personal history than most of the cabin dwellers who saw him along the trails. He had been born on September 26, 1774, in the New England rural town of Leominster, Massachusetts. His family had come on both sides from vigorous Yankee blood for several generations. His father, in fact, had been one of the "Minute Men" at Lexington and Concord, had fought at Bunker Hill, and when John was left motherless at the age of two, had been with Washington in New York and would be later at Valley Forge. John had probably grown up in Leominster, or perhaps in later boyhood near Springfield. But what else had happened to him during the years before he appeared west of the mountains in his early twenties as a full-fledged tree producer is still anyone's guess.

Colorful guessing, in fact, is exactly what John had the knack of inspiring from the very first, wherever he went in the West. People along the Allegheny heard that he had wrestled with snowstorms on the Appalachian plateau, and had once floated down the river asleep on a chunk of ice. There was no hardship he had not endured or emergency he could not face. By the time he was planting in central Ohio at the age of thirty, it would have been possible to trail his journeys, not only by his plantings but by the yarns he had left behind, for many of them would still be lingering from the Allegheny to the Mohican fifty years later.

The real legend, however, as we know it today, was just about to begin. North-central Ohio was to become the true Johnny Appleseed country.

By the time John reached the Licking and Owl Creek valleys just after 1800, he seems to have been interested in acquiring new, cheap land for himself so that he could settle down and live normally in a stable community. He bought two town lots in the newly platted village of Mount Vernon. And in the next few years he was involved with a long succession of purchases and leases in various parts of northern Ohio. There is evidence that he made clearings with the intent of establishing a home. He is even said to have proposed marriage on several occasions. In all, he spent about twenty-five years in the north Ohio counties now marked by such cities as Newark, Mount Vernon, Mansfield, Ashland, and Wooster— a longer period than he was ever to spend in any other well-defined area.

Whatever his other projects, however, he never abandoned his nurserying, and at the end of the quarter-century, when his little seed patches at various times had gradually spread into a network over at least nine counties, he was still just the itinerant apple tree man of the trails, with no home or any other adjunct of normal middle age.

But a miracle had happened—John Chapman, the Yankee nurseryman, had become Johnny Appleseed. And in spite of all his strangeness and abnormalities, he had won a huge place in people's love and fancies. Only a few people in many generations are ever so fortunate.

First there had been his colorful strangeness. There was no doubt about it, he was just queer, as the common run of people went. Although these Ohio settlements had grown up rapidly into progressive modern communities, John had remained always the borderer. He dressed like one. He lived like one. He preferred campfires and improvised shacks in the woods to firesides and modern houses. People talked, of course. They treasured anecdotes about his eccentricities, and as always happens they created more. Somebody had seen, or imagined he'd seen, for instance, John with a mushpot on his head, and the story spread that

the pot was his standard headgear—it still is, in the folk tales.

Then there was his religion. Somewhere, he had touched the beautiful idealism of Emanuel Swedenborg, had become an ardent convert, and was to spend the rest of his life more or less as a voluntary missionary in this faith. He distributed literature and talked the mystical doctrines to the frontiersmen. Few understood the subtle reasonings about material-spiritual correspondences, but they could understand the great humanitarianism exemplified in the life of kindly John Chapman. Consequently, Johnny's apple tree business was soon all mixed up in people's minds with his angels and with a host of quaint tales about his goodness to all of God's creatures, even the lowliest. He even put out his campfires, they said, when mosquitoes were perishing. And one day near Perrysville, after having killed a rattlesnake that had bit him, he was shaken with deep remorse for having taken the life of one of God's beings that had merely acted in self-defense.

Even more cherished were his kindnesses to people. When seventeen-year-old David Hunter near Mansfield lost both father and mother and was left not only with a farm to manage but with eight younger brothers and sisters to rear, John gave him enough apple-trees to set out a large orchard. It became one of the finest in the county. When a family near Spring Mill lost all their china in an accident, John stopped in at Sturgis' store in Mansfield and bought them a new set. Newcomers making their first clearings commonly found John at their doors, not only to advertise his nursery line but to bring a few plants of hoar-hound or catnip for the housewife's herb bed.

It was the War of 1812, though, that really touched off the heroic part of the gathering legend.

When the fighting with Britain broke out in the summer of 1812, the Indian border in northern Ohio had immediately become angry and dangerous. Chapman, who was freer than most men, promptly became a border scout and seemingly, on several occasions, did the settlements good service in warning of possible dangers. The climax came in August when the Indians began a series of terrible slayings in the valley of the Black Fork. On one especially fearful night, John, it was said, ran barefooted the entire dangerous thirty miles from the unprotected block-house in Mansfield to summon soldiers from Mount Vernon. He became the community hero after that, and seventy-five years later when the citizens of Ashland County set up a memorial to the people massacred in 1812, they inscribed his name on the stone—the first of numerous Johnny Appleseed monuments.

So, his apple trees, his kindly Christian idealism, his heroism, and downright queerness had combined to make a community folk character of Johnny Appleseed. People liked to think of him and his seeds as having been put into the American West for a divine purpose. They often referred to him as a sort of John the Baptist who had been sent to prepare the way in the Western wilderness for the advance of American democracy.

About 1830, people began to see less of John in central Ohio. His nurseries had been slowly extending west into Indiana. By the time the first earth was turned at Fort Wayne in 1832 for the new Wabash and Erie Canal, he was already making his western headquarters in the St. Joseph's–St. Mary's–Wabash region. It was new country for him again, just about to feel its first big rush of development, the sort of place where John Chapman had always felt most at home. Instead of traveling back to Pennsylvania each fall as he had once done to wash out his supplies of appleseeds at the cider presses, he had only to return to the communities he had helped found a quarter of a century before in central Ohio.

During the last few years of his life his older haunts saw him chiefly on his annual round of visits, which he seemingly maintained till the year of his death. Much of the cherished picture of the saintly gray-haired old man that has become firmly fixed in the popular story came from these last visits to Ohio.

When he died at the age of seventy one cold day in March, 1845, in a cabin north of Fort Wayne, he was still an active nurseryman. Since 1834 he had been investing his life's savings in canal lands and had finally acquired approximately 274 acres in Jay and Allen counties, Indiana. On at least two of his tracts, his estate papers show, he had apple tree crops in production. One in Jay County had 2,000 trees worth inventorying at two cents each; one in Allen County had 15,000 more worth three cents each. The rates were probably not far from the sale price he had been charging for the past half-century. In addition, he still owned small plantings in Ohio.

It is hard to estimate Johnny Appleseed's precise horticultural service to the Middle West. His activities had served in a unique way a huge segment of territory extending deep into new country. There is nothing like it anywhere else in the American story.

But he had left behind far more than apple trees. Even before the John Chapman of the flesh had passed on, the spiritual Johnny Appleseed had started an even greater sowing and harvest. Probably every last one of John Chapman's tens of thousands of seedling trees has long since grown and now disappeared from view (although local reports of their continuance may be heard all the way from Massachusetts to Illinois), but the planting of Johnny Appleseed—his lesson that the soil is to be used primarily for human service—has grown into a chain-planting of practical idealism that links the Atlantic to the Pacific. Johnny Appleseed today is not merely the patron saint of all American orcharding, but of planting and conservation and natural beautification wherever these services are in progress. He tends national forests, builds conservancy dams, beautifies roadsides, and tucks flower seeds into school gardens. He alone of all America's great legendary folk heroes now is primarily concerned with the extension of beauty and fruitfulness, with everything that leads forward the American ideal through wise management of natural resources.

JIM AVERY'S BIG OXEN

One of the minor unsolved mysteries of the live-stock world is what Jim Avery fed his cattle. Before antibiotics and hormones and high-protein mixed feeds were even a twinkle in the eye of a scientist, Jim produced the biggest cattle in the world; his prizes were Mack and Teddy, monsters whose weight went 'way beyond the two-ton mark. But Jim kept his mouth shut, and took his secret to the grave.

Jim Avery grew up in a neighborhood accustomed to superlatives and big records. His next-door neighbor, Will Wells, picked one hundred barrels of apples one fall day in 1900, a record that has never yet been beaten.

So Jim thought big, and he knew working cattle. Man and boy he had grown up with them, and had worked them in the lumber camps around Buckland, Massachusetts, where he was born. He was well along in years and making good money in the lumber business when he bought Jim and Joe, three-year-old Holstein steers. He saw at once that he had a pair of unusual animals, and decided to try out a theory of feed and feeding he had been turning over in his mind for a long time. He locked them in his barn and began his secret rituals. Both did well, beyond Jim's expectations in fact, and he was about to unveil them to the public when the near ox, Jim, up and died.

171

Jim had his eye on another fine ox, which he bought, named Jerry, and went on with his feeding. When they were bigger than any pair of oxen he had ever seen, he brought them out, weighed and measured them, and invited the world to come and marvel at what he had wrought. This, of course, for a price, for Jim had a Yankee shrewdness with a dollar. They were almost perfect matches—height 17 hands, girth 10 feet, length 15 feet, 11 inches. Both eventually went beyond two tons in weight. Each had a magnificent pair of curving horns, which Jim tipped with shining brass and kept in a high polish, and they had sleek, velvety coats.

Being a canny businessman, Jim took them around the county fair circuits in New England and New York, charging a dime a look, and cleaned up. In an era when a good deal of the work on farms and in the lumber camps was done by oxen, the Avery yoke at once became famous. The press used only superlatives in its accounts. The Boston *Sunday Herald*, May 30, 1897, exclaimed, "Search the farms of the State and visit every agricultural Fair, and you will not find the equal of this yoke of cattle. They are as handsome as they are large. Their black and white skin is clean and sleek and their long graceful horns are as bright as a mirror."

William R. Sessions, Secretary of the Massachusetts Board of Agriculture, said in 1895, "Their monstrous size and symmetry of form, together with the almost exact resemblance in size, form, color, and markings are truly remarkable. They must be seen to be appreciated and I would advise every man, woman, and child who has the opportunity to go and see them."

Joe and Jerry, big and famous as they were, did not satisfy Jim Avery. He thought he could do better. As his famous pair began to age, he kept his practiced eye open for promising young animals and settled on a pair of three-year-olds, also Holsteins, from the Wells Brothers Stock Farm at Wethersfield, Connecticut. His letter to the owner of the farm was short and to the point. *"If you have not sold the bulls, bring them to my place and I will give you your price, twenty-five dollars."*

A neighbor and contemporary, Dr. R. N. Shaw, a veterinarian who now lives in Shrewsbury, Massachusetts, remembers when Jim Avery brought his new pair of Holsteins to Buckland. "He waded them across the Deerfield River rather than go down to Charlemont to the bridge," he recalls. "This team was Jim's dream come true. He named them Mack and Teddy and they eventually became the world's largest oxen. Mack alone weighed 4,700 pounds.

"It was a big day when Jim loaded each one into a horse-drawn lumber wagon and drove four miles into Shelburne Falls where they boarded a train and headed for the fair circuit. The venture proved very profitable, even at the small ten-cent admission, as practically everyone who came to the fair went in to see them. They showed at Madison Square Garden in the show called Country Fair. The management made them unload at 2 A.M. as they had to walk to the Garden and they wanted as few people as possible to see them."

Mack and Teddy were shunted around the fair circuit in a Palace Horse Car which was leased for the season. A crew of three went with them. Francis Avery, Jim's nephew and one of the crew, remembers them today as the biggest eatin' cattle he ever saw. He says, "I never saw cattle that could eat as much as they did. Each one would eat a half-bushel of shelled grain at a feeding, and drink six pails of water, besides a pile of hay as high as your head."

Mack and Teddy were broad of back and beam. Three men could walk around comfortably on their backs, and a man in a rocking chair felt perfectly safe in dozing off. It was advertised that a bushel of corn could be emptied on Mack's back, and not a kernel would roll off.

No one knew how much Mack and Teddy could pull, since they never entered a contest. However, the manager of the Brattleboro Fair, looking for a special attraction for the last day, offered Jim Avery $100 if Mack and Teddy pulled a stone boat with an 11,000-pound load six feet. The two animals waited patiently while 11,284 pounds of stone were weighed and stacked on the boat. Then at a word from Jim they lowered their heads, flicked their tails, and walked away with the load. Jim had trouble in stopping them, as they were headed for the barn, and it was feeding time.

After the round of the fairs was over, Teddy and Mack went back to the yoke and worked regularly on Jim's farm.

When they were twelve years old Jim found Teddy dead one morning in his stall, victim of a probable heart attack. Mack made the circuit alone for three years, but when he was fifteen he began to have trouble in getting around, and Jim sent him to Bellows Falls to be slaughtered. He dressed out 3,300 pounds of fine tender meat. His hide, as soft and thin as a young steer's, weighed 190 pounds. Francis Avery took Mack on his last ride. Jim was getting old too, and he had a good deal of affection for the old ox.

People often asked Jim how he had grown the biggest cattle in the world. He'd always smile and change the subject. The only other person who might have known the secret was his old driver, Sandy Underwood, but Sandy wouldn't talk either.

Dr. Shaw may have a clue to Jim's feeding. He explains it this way:

"First, Jim Avery had very little education according to accepted standards, but he was a very smart man, a keen observer, and a hustler. His hobby was fine-looking livestock, especially working oxen. He made a fortune in the lumber business which started as a sideline on his farm, therefore he could afford to blow a little money on his hobby. He owned a herd of thirty-five or forty milking cows, the source of most of the income from his farm.

"Second, he operated in a period when there was practically nothing known about feeding as we know it today. Therefore, he could not have gotten any outside information. He had to figure it all out himself and use the feeds *available on his own farm.*

"Third, comes the question, 'What feed was he producing on his farm that could stimulate tremen-dous growth and isn't ordinarily used as a feed for oxen?' The answer quite obviously is *milk.* We all know that the average ox won't drink milk if he can get water. I believe Jim withheld water from them until they were glad to drink anything that was wet. After they had acquired the taste for milk I believe that was the only thing they were allowed to drink during their growing period. I expect he started with skim milk and later when he saw how well they were doing he changed to whole milk. He apparently fed them milk until they were full grown. He himself said, 'An ox will continue to grow until he is nine years old if you feed him what it takes to grow on.' "

Before and since the time of Mack and Teddy there have been various claimants for the title "Biggest Ox in the World." The famous Lincolnshire Ox, shown throughout England in the seventeenth century, was said to have measured twelve feet from head to rump. A few years ago Lon Wooley of Friendship, Indiana, claimed his two cattle were the biggest in the world. Mr. Wooley kept them around because he became attached to them as calves and regarded them as little less than brothers. He never had them weighed, but experts at guessing placed them around 3,500 pounds. Charles L. Acree, who operates the Fabulous Farm at Lake Wales, Florida, has made a strenuous effort to obtain the largest bovine in the U.S.A. His best animal weighs a trifle over 3,900, under Mack's weight, champion in 1900, and champion today.

THE WEATHER EYE

Some people think it takes a college education and a roomful of instruments to forecast the weather. This is simply not true. The old-timers did a pretty good job with what they had at hand—an assortment of corns and bunions and an eye for the sky, the conduct of their animals, and portents of various kinds.

A well-trained bunion was as good as any barometer and rheumatic pains, if you knew how to interpret them, always presaged weather changes. If the squirrels were observed to be working feverishly at nut storage, a hard winter was coming; and there was always the infallible groundhog to tell you what to expect in the spring.

To make the art of forecasting the weather simple and easy, there was an infinite variety of rhymes, ditties, and verses to fall back on. Take the matter of rain: Some believed, with the Indians, that the only sure sign of rain was "cloudy all 'round and pouring down in the middle." To others the shape and manner of clouds could be very revealing:

> In the morning mountains,
> In the evening fountains.

> If woolen fleeces spread the heavenly way,
> Be sure no rain disturbs the summer day.

> Mackerel sky five miles high
> Lets the earth go three days dry.

> If it rains before seven,
> It will quit before eleven.

The oldtimers didn't always agree. There's another involving the mackerel sky, "Mackerel sky, rain is nigh." You just had to be firm and make a choice when contradiction arose.

Everybody today quotes, "Red at night, sailor's delight. Red at morning, sailor's warning." Here are some variations:

> Thunder in the morning, all the day storming;
> Thunder at night is the sailor's delight.

> Evening red and morning gray
> Will speed the traveler on his way;
> Evening gray and morning red
> Will bring the rain upon his head.

> A sunshiny shower never lasts an hour.

Sailors, who had quite as much concern for the weather as farmers, backed up farm portents with some of their own. They believed, with farmers, that a rainbow was a storm signing off. This probably stems from Noah's rainbow, which came out at the end of the forty days' rain. Other sailor portents were:

> Rainbow to windward, foul falls the day;
> Rainbow to leeward, damp runs away.

> First the rain and then the wind,
> Topsail sheets and halyard mind;
> First the wind and then the rain,
> Hoist your topsails up again.

The presence or absence of dew was an eloquent sign for the farmer who wanted a good day for his hay. He could take his choice of these couplets:

> When the dew is on the grass
> Rain will never come to pass.

> With dew before midnight
> The next day will sure be bright.

> When the grass is dry at morning light
> Look for rain before the night.

What happened, weatherwise, on particular dates set the pattern for the year, or so the ancients believed. These dates were changed when the Gregorian calendar was adopted, which might be confusing unless you add eleven days to the modern version. One of the most important of these dates was St. Paul's Day, which falls on January 25, present reckoning:

> If St. Paul's day be faire and cleare,
> It doth betide a happy yeare;
> But if perchance it then should raine,
> It will make deare all kinds of grain;
> And if ye clouds make dark ye skie,
> Then neate [cattle] and fowles this year shall dye;
> If blustering winds do blow aloft,
> Then war shall vex ye realm full oft.

Personal fortunes and calamities as well as the weather were covered by some of the poets. The day on which Christmas fell was especially important, as the following will indicate:

175

If Christmas Day on Thursday be,
A windy winter you shall see;
Windy weather in each week,
And hard tempests, strong and thick;
The summer shall be good and dry,
Corn and beasts shall multiply;
That year is good for lands to till,
Kings and princes shall die by skill;
If a child born that day shall be,
It shall happen right well for thee:
Of deeds he shall be good and stable,
Wise of speech, and reasonable.
Whoso that day goes thieving about,
He shall be punished, without doubt;
And if sickness that day betide,
It shall quickly from thee glide.

St. Vincent's Day, January 22; St. Vitus' Day, June 15; April Fool's Day, April 1; St. Bartholomew's Day, August 24; All Saints' Day, November 1; and St. Swithin's Day, July 15, were also weather vanes:

Remember on St. Vincent's Day
If that the sun his beams display,
Be sure to mark the transient beam
Which through the casement sheds a gleam;
For 'tis a token bright and clear
Of prosperous weather all the year.

St. Swithin's Day if thou dost rain,
For forty days it will remain;
St. Swithin's Day if thou be fair,
For forty days 'twill rain na mair.

And there was our old favorite, Groundhog Day, which fell on February 2. This was also known as Candlemas Day and Purification Day:

When on Purification the sun hath shined,
The greater part of winter comes behind.

If Candlemas Day be fair and bright,
Winter will have another fight;
But if Candlemas Day be clouds and rain,
Winter is gone, and will not come again.

If Groundhogs see their shadows on February 2,
Men can take for granted, six more wintry weeks are due.

If St. Vitus' Day be rainy weather,
It will rain for thirty days together.

If it thunders on All Fools' Day,
It brings good crops of grass and hay.

If Bartlemay's Day be fair and clear,
We may hope for a prosperous autumn
    that year.

If ducks do slide at Hollantide,
At Christmas they will swim;
If ducks do swim at Hollantide,
At Christmas they will slide.

The vagaries of the weather in certain months might mean trouble ahead, or it might bring good fortune:

If you see grass in January,
Lock your grain in your granary.

All the months of the year
Curse a fair Februeer.

A February spring
Is worth nothing.

When April blows his horn [thunder],
It's good for hay and corn.

A cold April
The barn will fill.

And here we get off the subject of weather, per se, and go to bees:

A swarm of bees in May
Is worth a load of hay;
A swarm of bees in June
Is worth a silver spoon;
A swarm of bees in July
Is not worth a fly.

The moon has always enchanted the weatherman, be he amateur or professional. Here are some moon tunes:

Pale Moon doth rain,
Red Moon doth blow,
White Moon doth neither rain nor snow.

If the Moon shows a silver shield,
Be not afraid to reap your field;
But if she rises haloed round,
Soon we'll tread on deluged ground.

When the wheel is far, the storm is n'ar;
When the wheel is n'ar, the storm is far.

Clear moon,
Frost soon.

The Moon and the weather
　　May change together;
But change of the Moon
　　Does not change the weather.
If we'd no Moon at all,
　　And that may seem strange,
We still would have weather
　　That's subject to change.

The wind, too, was a powerful weather maker for Grandfather. We are all familiar with the ill wind which blows nobody good, and we all wet a finger now and then to gauge the wind's direction. Here is how to use the winds to gauge the weather:

A veering wind, fair weather,
A backing wind, foul weather.

When the wind backs, and the weather
　　glass falls,
Then be on your guard against gales
　　and squalls.

If the wind is northeast three days
　　without rain,
Eight days will pass before south wind
　　again.

Trace in the sky the painter's brush
Then winds around you soon will rush.

Winds that change against the sun
Are always sure to backwards run.

When the wind goes against the sun.
Trust it not, for fast 'twill run.

And now the fisherman's friend, the old familiar verse still in good repute:

When the wind is in the east,
　　'Tis neither good for man nor beast;
When the wind is in the north,
　　The skillful fisher goes not forth;
When the wind is in the south,
　　It blows the bait in the fish's mouth;
When the wind is in the west,
　　Then 'tis at its very best.

There are a few leftover couplets which might help in filling out the picture for do-it-yourself weather prophets:

Fog on the hill
Brings water to the mill.

Fog on the moor
Bring the sun to the door.

When the mists begin to nod,
Fisher, then put by your rod.

Rainbow at night, sailor's delight,
Rainbow in the morning, sailor take warning.

Thunder in spring
Cold will bring.

When the clouds are upon the hills
They'll come down by the mills.

Year of snow
Fruit will grow.

SPRING ALMANAC

When that Aprille with his shoures soote
The Droghte of Marche hath perced to the roote.
— CHAUCER

Give the kids molasses and sulphur for that peaked
　　look.
Air featherbeds and winter woolens.
Give the feet a treat; take them wading.
Cook a batch of dandelion greens with a ham hock.

Take down the storm windows; put up screen doors.
Store red flannels in mothballs.
Cull the lazy hens.
Stand an old broom outside the kitchen door for
　　muddy feet.

Make the hotbed early; use well-aged horse manure.
Stay up nights with lambing ewes.
Give the new-hatched chicks twelve hours behind the
　　kitchen stove.
Turn the compost pile and add lime and fertilizer.

Set broody hens with fifteen eggs; mark them well.
Take the leaf mulch off the bulbs.
Give the fruit trees a doorman spray.
Keep the cat away from the nesting robin.

Read the Bible.
Cut hay after a red sunset.
Tie up the dog; his fancy turns too.
Watch for spring sniffles; keep the feet dry.

Clean out the gutters.
Fill the mudhole under the barnyard gate.
Thin the blood with sassafras tea.
Buy a new bonnet with a blue ribbon on it.

Guard against the ravages of spring fever.
Look for morel mushrooms when apple trees turn
　　pink.
Set out rosebushes. Keep their feet dry.
Don't plow across gullies.

Prune grapevines; leave three buds to the twig.
Don't turn the cow on pasture until it has a six-inch
　　start. (The pasture.)
Plant radishes and lettuce early; frost won't harm
　　them.
Plant spring posies in flats; use plenty of sand.

Watch the heat in the brooder house; have substitute
    heat at hand.
Kiss all the June brides.
Keep young pigs from chilling.
Be patient during house cleaning.

Beware of peddlers of spring tonics.
Tie poultry wire around young fruit trees.
Keep away from trees during spring storms.
Take spring bath only after weather is well settled.

Look to the beehive. Perchance a new queen is needed.
Plant oats early.
Take the cow to the bull.
Change to summer oil in the tractor.

Watch for bloat in pastured cattle. Feed some hay at
    first.
Consult seed catalogues early, say, in March.
Follow markets and quotas in planning crops.
Prune fruit trees before the sap starts.

Control the gypsy urge.
Reset fence posts loosened by frost.
Seed the lawn; roll when not too soggy.
Nibble on a fiddlehead.

Do not spare the hoe in the young garden.
Look for the timid violet beside the mossy stone.
Go fishing.
Shore up the gullies against washing. Watch the top-
    soil.

Give orphaned kittens a home in the barn.
Plant cucumbers when the moon is full.
When the sap starts, slippery elm bark is prime.
Soften stiff boots with neat's-foot oil.

Pick the geese.
Trade roosters with a neighbor.
Stay off wet fields with the manure spreader.
Buy certified seed.

Watch bloat on the new grass.
Prepare for the equinoctial storm.
Return neighbor's snow shovel; borrow his lawn
    mower.
Secure floodgates against freshets.
Breed gilts for farrowing.

Plant the hybrid recommended for your county.
If your alfalfa fails try birdsfoot trefoil.
Set out strawberries and salt the asparagus.
Buy a straw hat; use last summer's for a scarecrow.

Oil machinery before using. Oil and store under roof
    when finished with it.
Swear not at the weather.
Help thy neighbor when he needs it.

179

SPECIAL EVENTS

A special event in the Good Old Days was special indeed for kids. We have some of the same events today, like Christmas and the circus, but there's nothing special about them now. Today's kids are fed up. They can see a circus or a big league ball game on TV, they have a special room full of toys, and they scarcely look up when an eight-engine jet flashes across the sky. In the old days special events were rare, and something to look forward to with pleasure; you dreamed about them and saved your money because the more special the event, the more money it took. ¶ Weddings were not special events. You couldn't enjoy a wedding because you had to dress up in a starched shirt and be "a little gentleman." Funerals were certainly not special events. A special event had to have a degree of regularity so that you knew what was coming and what to expect. A good example was the county fair, which was the most special of the special events, but Christmas was a very close second. ¶ It was lucky that special events almost always came just when you needed them most. The fair came after harvest, the Fourth of July when you were all worn-out with weeding the corn. ¶ Other special events when kids could have fun were family reunions and the Christmas program at school. You got an orange in your treat after the program, and an orange was indeed a treasure. Grownups regarded camp meeting, the Chautauqua, and the revival at the village church as special events. The grownups said they "uplifted you," but that didn't mean very much to kids. Eating sure helped to make a special event special. ¶ Minor special events were Thanksgiving, when all the kinfolk got together for a big dinner, and Easter, when the women got new bonnets and the kids had an egg hunt. ¶ The circus was a very special event, and it was more fun for both young and old than anything, but you never could depend on it. It was usually at the county seat and it cost a lot of money for the whole family to go. You got up early in the morning and drove twelve miles and you got back after dark, with the chores to do. Sometimes the circus came along during the harvest, and you had to look at the posters on the barn instead of going. ¶ Birthdays, a new pup, when you took off your shoes for the summer, and your first long pants were strictly not special events, but very fine nevertheless. Parents regarded the arrival of a new baby as a very special event, but it bored kids. ¶ The more special events you had, the less you enjoyed them and some of them were not very exciting when you grew up. Christmas was not nearly as much fun if you didn't believe in Santa Claus. But you never got tired of the county fair, and while you often wished it would last a year instead of six days, you knew very well you would get fed up with its thrills, as kids do now with a special event happening every day.

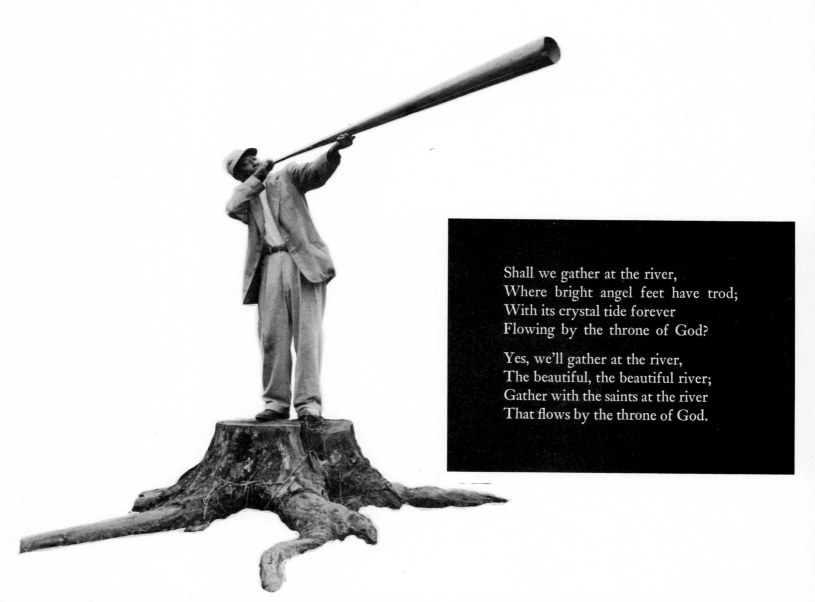

WE'LL GATHER AT THE RIVER

The last hymn is sung and there is a hush as the solemn words of the benediction are spoken. The crowd files slowly into the starlit night and in little knots disperses to the tents set in a semicircle among the trees. Soon the campfires are going, one in front of each tent; seats are ringed around the fires and the talk begins. Families separated by time and distance gather here again, friends renew old ties. Someone brings a jug of sweet cider and a tray of doughnuts from another fire; couples wander off into the shadows, and children watch the sparks as a fresh pine log is thrown on the fire. This was an old-time camp meeting.

Isolated by the trackless forests and bad roads, the early settlers had only the rare itinerant preacher to bring them the word of God. God-fearing men all, the promise of heaven and the penalties of sin were very real to them, and they needed more than the rare visits of the circuit rider to keep alive their zeal.

The camp meeting originated in the hills of Kentucky in Daniel Boone's time and spread rapidly north, west, and south. The Presbyterian Church organized and conducted the first meetings, but other sects, especially the Methodists, followed until every community was served, near or far, by an annual meeting.

Camp meeting sites were chosen with care. A grove of trees for shelter, a free-flowing spring for water, and a central point accessible to people over a wide area. The meetings were usually a week long, or from Sunday to Sunday. The worshipers came by wagon, or horseback, or on foot. They brought with them food for the week, blankets for their beds, and their long rifles for protection. They built rude shelters, made their cooking fires in the open, and slept on straw on the ground.

There were usually three services a day, a prayer

service in the morning, sermons in the afternoon and evening. The sermons were interminable—often two hours long, delivered by the golden-voiced orators of the church who preached damnation for sinners, the rich rewards of heaven for the faithful. There were shoutings and mystic seizures, and the unsaved were invited to hit the sawdust trail.

The meetings filled a great social vacuum, for in the evening after the services ·great bonfires were kindled, and there was visiting and talk through the night. The youngsters had a holiday, and there was romance, too, and many a young swain returned to his cabin in the wilderness with a bride courted and won at the meeting.

The institution of the camp meeting flourished all through the nineteenth century and on into the twentieth. However, as churches were built, population grew, and religious services became a weekly affair, the spiritual need for the camp meeting waned. First inspired by a religious need, they soon became as much a social institution as a religious meeting. Family reunions, recreation, and social intercourse usurped much of the religious intensity of the early meetings. The services were modernized, as the thinking of a new era relegated the "old-fashioned religion" to a dead past.

But the camp meeting had become a community and family tradition, and such traditions die hard. A few survive, among them the Indian Field meeting, held each year at Indian Field, South Carolina.

An institution of a bygone age projected into our twentieth century, the Indian Field meeting has changed with the years and times. Originally a rip-snorting, hell-fire-and-brimstone religious revival, it is now conservative and somehow more reverent.

The first Indian Field meetings, from 1800 to 1838, were held on a campground near the Indian Field church. Demand for larger space resulted in a move to the present site, several miles away, in 1838. The grounds were incorporated in 1879.

The Indian Field meeting is held during the week ending with the first Sunday in October under the auspices of the Conference of the Methodist Church. The land is owned by the South Carolina Conference, but the houses belong to the families and the owners are not interfered with as long as the buildings are kept in reasonable repair and the household conducts itself with the proper decorum. If a family ceases to use its house, it may be sold or it reverts to the trustees. The grounds are under the management of a board.

The Indian Field campground is about a mile off Highway 15 near St. George in a grove of the rare longleaf pines, whose needles make a soft cover over the wide circle formed by the ninety-nine houses. These are still called "tents," a designation which dates back to the early times when temporary shelters were used. An early writer describes these "tents": "At first tents were built of pine poles with a partition

through the middle of a loft above, reached by a ladder, for the gentlemen's sleeping place."

These early "tents" have been replaced by rustic two-story houses, all very much alike, with dirt floors. The fronts of the houses face the inner circle. A porch and an outdoor oven at the back of the house serve as a kitchen. A porch on the front is the sheltered sitting-out place; upstairs are two large sleeping rooms, one for the men and one for the women. The beds are mattresses, a modern innovation, laid on rough bunk frames. Until recent times, the campers slept on straw on the floor.

On the ground floor is the dining room–living room, a room for the servants, and a small bedroom. This small bedroom is traditionally used by the old and infirm who cannot climb the steep stairs.

There are ninety-nine houses spaced evenly around a circle a half-mile in circumference. One house is owned by the Conference and is used by visiting clergy. Ninety-eight of the houses are owned by individual families and are passed down from one generation to the next. It is rare that the title to a house passes out of the family, but title can be bought and sold.

In the center of the circle stands the tabernacle, a rough structure seating twelve hundred with standing room for many more. It was built more than a century

ago of hand-hewn longleaf pine timbers, pegged together, and is in a remarkable state of preservation. The dirt floor is covered with aromatic pine needles for each annual meeting. Electric lights and a public address system have been installed in modern times.

The day starts early, with the blowing of the ancient, six-foot, homemade trumpet that was modeled after Gabriel's mythical instrument. The first trumpet sounds at 7 A.M., immediately after breakfast, and calls the people to the first meeting of the day, which is a prayer service. Then it calls them to preaching at 11, and again at 3:30 and 7:30 P.M. The Conference sends well-known preachers from far and near to deliver the sermons and conduct the services. The exhortations and shouting of an earlier frontier religion have given away to a more conservative and thoughtful approach. A well-trained choir leads the singing. Sermons have been shortened from an hour to half that and there is rarely a mourner's bench.

After the evening services the people walk in meditative silence back to the campfires that flicker and beckon in a great circle in front of the tents. Here fellowship approaches a religious significance. Easy chairs from the tents are arranged around the campfire and there are good talk, tall tales, and the understanding that comes with a common background.

THE CHRISTMAS PROGRAM

Before Thanksgiving most of us at Loon Lake School had our Christmas pieces memorized. For weeks we happily drilled and rehearsed. Classes were cut short for practice, and the last few days before the grand finale they were abandoned.

Outside talent was invited to take part in the program—fact is, you couldn't keep it out. Little brothers and sisters, too young for school, were given pieces or had stand-in parts. And on Program Night, no matter how inaudibly they lisped their lines, it was they who stole the show.

As the great day grew nearer marvelous changes came over our bleak schoolroom. Cloakrooms became fascinating dressing rooms. Piled high on the lunchbox shelves were Santa suits, Mother Goose costumes, brownie outfits, wigs, masks, angel gowns, and mysterious scenery props. Our lunch pails were stowed on the floor amid the dripping boots and overshoes.

About the curtainless windows dangled paper chains, and red and green ribbons festooned the ceiling in intricate loops, braids, and swirls. The blackboards had a bright border of poinsettias, laboriously cut out, colored, and put up with flour paste.

George Washington's portrait was gaily fringed with boughs of evergreen and President McKinley's heavy-browed visage stared from among clusters of silver icicles. On the back wall the big clock's dignity, though not its face, disappeared in a tangle of tinsel.

The trimming of the tree, dragged in by the older boys from a nearby woods, was an all-grade activity. And proudly the graceful green boughs of the tall hemlock bore their burden of baubles, tarnished tinsel, and strings of popcorn and cranberries.

The tree-trimming, though tremendously important, could not compare with the building of the plank platform. The noise of those pounding hammers was more than music to our ears! It was the roll of drums presaging our wondrous affair.

Then the bed sheet curtains were put up, strung on a taut wire with safety pins. The teacher selected the most reliable sixth-grader in the class to draw the curtains that night. He was envied by all.

There was tension in the very air. The last day or two before the Night it almost reached the breaking point. Youngsters became a bit hysterical and the teacher turned on all her self-control. She usually broke when some young performer, after rendering his piece, made a graceful bow, and forgot he was standing on a platform.

But along in the late afternoon everything settled down to a tense calmness. We bundled up for our walk home, turned at the door and looked back on the exciting scene where soon a great drama was to unfold. "See you tonight," we said to our friends. Our words were intended to be heavy with portentous meaning. For were we not, all of us, conspirators on the brink of a great adventure?

At our homes we rushed through supper and barn chores with unusual speed. Then, in the starlit darkness, the whole family piled into the straw-filled wagon—"The Night" began.

A stray Christmas angel hovering over our Loon Lake School District could see, through the falling snow, a dimly lighted one-room school as a sort of hub of a wheel. Converging on the dim light from all roads were slow-moving buggies and wagons. If the roads were covered with snow, there were sleighs in the procession.

Wondrous to see, through the falling snow, the unfamiliar sight of a lighted schoolhouse! This was the only occasion when our school was not deserted-looking at night. As we neared the beautifully lit building, anticipatory thrills ran up and down our spines and the magic of "The Night" deepened.

We took our assigned seats, where we looked upon each other with speechless awe. Everybody was in his Sunday best. The girls had ribbons in their freshly curled hair and the boys wore their best suits, with white shirts and ties.

Our teacher was everywhere at once. The hint of hysteria of the past week was replaced by a calm assurance of a successful accomplishment. She played the pump organ for our opening song. The old organ didn't like the cold, and some of the keys stuck, but the melodies were familiar and we hardly noticed.

Backstage, miraculously keeping track of the books and magazines in which were our pieces and plays, the teacher cued lines while helping us don our costumes. Pillows had to be stuffed into the yawning cavity of a youthful Santa's trousers. Angel wings had to be ad-

justed, burnt cork applied to the unprotesting faces of comedy-act performers, crepe paper Mother Goose costumes were pinned just so. Stage business was managed with military precision; we knew just when to leave our out-front seats to be ready for our on-stage parts. Each of us had been assigned younger pupils whom we were to help. The big kids helped the little kids, on down the line. We talked in whispers—to make a noise would destroy the illusion out front. And out front, all was expectancy, and the hush before the first curtain.

Between acts the teacher kept a sharp eye on those delegated to removing and bringing on scenery and props. And she often paused to hold the trembling hand of a timid first-grader as he quavered out his long-practiced piece. To forget a line would have broken his heart and disappointed his parents, yet to venture on stage in front of all those people was impossible without a little moral support.

So "The Night" wore on with the teacher playing her role of musician, stage director, make-up man, prompter and instiller of confidence.

Just as the heavy eyelids of the weary preschoolers were drooping, a jingling of sleigh bells was heard outside. A thrilling happiness vibrated through the air, touching young and old. The masked, white-bearded "school-board Santa" became the real, living Christmas Spirit. Those of us who knew Santa stuff

was make-believe knew also that this night our souls climbed to dizzying heights of happiness. Santa passed out the treat, a bag of candy and an orange, and was gone again into the night.

Perhaps that stray Christmas angel hovering low over our little school may have folded his wings and crept quietly inside. Somehow we really felt like being "kind one to another, forgiving one another."

Program Night ended with the "Star of the East," sung by a nervous soprano borrowed from the church choir. I know now she wasn't much of a soloist, but to me then the yearning, muted notes rose and fell in sweet sadness, flooding the air with a mystical cadence. Then the old organ, its unpredictable keys either warmed by the stove's heat or perhaps awakened from silence by the spirit of Christmas, released lovely, mellowed music.

Of such power was the spell woven about us that we not only forgave each other, we even forgave our teacher, her sternness and her impatience. After all it was she who had brought us a little nearer the angels, kings and queens for a night.

Whether we faltered in our lines or carried them through without a break, we were all part of a glorious thing. And our parents, smiling encouragingly, applauding, were each in their hearts saying as we appeared on the flimsy stage, lighted by flickering lanterns, "That's my son, that's my daughter."

HEIGH HO, OFF TO THE FAIR

One of the high spots of the year when I was a boy was the county fair. This usually came along about the first of September when the crops were laid by and there was a slack time. The fair that I attended as a boy was not officially a county fair—there was no such thing in our county at that time. It was just a plain country fair. It usually lasted three days— Thursday, Friday, and Saturday—and a good many people made all three days. Those who were within driving distance by horse and buggy or wagon drove back and forth each day. People living further away sometimes made tents out of tarpaulins and spent the entire three days on a sort of picnic.

The "fair" part of the fair was pretty sketchy. There were a few livestock exhibits, mostly of good working farm animals cleaned up and brushed. The horses had their tails and manes braided, and the sheep had the burrs combed out of their wool. The biggest display was of jellies, jams, and preserves, canned stuff and baked goods brought in by the women. There was a good deal of rivalry in this section as well as some political shenanigans. People thought too many winners were kinfolk of the judges.

I had a tremendous sweet tooth like all boys, and the "sugar and sweet" section of the fair colored my whole life. It even stimulated a rather peculiar ambition. Unlike my friends, who yearned to be either Indian fighters or streetcar conductors, I wanted to be a big enough man someday to get on the fair board and judge the pies and cakes. I used to stand around with my mouth watering, watching the judges nibble here and nibble there on the best cakes and pies in the

county. There were also a few displays of fruits and vegetables, especially watermelons, which were ripening about that time. That's another thing I wanted to be—a watermelon taster, and to heck with fighting Indians.

My first visit to the fair was when I was a babe in arms and I'm told I bawled all day from fright. However, when I turned six and was looking forward to my first year in school, I had toughened up somewhat. That was the year my mother gave me fifteen cents to spend. That wasn't fifteen cents a day, but fifteen cents for all three days. I can tell you that I had to husband that wealth to make it stretch over three days. As soon as I put it in my pocket it got red-hot and it stayed hot.

Those were the days when a good hand could be hired for a dollar a day, and fifteen cents was an hour and a half of sweat for a grown man. If your father was a working man he looked a long time at that much money, and if he hired hands himself, he took an even longer look.

That fifteen cents was a sacrifice for somebody, and I wasn't allowed to forget it. Nevertheless, I blew five cents just as soon as I could scurry to the peanut stand. Near the peanut stand was a taffy pull stand, and that was tempting. But we sometimes had brown sugar taffy at home, and peanuts were hard to come by except at Christmastime. So I invested my quota for the day, five cents, in a bag of peanuts. Later I did some trading with a friend who had decided on taffy. The second five cents went for a merry-go-round ride the next day. I was completely wiped out on the third day when I invested in a sheet of transfers at a knickknack stand.

When I was in my early teens and making my own money I splurged like a drunken sailor. I remember one summer I had two silver dollars and some small change from debugging a field of potatoes. I never stopped eating peanuts and I didn't wash them down with plain water either—I washed them down with lemonade at five cents a glass. Most of the two dollars-odd went down my gullet and the consequences were unfortunate. On the Sunday morning after the fair I woke up with a fever and other symptoms, one of which was diarrhea. My mother thought at first it might be the flux. A gallon of buttermilk cured it.

Scattered among the trees was a variety of temptations for the gullible country boy. Among them were the dog-faced boy, the biggest boa constrictor in the world, and the bearded lady. The bearded lady was often discussed around the stove at the grocery store on winter evenings. Many doubted that she was really a lady at all. Some said she was a man, padded in the right places, and too lazy to do a man's work.

"The Cane You Ring Is the Cane You Get" was always a popular game at our fairs. This was because tied to the heads of a few special canes were several fine, extra prizes. One year a cane had a nickel-plated revolver tied to it and that was worth spending big money to win. One customer spent an afternoon and a whole week's wages trying to ring that one cane. He finally suspected skullduggery and got the sheriff. Sure enough, the ring couldn't be forced over the cane and pistol, much less dropped. There was a lot of excitement and the game was closed. But the next day it was going again and everybody was trying to ring a hunting knife with a wide leather sheath.

There was a shell game too, which was a "now-you-see-it, now-you-don't" in more ways than one. The pea disappeared when the money was around, the shellman disappeared when the sheriff was around. Keeping one eye on the pea and one on the sheriff just made things more interesting.

Would-be baseball players of the county could not resist "Dunk Roscoe." This attraction was a hundred-gallon stock tank above which was suspended a chair. Beneath the chair was a twelve-inch circular target which, when whacked by a baseball, released the chair, dumping Roscoe into the tank. Roscoe was authentic. He was Roscoe Bates, a local drifter, who had been dunked for so many years he became an institution. It was said to be the only time Roscoe drank water. In our community a baseball player could receive no higher praise than "He's good enough to dunk Roscoe!" Roscoe received three cents for each dunking, nothing for a miss. This arrangement made him an admirer of the expert thrower. On good days he made as much as three dollars.

I cannot, even now, speak of our country fair peep show with candor. Those were the days when a leg was never a leg but a limb, and no genuine lady ever showed her ankle in public. I know now that the peep show was not the den of iniquity which I heard my mother call it. Looking back I can see four fat females, their bloom long since faded, sweating in the summer sun while a spieler described their charms and accomplishments. It was a tough job they had, standing in the dust and heat, trying to look seduc-

tive. I heard one man say they were veterans of Roosevelt's Rough Riders. Mother considered them fallen women; Father never did say, not at least within the hearing distance of a big-eared kid. Like all good wives, Mother shunned the vicinity of the peep show. But she always knew where it was located and her intuition told her when Father began to stray in that direction. It was the bachelors, being less restrained, who patronized the show in numbers. Married men had to resort to trickery and sneak visits.

All this I knew from eavesdropping and hearsay. The four tired sirens and our fair vanished with the horse and buggy, long before I reached that devilish age when I could plunk down my two bits and walk into that fascinating den of vice.

By far the most important event of the fair was the balloon ascension. It overshadowed everything, even the peep show and the dog-faced boy. The balloon ascension took place every afternoon at four o'clock, and people who couldn't make the fair for anything else suspended harvesting or seeding to show up for that event.

I doubt if anybody younger than a grandfather remembers a hot air balloon ascension. This was long before the time of the flying machine, and to see someone get up in the air in any way whatsoever was a thrill which tickled the innermost yearnings of earth-

bound man. The balloonist was just an ordinary fellow, I know now, who probably was a blacksmith or a barber during the off season, but to me he was a superman. He walked around the fairgrounds like a god and people hung on his words. Next to being a watermelon taster, I thought possibly I might go into the balloon business.

His property and paraphernalia were simple: a balloon of light canvas, perhaps thirty feet in diameter, grimy and much patched; a rope for hoisting the balloon over the fire pit, a parachute, and a simple swing-like trapeze beneath the parachute. That was all.

A rope was stretched between two tall trees on the fairgrounds, and the balloon was suspended from this rope by a simple arrangement which allowed it to release itself when it ascended. The open end of the balloon was immediately over a fire pit. The fire pit was a rough trench ten or twelve feet long covered with old metal roofing and six inches or so of earth. A crude chimney made also of metal roofing projected into the open end of the balloon.

As the time for the ascension neared, the balloonist appeared from somewhere with a train of small boys. Some of the boys were proudly carrying buckets of kerosene, a menial job which the balloonist disdained. In this procession also were a dozen men engaged beforehand to man the guy ropes which held the bal-

loon away from the flame and also secured it until the moment of take-off. They were solemn and dignified, properly conscious of the trust placed in them. The balloonist stationed the men around the balloon (at the ropes) and gave each a few words of instruction.

Beside the fire pit was a pile of old barrel staves and scrap lumber. The balloonist stacked a heap of the kindling in the fire pit and threw a bucket of kerosene over it. Then with a majestic gesture he balled up a newspaper, backed off about ten feet, lit the paper, and threw it into the pit. There was a soft explosion as the kerosene ignited and the kindling started to burn with a crackle and a roar. The balloon began to bulge out with the hot air; the balloonist kept feeding the kindling to the fire, adding a canful of kerosene from time to time to keep it going briskly. Soon he was black with soot and sweat, and looked not unlike a hard-working devil as he climbed back and forth out of the hot pit.

When the balloon was almost full and had begun to strain at the guy ropes, the balloonist paused long enough to adjust the ropes which were suspended from the bottom ring of the balloon, and to secure his parachute very carefully to these ropes. A trip rope to release the parachute was tied loosely to the trapeze bar. Finally the big moment arrived. The balloon was entirely full now. Smoke seeped from its seams and it heaved and lunged against the ropes like a captive monster. The balloonist donned a red satin jacket which he unwrapped from a newspaper, seated himself on the trapeze bar, grasped the two ropes, and backed away so that the parachute was stretched free of the ground. He held up his hand for silence, which was quite unnecessary, because everyone was holding his breath and you could have heard a pin drop a hundred yards away. Here a man was defying death right before their very eyes. He warned everybody to stand back. Those in the front rows pressed backward. "Now," he shouted, "when I count three, let 'er go." He paused dramatically, "One . . . two . . . three!" With that the anchor ropes were cast free, the balloon shot skyward with a tremendous rush, and the balloonist was jerked upward into the air. The balloon ascended straight up for several hundred feet; then it was caught by the prevailing breeze and began to drift slowly and majestically toward the east, growing smaller and smaller. The tiny figure, suspended by invisible lines below the parachute, seemed lonely and somewhat doomed.

The crowd stood frozen and silent; every eye was glued on the balloon; every mouth was open. When the balloon had shrunk to the size of our backhouse, the speck beneath was seen to wave. The parachute dropped free, bellied out, and floated earthward. It was almost as large as the balloon, and the crowd watched its swaying descent until it vanished among the trees on a distant hillside. As soon as the parachute was released, the balloon turned over; spewing black smoke, it finally collapsed, plummeting straight down to the ground.

Someone hired for the purpose was standing by with a spring wagon and a team of fast horses. As soon as the driver had determined the approximate place of landing he galloped his team through the fairground gates, and set out to find the balloonist and the balloon. I hung around the gates for hours one afternoon waiting to see his return. Finally the spring wagon emerged from a cloud of dust in the distance. The balloonist was sitting on the folded balloon, smoking a cigar, looking tired and bored, and not very romantic. I concluded one got that way going up in a balloon, day after day, during the fair season. Fame had long since lost its glitter.

One balloonist took his wife up with him, and another suspended a monkey in a small parachute below his own. This innovation was short-lived, as the monkey was hard to find. One lucky monkey came down in a tree covered with wild grapes, not quite ripe, and was sick for several days, missing his performance.

After the season, barring accident, the balloonist went back to his barbering or blacksmithing. But barber or blacksmith, the balloonist was a man of courage and daring. It took a lot of nerve to jump into space with a homemade parachute over unknown countryside. And there was always the chance that some clumsy spectator might foul up the guy ropes or the parachute. One balloonist in particular I shall never forget. He had a very dark complexion and some said he was a colored man. Others said he was an ordinary white man who had been permanently stained by the smoke and soot. Late that year at a country fair far away, his parachute failed to open.

The automobile and the airplane came along, and both our country fair and the hot air balloon vanished into history. I wonder if the first man to shoot the moon will give small boys the same chill of excitement as did the balloonist at our country fair?

SHIVAREE

The brief ceremony in the Featheroff parlor was over and Alice Featheroff was now Mrs. Dan Hoffman. As she sat beside her husband at the wedding dinner she looked across the table at her cousin Abel, who could laugh and eat at the same time. "How can he act like that?" she thought. "This is my wedding day and it's not right to laugh about it." Dan had been her first and only beau.

To Alice, marriage would be a career—she would keep a good house and take care of Dan and have children. Most of all she wanted children. When she thought of children she blushed, for she knew little about the mysterious processes by which children were conceived and born. Her blushes deepened, for unbidden, and out of nowhere, came the thought that tonight in Philadelphia she would be alone with Dan.

"It can't be bad now," she told herself. "We're married." But the thought of her wedding night filled her with a not unpleasant mixture of fear and anticipation. She was relieved when Dan pushed back his chair and with a great show of casualness announced, "I think I'll go hitch up. It's going to be a long trip to Philadelphia."

With her chattering helpers Alice went to her room to dress for the journey. In a few minutes Dan came back from the barn, clomped upstairs, and knocked timidly on Alice's door.

"You don't need to hurry, Alice," he said. "We don't go to Philadelphia today. We get a belling tonight—somebody got a wheel off our buggy."

Stoically Alice unpacked her valise.

By evening the grapevine had carried the news of the belling to every farmstead around Emaus—there would be a gathering at Groot's grocery store on the Bath road—the bride and groom were holed up at old Gus Featheroff's—one of the Hinkle boys had taken a wheel off their buggy and it was certain that no one would lend them a rig.

Soon after dark a half-dozen boys wandered into Groot's store and sat down around the pot-bellied stove. Then some young men, a few with their girls, showed up, and finally there came a sprinkling of older people. They carried an amazing variety of gadgets designed to make noise—horns, pots and pans, gongs, cymbals, and bells—cowbells, sheep bells, sleigh bells. The Hinkle brothers had taken down the 150-pound dinner bell from the milkhouse and carried it on a pole across their shoulders. There were a few of the lustier instruments from the Bath Silver Cornet Band.

Soon the store was crowded. Mrs. Groot took up a strategic position where she could keep one eye on the small boys and the other on the open cracker barrel. The young bucks pinched the girls and the small boys tried out their bells and horns on each other. In the bedlam and confusion the flames danced in the kerosene lamps and the new pots and pans rattled on the shelves.

Finally Jake Hermann, an old hand at bellings, mounted a chair and shouted for quiet. "Dan and Alice ought to be in the feather bed by the time we get there," he said. He elaborated on the plan of attack and warned that the least noise would be punished by a bust on the nose. "You kids had better be quiet or we'll send you all home," he added. "Now let's go."

By the light of a full moon they started on the two-mile walk to the Featheroff farm, the crowd of fifty or more stringing out along the country road. Jake, with one or two older men, was in the lead, the better to restrain the small fry. Then came a tight knot of girls making a giggling pretense of ignoring the heckling troop of young men, and bringing up the rear, the bolder youth, each with his girl.

There was a crunch of feet on the gravel road, the half-repressed shouts of the small boys, and once a metallic thump as someone dropped his cowbell. There was speculation on what was going on now in Alice Featheroff's upstairs bedroom. Far in the rear someone shouted, "Hey, Mary, how would you like to be where Alice is!"

"Shut your big mouth," ordered Jake. "We're gettin' there."

When the bellers came within sight of the Featheroff home they saw the light of a kerosene lamp reflected against the shade of an upstairs window. A wisp of smoke from the kitchen chimney curled lazily across the face of the moon. The light was in Alice's room, an informed source announced, and it

was assumed that the happy couple were preparing to retire.

Alice had persuaded Dan to wait up for the bellers, hiding that fearful expectancy with which she looked forward to her wedding night. But Dan had no such delicate qualms. "I'm sleepy," he said. "Come, we'll go to bed."

At that moment the bellers were surrounding the house. Gus Featheroff's old bitch, who slept back of the kitchen stove, was deaf—there would be no trouble from her; this would be a complete surprise.

"We'll wait until they get good and settled in bed," Jake Hermann ordered. "When I shoot off my shotgun, let 'er go."

Shadows moved back and forth across the window shade within the lighted room. Because he understood that to small boys a belling is the most fun of anything, Jake stationed himself among them. The noise hadn't started yet and the boys at the Featheroff belling did not like to wait. It was a brisk night and the cold began to nip the feet and hands. Jake was prepared to squelch any signs of a premature attack.

Finally Dan Hoffman's figure converged on the lamp and the light blinked out. "Wait till they get snug and warm," warned Jake.

A few minutes later a double shotgun charge split the darkness. There was a sudden blast of noise from horns, bells, and kitchenware, accompanied by howls and catcalls. The terrific clatter penetrated the deaf ears of Gus's bitch, who set up a frenzied barking. A treeful of guineas on the far side of the barn woke up and gave the alarm in their rusty-gate cackle. The echoes bounced off the far hills of the valley.

The noise swelled up and died down and then rose again, but all was darkness and silence within the house. For a half-hour the clatter continued; then the bellers began to lose patience. There was a shower of gravel against the window; someone shouted, "Let's smoke 'em out!"

Jake boosted one of the Hinkle boys to the roof of the lean-to kitchen and Felix Groot brought an armful of grain sacks from the barn. These were stuffed into the kitchen chimney and the crowd retired to await developments. These were not long in coming.

The glow of a lamp appeared in the bridal suite, the shade went up, and both Dan and Alice thrust their heads and shoulders out of the window. Smoke curled around them.

They were gasping and coughing, and Dan was mad. "Go 'way!" he shouted. But the bells and horns broke out anew and a handful of corn rattled off the house. Dan revealed his horse sense by not flying in the face of fate. He called out, "All right, all right, we'll be down."

Soon he and Alice appeared at the front door, Dan's hairy legs silhouetted inside his nightshirt. Alice's plump figure was wrapped in a voluminous robe.

"Kiss your bride," someone shouted. Dan dutifully leaned down and pecked Alice on the top of the head. From beyond the circle of light round the doorway, Dan's friends shouted their lusty comments. "Got a family started yet, Dan?" "I forgot to kiss the bride; how's about another chance?" "Has she chased you with the rolling pin yet, Dan?"

A small boy whispered plaintively to another, "I wish he'd give us our candy pretty soon. My mom said I had to be home by eleven o'clock."

Alice buried her face in Dan's shoulder. Recalling how long it took for him to calm Mrs. Hermann after their own belling, Jake stepped up on the porch, reached for Dan's hand, and recited, "Your friends congratulate you both, and wish you happiness."

"Thanks," said Dan. "Here's something for a treat. Don't forget the kids." He handed Jake five dollars.

Back at the grocery store Jake bought a box of good five-cent cigars for the men and ten pounds of hard candy for the women and kids. It was late; they were happy and sleepy, but Dan and Alice were now members of the community, in good standing, as a married couple.

It was among the Pennsylvania Dutch that the shivaree, or belling as it was called in those parts, achieved its full flower. Around Emaus, in the Lehigh Valley, the belling of Dan Hoffman and Alice Featheroff was an event of the spring season of 1901.

Webster prosaically defines shivaree as a serenade of a newly married couple. But it was usually more than a serenade; it was an initiation, a ceremony which introduced a new family to a community. As a social affair it was subject to local embellishments and variations limited only by the imagination of its self-appointed leaders. It could be, and often was, a dreaded event for the young couple, an ordeal which clouded their wedding day. In spite of Webster, there was often more horseplay than harmony at a shivaree. The harmony was lost in history.

The lustiness with which a shivaree was carried

forward was a good barometer of the popularity and social standing of the new couple. A well-liked young man could expect all his friends to be present to express their affection in cruel and unusual ways. On the other hand, if he had enemies in the community, or was not generally well liked, the shivaree offered an excellent opportunity to settle old grudges under cover of darkness and numbers. Whether given in fun or spite, the shivaree was no trivial matter for the bride and groom.

But not to be shivareed at all was a fate even worse. To be ignored marked a couple as so utterly unimportant that never could they expect to attain any sort of social standing. People would always say of them, "They weren't belled, you know."

Not all shivarees came off as smoothly as Dan Hoffman's and Alice Featheroff's. A gentle, kindly man often deteriorated during the ordeal of his wedding. He might carry nerves into the wedding night and become extremely stubborn when the shivaree showed up. A Greensburg, Indiana, bridegroom refused to present himself and was taken, kicking and shouting, from his bridal bed. A sack was tied over his shoulders and he was stuffed, willy-nilly, into the turtle back of a Ford roadster. One of the abductors had just captured a skunk and the varmint was tossed in with the reluctant bridegroom. After a wild ride over back country roads he was returned to the arms of his bride. The skunk was exhausted; and the bridegroom's contribution to the scented bower of love did not please the bride.

Ingenious ways to render the groom *persona non grata* to the bride have gotten many a marriage off to a slow start. In the West the groom was plied with hard liquor by his well-wishing friends until he was highly unacceptable in the marriage bed. Among the rugged folk of the mountain country of Kentucky and Tennessee it was customary to abduct the bride or groom or both, on the night of nights, and to keep them apart and awake until both became thoroughly disgusted with the whole institution of marriage. This often led to violence. Near Hazard, Kentucky, a shivaree crowd was peppered with birdshot when an irate groom discovered a party of his friends making off with his bride.

The common denominator of shivarees everywhere was a ransom given either in the form of money, food, or wine to buy peace and privacy. This was an attractive feature for small boys, who often outnumbered grownups at shivarees, more concerned about the treat of candy than about wishing the new couple Godspeed on the journey of life. Knowing a good thing when they found it, the younger set in a community might shivaree a couple night after night until patience and pocketbook were exhausted. In New England in the old days the serenaders were invited into the house for doughnuts and pie, preparations being made in anticipation of their visit.

It was customary in some parts to grant immunity in case the belling could not be held on the night of the wedding. Elaborate strategy was planned to evade the bellers, who set up a system of spies, counterspies, and stool pigeons to track down the fleeing couple.

The shivaree dates from the Middle Ages and probably originated in France. There it was known as the *charivari*, from which our word "shivaree" has been corrupted. It is probably a survival of a primitive ceremony to exorcise the evil spirits which sought to plague newlyweds.

By modern times the custom had lost its superstitious implication and had degenerated into coarse horseplay. In some countries the shivaree is an expression of disapproval of a person married the second time. In others it is community punishment for having neglected certain conventions.

The institution was brought to North America by the French by way of Louisiana and Canada. It soon spread all over the country under various names—horning, rouser, wake-up, belling, jamboree, tin pan shower, skimmerton, callithumpian serenade, and others. In Germany the serenaders wear masks; and they call the ceremony *Katzemusic*—cat's concert.

The shivaree is a rare event today. Country newspapers in the Ozark and hill country of Kentucky and Tennessee report an occasional revival, but in most places, like those fine old rural institutions, the husking bee and the quilting frolic, it is rapidly becoming only a memory of youth. This is indeed unfortunate. There is nothing like a shivaree to get a new couple off to a good start.

CHRISTMAS ON DUTCH FORK

Christmas in the Dutch Fork when I was a kid some three score years ago had a quality about it not found elsewhere. Our isolation and simple life on a hill farm in South Carolina gave it a special importance, and a special kind of observance. Santa Claus made his visit, it is true, and he brought us simple, but highly prized gifts. But in the Dutch Fork, Christmas was not primarily a time for gift-giving—the big event of the season was the family reunion, dearer to our hearts, in our remote valley, than any gift.

The elaborate preparation for the reunion started in late fall with a round of letters from distant kinfolk who would return to the ancestral homes there in the Stone Hills for the magic season. Long before Christmas we knew what trains to meet at White Rock, three miles away.

To the boys of the family fell the chore of getting in a good wood supply. We did that on Saturdays when out of school, for we didn't want to be bothered with that when the holidays came. In addition to plenty of small dry wood for the cookstove, which was cut during lay-by time the previous summer, we

needed a lot of green, long-burning wood for the fireplace. All-dry wood made too hot a fire and burned up too quickly. A generous sprinkling of fresh green hardwood lasted longer, and it sizzled and sang as it burned, and cast soft, dancing shadows on the floor and walls on through most of the night. And a lot of big backlogs was essential, so we wouldn't have to be putting on wood so often. Some of these backlogs took two men to wrestle into the wide fireplace. But once bedded down there, and with smaller kindling under and around it, that log would often last all day and into the night, a gentle, steady fire that we liked. And when we went on the hunt by day, we knew at least its dying embers would still be red with warmth when we returned. A cord of wood was stacked in the sheltered end of the porch, handy and dry for the women in the kitchen.

The first big event of the season was the closing of school for the holidays. When that came we knew the glorious days were at hand. On the last day we took the teacher little, useless, homemade presents, and she gave each of us little bags of fruit and candy. That last day was long, but finally we heard the magic word, "Dismissed," and we ran from the room, calling "Merry Christmas" to the teacher as she poured what water was left in the bucket on the dying fire in the big rock fireplace.

The group became smaller and smaller as the paths divided up the valley and over the ridge, and at last we were home—two delightful weeks lay ahead. We put our books securely away, pulled off our school clothes, and put on our everyday ones. That was the perfect moment, when everything was right with the world. We were happy to be alive, for the greatest season of the year lay ahead.

We eagerly watched for the mailman every day. We waited for his horse and buggy to round the bend below our place, and ran up to the house with the letters from our kinfolk, informing us when the clan would gather.

About that time we'd butcher, too. The thrifty Dutchmen of the Stone Hills know how to make many good things from a hog. And those who had drifted to far places were specially hungry for hog makin's they knew when they were young. Sausage! Nowhere else did it taste the same. Real sausage, to us, took a lot of seasoning; sage, garlic, onions, and the like, in addition to salt and pepper. And we didn't eat much of the sausage fresh. It would keep well and improve with age. We'd hang the sausage in the smokehouse, let it dry out a few days, and then smoke it with green hickory and corncobs. Then it would be dry and stand like a walking stick.

For variety, hens and a goose or two were fattened in a coop, and the big Tom turkey which roosted in the tree beside the barn was destined for the Christmas table. There would be wild meat, too—rabbit and 'possum and quail, with all kinds of vegetables from mother's summer canning, and from the root cellar. Not the smallest reward of the season was the eating.

Every meal during Christmas week was a big one, but the table literally groaned on Christmas Day. Christmas dinner was at noontime. There would be a turkey and several other kinds of meat, both fresh and cured, every kind of vegetable possible, two or three kinds of pie, two or three kinds of cake. The kids ate until no more would go down. Food was pretty rich, and we weren't accustomed to that, and so for a long time after Christmas week we craved the simpler things. The day after our last company left we waded into a pot of sauerkraut and baked potatoes, and then we would vary that with cow peas and corn bread. Those things went well together, and our parents told us they were easy on the stomach and good for what ailed us.

It was some days after we got out of school before the company started to arrive. It was always by train, for there was no other way. The train into Dutch Fork came at 6 P.M. At Christmastime, that's after dark. I liked to drive the wagon out to White Rock station. We always wanted to get there an hour early. In that way we wouldn't miss, if our clock at home was wrong. So that put me out there by dusk, otherwise when I was young, they wouldn't have let me drive. And one of the visiting men drove back.

When we drove old Frank we had to hitch him in a pine thicket away back up there on the knoll, away from the station, near John Richardson's house, for he was terribly afraid of a train. Even up there, from the distant sound of it, he would still be in a quiver when we went to get him. And, as we drove back down to the station, he was hard to handle. Didn't even want to go that way. And we had to hold him by the bridle while the luggage and folks were loaded on. The one that held him had to leap on as the wagon came by, for old Frank was off and galloping, smelling of cinders from the old wood-burner.

On the way home we had to go through a bog hole in Julian's woods. The whole road was a quagmire, but that bog hole, several hundred feet through, always frightened me. We could easily break a trace or a singletree or bog down in the hub-deep mud. I didn't try to direct Frank through the bog, just gave him the lines and let him go. He had a sort of sense that we didn't have for finding the best way through. When we got through, I was relieved, for from there on, the horse could trot some. And old Frank was thinking about that feed in his dry stable. We had in mind the good things we knew were being put on the table, for our folks could hear the whistle of the distant train and knew about how long it would take us to get home.

We were a sort of colony up there in the Dutch Fork. There were six houses of us there at Spring Hill, and the womenfolk worked out where each visitor was to eat and sleep, with later rotations. There were late arrivals and early leavers, and the schedules worked out for each home were complex and confusing, except to the women.

The shank of the holiday season was "between the

a most spirited game of cards every night, often into the small hours. The play was hard, but there was much teasing and joking, all in good humor. The women sat in a great circle around the wall and talked and changed about to get with the others. Most of them had embroidery, quilt patches, or other needlework that kept their unconscious hands busy, while their tongues wagged.

On the floor, between the circle of women and the card group in the center, we kids played. Most of the time we were fretting to go out and shoot firecrackers, which for some reason were a part of the Christmas tradition in our part of the country. We never saw them at any other time, not even on the Fourth of July. They were very scarce, and we husbanded them closely. When one of us decided to give up one of his treasures, everybody wanted to hear the bang. So the men lay down their cards and the women their handwork and out in the dark night they went. One of the men brought a shovelful of burning embers from the fireplace and put them in a little pile in the red clay yard. There we kids shot a few of our precious firecrackers each night. Wild ones among us would chase each other with Roman candles, shooting sizzling balls of fire at our companions as they scurried all over the yard and took refuge down behind the woodpile.

One night during Christmas week was set aside for Christmas exercises at the church. That was when we kids showed off. Our teachers and parents coached us for weeks in our little pieces and songs. We always had a large cedar or holly tree that filled one corner of the church. On it was draped long strands of bright red holly berries and popcorn that we strung for that purpose. They were the only tree ornaments we knew. Our lights were candles, saved from one year to the next. At one point in the program, the oil lamps that hung from the ceiling were put out and the candles over the tree lighted. Then we sang "Silent Night." Soon the lamps were relit and the candles blown out to save them.

I always dreaded saying those pieces, and I somehow escaped until up some size. I'd beg out in some way. But all of the other kids were showing off, so my folks felt embarrassed and urged me to try. They taught me a little four-line verse, which took several weeks. I was to be one of a group of five, two boys and three girls. They put me in the center, as I was a lot bigger than the others. This was purely primary stuff, but it was heavy for me. The first two on my

two Christmases," that is, the week between Christmas and New Year's Day. The intensity of the reunion built up before that and frazzled out after it. The routine was rather fixed. For the men it was the hunt, mainly by day, but occasionally a group wanted a 'possum hunt too, and that called for night. Game was plentiful. The favorite was quail, and they brought in bags full, as there was no limit.

As fine as the days were, nights were even finer. Then we all met at the ancestral home, known to all as The House. After supper all took the winding path to The House. On old maps The House is shown as Veal's Tavern or Eleazer's Tavern, and still stands. For it was there the stagecoaches stopped in an earlier day, and herdsmen from what was the frontier then across the mountains in Tennessee put up for the night, with their herds and flocks.

The living room, then, was not crowded even when the whole clan gathered. At the east end was an enormous fireplace, the only source of heat, but ample enough to make the large room comfortable. The set-back table was placed in the center of the room. There the "gambling element" of the clan had right rattled their verses off without a hitch, but I got more and more scared. When it came to me, I turned to stone. I couldn't think of that first word. Not only that, I doubt if I'd have known my own name then. There was a long and painful silence. My sister was the organist and sat right down in front of us. She tried to prompt me with the first word. It was "Remember." But it didn't mean a thing to me. I wondered why she was whispering "Remember, remember" when that was all I was trying to do.

Each day had its own special event, but of all of them Christmas morning was the one that reached the peak of excitement and anticipation. Our parents got up before dawn on Christmas morning and made a roaring fire and then called us. We were dressed and ready, huddled quietly on the stairway.

Our gifts were mostly of the useful kind—knitted socks, gloves, scarves, and sweaters. There might be a homemade rag doll for the younger girls and a few ten-cent presents from the variety store in Columbia. Ten cents would buy a pocket knife or a doll that would cost a dollar now. Sometimes gifts were ordered from J. Lynn & Co. of Chicago, which got out a catalogue full of wonderful things. My folks once ordered me a knife with a chain on it, the most treasured possession I ever had. I don't know why I remember the series of little pewter birds that you filled with water. If you blew on them they would gurgle and sing, and every Christmas someone got a pewter bird.

No Christmas week could pass without a minor or major crisis. One year we had a major crisis the day before Christmas, at least it was major for us kids. That was when a chronic drunk, from further down the road, got all liquored up and came whooping and yelling up our way. We kids were deathly afraid of him; we feared he'd stop, and he did. He came from Chapin, reeling and rocking and beating his lathered horse. He stopped suddenly in our yard. And before we could run and hide, he saw us and called us to him. I've never been much more scared than that. In fear and trembling we went up to his buggy. He got out, staggered to the back, pulled the boot up, opened a sack, and from it gave each of us a coconut and a can of sardines. He said, "These are yours, and don't let your mammy have 'em." With that, he climbed back in the buggy, gave his horse a whack with the whip, and with a jerk that almost broke the singletree and all but threw him out, he was off down the road. We later learned that he had sold his last bale of cotton that day and spent it all for sardines, coconuts, and liquor. And that is what his wife and children had for Christmas.

All too soon the magic week was gone. Each day after New Year's our group grew smaller. We took them to the station and there was much kissing and waving of good-bys, and yelling words of parting to those returning to distant parts. As the old woodburner pulled out, I'd get under the shed away from the shower of sparks, as it puffed away carrying our kinfolk into the night. We would follow the glow against the night sky for a while. But soon darkness took over again and we walked back up in the pines beyond Mr. John's place, where we found old Frank with his eyes bulged out with fright. Christmas was over! And we kids faced school again next day, and a bleakness that looked like eternity, before the magic season could come again. The new calendar was hung on the wall and a new almanac from the nail on the edge of the mantel there over the fireplace. Both of them looked mighty sad with Christmas covered by eleven deadly pages!

FIND THE RED EAR

A shrewd Yankee farmer thought up the husking bee to get his corn husked free. His was a simple idea, but the fascinating by-products soon got out of hand and the husking bee became a social institution which spread to all parts where corn was grown.

It was the custom in old New England to haul the corn out of the field before the winter set in and store it in the barn. The farmer husked it at his leisure, protected from the elements.

Husking bees were usually held in the late fall before the weather got too cold for comfort in an unheated barn. Neighbors gathered, sat on stools, and husked the corn, throwing the ears in the center of the floor. Near the door was a table laden with plates of doughnuts and cookies, and jugs of cider. Constant reference was made to these refreshments by the huskers. If the cider was hard, a good time was had.

A gentleman finding a red ear of corn was privileged to kiss the lady of his choice. This custom was sometimes abused by unscrupulous swains who smuggled red ears to a husking under their coats and brought them out at the strategic moment. Many a troth was plighted at a husking bee.

At the better husking bees the evening was rounded off by a square dance. This was the ancestor of the effete barn dance of modern times, a pale substitute for the real thing, which not only provided a good time, but got the corn husked as well.

205

SOLD

Ike Newman was feeling his years of work on the farm but he had enough salted away, he thought, to do him. He'd sell out and go to California where life was easy; he'd have an auction and let everything go, lock, stock, and barrel.

Ike had lived for sixty years on the farm his father left him. The attic, sheds, and lofts were stuffed with a lifetime collection of personals which only an auction could bring into the light of day. Ike's machinery and livestock were above average and his wife had furnished their home with solid pieces. It would be a good auction.

Ike decided to hold his sale in late June. His neighbors would be glad to have an excuse to take a day off from cultivating corn and making hay to come to the sale. Ike drove into Plainfield to have a talk with

Colonel Woodrow Boone, reputed to be the best auctioneer in the county. The Colonel asked 5 per cent for selling the farm and a flat 2½ per cent on livestock, machinery, and household goods. Ike made a quick calculation and decided that Colonel Boone was making too much money for one day's work.

But Colonel Boone refused to haggle. He pointed out that 5 per cent on the farm was the regular commission charged by realtors. The 2½ per cent on the chattels and household goods was low, he said. "Up in New England they're getting as high as 10 per cent." Ike reluctantly gave him the job and they set June 26 for the sale.

A few days later Colonel Boone drove out to Ike's place to "write up" the sale. He listed the household goods, farm tools, and livestock, and wrote a glowing

description of the farm and buildings. He carefully examined everything that would go on sale, noted its condition, and made a mental note of its probable value. He picked up bits of history about the older pieces of furniture which he would recite at the sale. He had Ike and his wife arrange and classify everything, packaging small items in lots, each with a "come-on" article to tempt the buyer looking for concealed bargains. Bills were printed and an advertisement appeared in the Plainville *Courier*. The bills were tacked up at vantage points around the county —in the post office, hardware stores, feed dealers, on fence posts at crossroads, and on an old tree near the covered bridge across Walnut Creek. For fifty years this old elm had been used as a billboard for sale bills and election posters and farmers always stopped there to read them. Ike was charged for the printing, but the distribution was part of the service offered by the auctioneer.

In addition to the listing, the bill gave the information that the sale would start at 9:30 A.M., the terms would be cash on the day of the sale, and the Ladies Aid Society of the Baptist Church would serve lunch.

The day of the sale dawned cool and clear, one of those June days the poets like to write about. Long before the time for Colonel Boone to open the sale, cars lined the lane leading up to Ike's house. The Baptist ladies had taken over the milkhouse stoop and were already selling coffee.

Everybody expected to pick up something for less than it was worth, and Colonel Boone knew that Ike and his wife expected him to sell it for more than it ought to bring.

Colonel Boone was there, too, directing his assistants in last-minute rearranging of the household goods on the lawn. In singles and groups the men examined the machinery and livestock; the women poked into boxes and opened drawers among the household goods on the lawn. One prospective buyer for Ike's tractor had started the engine and was discussing a knock with a group of self-appointed experts.

Promptly at nine-thirty, Colonel Boone mounted Ike's manure spreader and shouted for attention. "I know I am speaking from the Republican platform," he said, "but I'm not going to make a political speech. Just want to tell you the terms of the sale and something about the fine articles we are going to sell."

He sold the smaller pieces first, from the manure spreader, at the rate of four sales a minute. Each object was brought to him and held up so that it could be seen by the crowd. The first sale, a pitchfork whose handle had been polished by twenty-five years' wear from Ike's horny hand, was knocked down to the first bidder for ten cents. Ike stood a distance away so he couldn't hear. He hoped that in an hour the crawling that was going over his skin would stop. The first sale is usually a "bargain," going quickly to warm up the crowd.

Then larger pieces of machinery were sold, the crowd following Colonel Boone from piece to piece.

By noon the livestock had gone and Boone was ready to sell the household goods. The Baptist ladies had been doing a rushing business in coffee, mince pie, hot dogs, and soft drinks. Babies cried constantly and there was a long waiting line at the backhouse in the garden.

Standing in the background, Ike and his wife watched their old familiar things pass into new hands and new homes. They spoke little for this was like an invasion of their privacy. When Mrs. Ike saw that her cane-bottom rocking chair, the one she got from her mother, was about to be sold, she rescued it and brought it back to where they were standing. "We'll take it with us," she said. "Sure, Ma," Ike smiled.

Once a bidder complained that his last bid had not been heard and Colonel Boone put the article up again. It brought fifty cents more than on the first round. Ike had a bad time when a cow brought twenty-five dollars less than he had paid for her a year before.

The clerk listed each article, with the buyer's name, as it was sold. Some paid for their purchases at once; others waited until the end of the sale.

Last of all the farm was sold. For this event there were exhibits of ears of corn and sacks of oats grown last year. Ike was called on to give a few words of testimony to the high yields that the place had always produced. Mrs. Ike told how the well could be called on to do three washing-machine loads every Monday and the cows could still be given all the water they wanted—"even at the end of a dry summer." The buyer turned out to be Jake Clark's boy, Joe. He was backed up financially by Jake, folks said, and there was no question of the moral support. His bride of last June was all smiles.

Buyers stowed small articles in their cars; some of the livestock was being loaded on trucks, and the young farmer who bought Ike's tractor drove it

AUCTION!

Saturday, May 18, 10 o'clock, A. M.

Will be sold at Public Auction, at the present residence
of R. B. KELLOGG, in Windsor, the following described
property, consisting of

HOUSEHOLD FURNITURE,
and Farming Tools.

One Bureau, one Sofa,
Lot of Mirrors and Chairs,
Dining tables, Center tables,
And pictures in pairs.

One nice Stewart stove
Which cannot be beat,
For a family to use
To cook what they eat.

And several other Stoves,
And pipe in connection,
Which you can't tell from new
But by close inspection.

All the things in the pantry,
Tin pans, jars and jugs,
Tin pails, plates and platters,
And white earthern mugs.

Demijohns, butter firkins,
Ball boxes and trays,
Which you know to be used
In a great many ways.

One barrel of Cider,
And empty barrels, too
Four kegs, a lot of bottles,
We shall offer to you.

One barrel of pork
We shall sell on that day,
And some one will buy it,
But who, we can't say.

One wheelbarrow, three axes,
Two hay-saws, three hoes,
One spade fork, two shovels,
And manure fork, goes.

Two hay-cutters, two forks,
One feed-box that's pine,
One express sleigh, four halters
And flour barrels, nine.

Five harnesses, two robes,
And straps without number,
One Mexican saddle, 2 bridles,
And a small pile of lumber.

Two bitting bridles, two martingales,
Open headstalls, three,
Six surcingles, three blankets,
I want you to see.

Two monkey wrenches, one crow-bar,
One refrigerator new,
One nice sleigh-pole & fixtures
I'm keeping for you.

To one two-horse wagon
I now call your attention,
And a great many things
I don't think to mention.

Now come one and all,
That I may be blest
With a call from my friends
Before I go West.

R. B. KELLOGG.
A. B. BURKE, Auct.

Windsor, Vt. May 10, 1867.

Sale attenders rarely buy anything. They go to sales for the same reasons they go to fires, funerals, and the theater. The professional attenders come early, find easy chairs near the auctioneer, and remain spectators. They are careful to keep out of the bidding, knowing that once caught up they are at the mercy of forces far beyond their control.

Each sale is a contest between the auctioneer and the bidder. The odds are against the bidder, for the auctioneer is an older hand. He warms up two bidders, pitting the greed of one against the pride of another. Both may have wanted the article in the early stages of the bidding, but soon the desire for possession gives way to the elemental desire to beat the other fellow, regardless of the value of the article or the cost to themselves. This is pay dirt for the auctioneer. Each bid made in frustration or anger boosts his commission and bolsters the well-known saying that an auction sale is a trap for suckers who pay more than it's worth for a piece of junk they don't need.

A vase bought the week before at the five and ten sells for eighty cents; a rusty saw sells for more than a new one costs. Auctioneers say a farmer is a sitting duck for a box of old scraps, nuts, bolts, rusty hinges, broken tools, spare parts of old and obsolete machinery. He may have his shed full of boxes bought at other sales or collected himself, but he'll always put in a bid for one more, storing them away like a chipmunk. He's pleased if he finds a good wrench or a new pair of hinges in a blind package, but if he doesn't he is philosophical—"You never know when you'll need a handle for an apple peeler," he says.

Women have a weakness for doilies, grab bags full of cloth remnants advertised as quilting material, and prints in gilt frames of "Rock of Ages" and "The Stag at Bay."

Anything will sell at a country auction, chiefly because the buyer doesn't want the other fellow to have it. Articles which can't be given away sell readily. George Bean, a Connecticut auctioneer, received a few desultory bids for a gadget the use for which he frankly admitted ignorance. When someone in the crowd explained that it was used to extract apples from the throat of a cow, the bidding went up. The farmer who bought it said he had never known a cow to choke on an apple on his farm, and he had no apple trees himself "but it might come in handy."

Auctioneers report some amazing sales. J. A. Bissantz, of Willamsburg, Ohio, once sold a corset and

noisily out of the barnyard. When the last car had gone and the clerks tallied up their books and turned over the cash, it was sundown. For the first time in their lives Ike and his wife had no chores to do. Mrs. Ike sat down in her mother's chair in the bare kitchen, and set her face in a frown to squeeze back the tears. Ike walked slowly out to the barn. Honey, the old Jersey, was in her stall—her new owner said he would come for her in the morning. Ike gave her some hay and broke a half-dozen ears of corn into her feed box. She had always been his confidant. "Honey," he said, "it's too late to back out now."

In addition to those who go to an auction sale to buy either something they need or something they have no earthly use for provided it is a bargain, there is always a sizable delegation of professional sale attenders, or lookers.

singletree (in combination) for sixty-five cents. "I sold a beaten-up bass fiddle used in the orchestra in Ford's Theatre the night Lincoln was shot," he adds. "I've sold cats and old pajamas and a treadmill thresher. I once sold a piano for ninety-five cents. The only thing I haven't sold is a coffin—but I did sell a tombstone and a set of false teeth."

In addition to the local professionals there will be a sprinkling of another breed of attenders, the antiquers. There is no region so remote, but has someone who buys, trades, and sells antiques. These will be at the sale and with them buyers from the big cities who spend their summers traveling from country sale to country sale. They dress like farmers, stand unobstrusively in the fringes of the crowd, and edge in their bids. Before the sale starts they have inspected everything carefully and when an article of antique value is put up they swoop down like vultures.

For the antiquers, the pot of gold is a "sleeper." A sleeper is junk to the owner, but priceless to a collector. It may be a spoon holder which has miraculously escaped the hazards of time while serving its mundane function of holding spoons on the kitchen table; or it may be a rickety old table, bearing several coats of paint, used for many years as a stand for the washbasin on the back porch. The expert antiquer hopes that no one sees what he sees—that the spoon holder is genuine Sandwich and the table is solid cherry put together with wooden pegs by a country craftsman a century ago. He dulls the gleam in his eye and bids fifty cents for the table. He may buy it for seventy-five cents. The nemesis of the antiquer is the local housewife who has been bitten by the antique bug and is refurnishing her home with "pieces she picked up for a song" at sales in the neighborhood. She knows enough to suspect that anything old might be a sleeper, but not enough to be sure. So she bids on everything suspect.

Another type of sleeper is what is known up and down the Wabash Valley in Indiana as "Aunt Minnie's Chicken Money." It seems that an early farm family along the Wabash took in Minnie, an orphan girl, to help with the household chores. Minnie wasn't paid a wage, but she was permitted to sell a few eggs or a hen or an orphan lamb now and then. She was frugal, and her wants were few. She wore the cast-off clothing of the family; once a year she went on a spending spree at the county fair, blowing ten cents for admission and fifteen cents for three bags of peanuts. Being shy and a little tetched in the head she had no boy friends, and never married. As she grew old she kept to her room under the kitchen eaves, spending her days darning and mending shirts. Everybody called her Aunt Minnie. When the children and grandchildren came for a visit they slipped her a dollar or gave her a pair of cast-off earrings which she never wore.

There was a casual curiosity among the family about what Aunt Minnie did with her money, but when she died none could be found.

Soon after her death the old folks decided to leave the farm. Everything went on the auction block, including the pathetic contents of Aunt Minnie's room.

Mrs. Cyrus Gilpenny bought Aunt Minnie's sewing basket, chock-full of a half-century's collection of bits of yarn, for sixty-five cents. When she got it home she found a wadded bill at the center of each scrap of yarn—eight hundred in all. The family sued Mrs. Gilpenny, but the courts held she had made a bona fide purchase of the basket "and its contents."

To this day, any sewing basket full of scraps brings a high price at country sales along the Wabash.

TRANSITION & DESTINY

Eli Culver sold his little farm in the Mohawk Valley of New York in 1798, loaded his family, household goods, and farm tools into an ox wagon and went out to Illinois. With a half-dozen other farmers he built a raft in Pittsburgh and floated down the Ohio to Cairo. As a veteran of the Revolution, Eli took out a homestead of 640 acres of bottom land. ¶ Eli took with him a wooden moldboard plow, a pitchfork, a scythe, and a hoe. After he had his cabin up he built a hickory split buck rake and a harrow. With very little improvement or variation these were the tools Eli, his son and grandson used until just before the Civil War, when Eli's grandson bought a horse-drawn drill. Horse-powered threshers appeared about mid-century and in the 1870's Eli's great-grandson bought the first reaper in Illinois. The crops had been, since 1798, wheat, corn, oats, and grass; horses had replaced oxen. The cattle were shorthorns, descendants of Eli's first ox team. The hogs were just hogs. ¶ For four generations Eli's descendants learned little about farming. They did learn about the soil on the Culver farm, its limits and possibilities, but by and large, what was good enough for grandfather was good enough for grandson. The Culver family helped build the church and the school, the sons and daughters married sons and daughters of neighboring farmers. They observed Christmas and Thanksgiving, suffered from the ailments of the time, died and were buried in the family cemetery. In later years they leaned heavily on the mail order catalogue for their wants. Education was generally limited to the three R's. With few exceptions the boys became farmers, the girls farmers' wives. ¶ Then, about the turn of the twentieth century, a great wind blew about the world, and there was an awakening. The telephone came, and good roads, and World War I, which was the death of the Old Order. Soon followed the tractor, the combine, new crops and new breeds of animals, electric power, antibiotics, and political controls. The tempo of life quickened, new ideas were accepted; farm people entered the stream of life of the world. ¶ Sons and daughters became lawyers and doctors and teachers and married lawyers and doctors and teachers. Only one in five stayed on the farm. The 640 acres which Old Eli took out in 1798 had shrunk in 1945 to 120 acres. Of the multitude of his descendants, only two were farmers. Eli IV, on the home place, discovered that 120 acres could not support his family; he took a part-time job in town. A cousin, choosing to remain a farmer, bought the fields around him, increased his holdings to 800 acres. He sends his children to the best schools, owns a Cadillac, and his women buy their finery in New York. He is not horny-handed, as the Culvers before him had been; as a modern farmer he has a working knowledge of chemistry, genetics, engineering, mechanics, and accounting. ¶ This has been the destiny of farming. The transition is almost complete. The small farm has all but disappeared; farming has become big business. Old Eli Culver could not live in this new world; he was too specialized, too isolated, and he loved freedom too much to be a modern man. The Good Old Days are gone forever.

THE LOST SARAH

Every old-time community had somewhere in its environs a queer one. Old Mart Wolley was our queer one, a hermit or a shy one, or just balmy, as some folks said. He lived alone in a log house his grandfather had built as a pioneer on a dead-end road at the head of Bear Creek. The old logs had crumbled and grown tired, and the house seemed to want to sit down against the steep slope. It barely showed its curling shingle roof above the tangle of lilac and burning bush that had spread around it.

Old Mart was born there and he took his bride there when he came back from the Civil War. She was an orphan girl; her name was Sarah and she had no kin. They lived there together for fifty years, working the thin acres, living mostly on Mart's pension. They had no friends; never attended church, and no one ever saw either of them except on rare occasions at the village grocery, and when Mart was brought out to witch a well. He was the only water witch in that end of the county, and he was a good one. His fee was two dollars or a ham or a side of bacon, whichever was the handiest.

When his wife died Old Mart sort of went haywire, as people said. He followed the hearse on foot to the cemetery, watched the clods drop on Sarah's coffin, and then walked back through the fields to Bear Creek. No one saw him for a long time.

Then one day he appeared at the back door of Mrs. Mary Cummin, a widow, a good two miles away from Bear Creek. Mrs. Cummin hardly knew him. His beard and hair had been long neglected. She said later that it was very plain that he hadn't had a bath since his wife died. He stood there for a long time watching her silently through the screen door.

"What is it, Mart?" she asked.

In his cracked old voice he asked Mrs. Cummin if she had seen Sarah. "She's been gone for a long time," he said. "I thought she might be over here."

The Widow Cummin was frightened and went at once to the sheriff. "He ought to be taken away and penned up," she said.

"He's harmless," the sheriff assured her. "Been looking for Sarah for a year or two now, but never hurt anyone."

During the years following, Mart turned up from time to time at neighbors, and in the village, asking about Sarah. Then one fall a hunter stopped for a drink from Mart's spring. He found him sitting in front of his door, almost blind and quite feeble; there was no food in the house.

The sheriff straightway took him to the County Home. There they fed him, cut his hair, combed out his beard, and gave him a bath.

The next morning they found him dead in his bed. Some say it was just old age, but the Widow Cummin claims that if they hadn't given Old Mart a bath he'd still be alive. Whatsoever the cause of his death might have been, there was a good deal of heartfelt satisfaction in the community. Folks said old Mart Wolley had at last found Sarah.

THERE WERE GIANTS
IN THOSE DAYS

There were giants in those days, roaring over the land. The tractor was young and people weren't sure whether it was going to be merely another kind of traction engine or an entirely new creation. The combine was just beginning to come out of the West. The few "horseless farms" were curiosities and doubtful experiments, and agricultural leaders were verbose about the "rural depopulation peril and the problem of keeping the boy on the farm."

Back there almost fifty years ago, when the agricultural prophets said "power farming" was the solution, they were right about it—but too often in the wrong way. Their courage and flights of fancy often outran their common sense. They confused size with strength, and the tractor giants of old, impressive in their bulk, carried far too much avoirdupois for their power, and were too elephantine for agility. Speed and ease of handling were chapters in a dream book

At the Winnipeg plowing contest of 1908 the average weight of the contending tractors was 537 pounds per rated belt horsepower, and in 1910 it was 504. Compared to modern tractors weighing around 200 pounds per rated belt horsepower, those early fellows carried enormous loads of useless metal.

It was a long, long time ago that the germ of the tractor idea incubated in human imagination. Way back in 1618 (in Europe, the Thirty Years' War was just beginning: two years before the Mayflower sailed for New England; nearly a century before the Frenchmen, Savery and Denis Papin, invented steam engines, 1698 and 1707; over a century before Watt's invention, 1765; and two centuries before Trevithick's locomotive, 1804) one David Ramsay patented in England "a system for replacing the labor of horses and oxen by inanimate motors for plowing the soil." In 1767 Francis More patented his "fire pump," as the steam engine was then called, to supplant horses, not only in working in the fields, but in the traction of vehicles. But they were but the visions of geniuses born centuries too soon.

Not until after 1830 did the mechanical tillage of the soil approach practical realization. This was largely due to the invention of the tubular steam boiler by the Frenchman, Marc Seguin, in 1827. In London in 1833 there was organized a "society for the encouragement of the popular application of steam power to transports in general and especially to the needs of agriculture." This was the beginning of the age of steam carriages, crude amalgams of stage-coaches and traction engines, early ancestors of the automobile that went chugging and lumbering over the roads of early Victorian England, frightening horses and little children.

Those were days of awakening inventive genius—the sewing machine, telegraph, the reaper, all were coming on the scene and the idea of automotive farm power struggled bravely under the heavy burden of the crude steam boiler. In many particulars these old steam plows and tillers were strangely "modern," with features analogous with machines to appear the better part of a century later. The early spiral rotary plow, and the tilling member of the British Rickett rotary plow of 1859, are very similar to the French Maillet tiller of 1914, the Bagan rotary plow developed in Canada in 1932, and the new Rototiller.

Plainly the irredeemable fault of all those early steam-powered machines, even as those of a later date, was their enormous weight. Successful farm power had to await the evolution of a lighter and more agile motor. For a half-century, particularly in Britain, inventive genius sought to side-step the problem of great weight in another way—by the cable plowing and tillage system. The Fowler cable haulage plowing system was first exhibited at Lincoln, England, in 1854. In this system a gang plow with both right- and left-hand bottoms was pulled shuttle-wise across the field between two engines at opposite sides of the field. This was sometimes modified to require but one engine with an anchor at the opposite headland, a type more frequently used in France and Italy. In the "Howard" or "round-about" system a single engine fitted with a winding drum was stationed outside the field and the cable was worked over pulleys at the corners of the land to be plowed.

The cable systems got away from the problem of the excessive weight and the power loss of locomotion of the steam engine, but they brought no great saving in man labor, and their first cost was prohibitive for anything but large-scale operations under favorable conditions. Nevertheless, they had a moderate success, particularly in England and Germany, where there were several hundred outfits in use. A few modernized versions are in use today. There have been some curious and fearful modifications of the idea. At Toulouse, France, in 1926, an electric-powered cable tillage system was tried out and there were others using horse-powered winding drums like a house-mover's capstan. The original makers of the British cable plowing systems are still in business, but their main product is a track-layer Diesel tractor.

Though the steam- and electric-powered cable system was a giant, it was an earthbound giant, and the extensive use of automotive power in agriculture still had to await the development of the lighter and more adaptable gas engine. The manufacturers knew that something had to turn up to make farm tractors prac-

tical. It was the gas engine, but when it first appeared they didn't recognize it as their savior. Early gasoline tractors merited about all the ridicule which the steam engine makers and threshermen heaped on them. The cannonading of their big cylinders shook the earth and wakened babies in their cribs miles away. There was a whirring of big flywheels and grinding of gears as the clumsy giants thundered along at a turtle's pace. Rated at a road speed of about two and a half miles an hour, possibly correct on a downgrade, a bump in the road might stall them cold. And instead of a streamlined radiator, on their front was a contraption that looked like the result of a love affair between a shower bath and a peanut roaster.

But their development, if slow to start, soon became rapid. During the summer of 1892, in the shade of a village store in Iowa, John Froelich built the first gasoline tractor that propelled itself either forward or backward. The J. I. Case Threshing Machine Co. made an experimental gas tractor in 1892, but the first commercial manufacture of a gas engine tractor is believed to be the one made by C. W. Hart in 1896, the Hart-Parr, now incorporated in the Oliver line. But it was not until 1903 that the tractor began to be a real commercial success. In 1916 *The Farm Implement Review* listed 96 active makers with 137 designs. In 1918 a trade directory, *The Tractor and Implement Blue Book*, listed 130 makes of tractors exclusive

of garden tractors and cultivators. This figure included only those having considerable commercial production and sold by dealers. The number of adventurers in the tractor field at the crest of the power farming spree was far larger. One authority, Harry G. Davis, of the Farm Equipment Institute, lists 593 establishments in the United States that attempted to manufacture farm tractors. There was an additional list of 169 British, French, German, Italian, and other foreign machines. A French work of 1920, *La Motoculture Pratique*, describes 116 makes.

Many of these ventures were little more than get-rich-quick schemes of selling stock in nebulous companies, like the one whose unworthy product had to be towed from the rented shop where it was assembled, to be photographed posed before a plow it had never pulled. But the sorry thing was that so many of these premature mechanical mushrooms, fated soon to perish in the hard soil of practical farmer trial, were honest and worthy products, the conceptions of courage, optimism, and considerable mechanical genius.

Of the two main influences of tractor design, the automobile and the traction engine, it is obvious that the former is now four-fifths predominant, but it was the latter that had the most influence on the early designs. Because the first ventures into the tractor field were made by the manufacturers of steam-traction engines, their first efforts all looked like a steam engine had sired them. The engineers who designed them were not lacking in vision, for they quickly saw the writing on the wall, but they could not get the traction engine idea out of their minds. To many, the idea that a tractor should weigh less than ten tons was almost heresy.

It was these men, trained in the traction engine tradition, who brought out the big ones—giants of those days. In 1918 the heaviest tractor listed in the *Blue Book* was a 35-70 hp job weighing 30,000 pounds. The most powerful was a 60-90 hp outfit which was, oddly enough, a ton lighter. But these giants with their six- and seven-foot drive wheels, with three- to six-foot rims, were dwarfed by the mastodonic steam engines they were about to supersede. They looked like toys beside the three-wheeled steamers of California that sometimes had a tread or over-all width of more than thirty feet. Possibly the nearest approach to this in the gas tractor was a 200 hp machine brought out by a West Coast maker.

Though many made money for their owners, all were heavy on the farmer's land and on his pocketbook, which they flattened out under prices of $3,000 to $7,500 or more. And some flattened their makers, for those were the days of incautious optimism, riotous showmanship, and profitless exhibitions. Everyone wanted to see who could make the biggest mousetrap as well as the biggest tractor. If one manufacturer assembled an outfit of a fifty-five bottom gang plow pulled by three of his tractors, his championship was short, for soon another had a sixty plow assembly "turning over an acre every three minutes," as the enthusiastic salesman put it, conveniently forgetting a few seconds of the actual time.

But the giants were not race horses—if their makers were intoxicated with visions of size and power, they scarcely thought of speed. In 1918 six miles an hour was the highest-rated speed of any American tractor—far indeed from the 1956 daredevil record of over sixty-five. The idea of pneumatic or even hard rubber tires for tractors or farm implements would have been laughed at here in America, but rubber "tyres" were being placed on steam wagons and tractors in England. One American company in 1913 and 1914 startled the market by advertising a farm motor truck fitted with wooden peg tires!

If the pioneer tractor prospect was awed by magnitude, he was also bewildered by diversity. Traction, then the big problem in the tractor designer's mind, was multiplied in amazing ways. Drive wheels, one, two or four, were placed anywhere the maker thought they looked good. Some had large-diameter drive wheels running in the furrow, and some single, wide-drive drums or rollers. One of the latter, the Knapp "farm locomotive," a New York State invention of 1912, was in some respects of advanced design, with a "modern" front hood and a radiator like an automobile. Some makers furnished interchangeable round wheels and track-layers, and a French machine carried, in addition to its ordinary drive wheels, auxiliary track-layers to be let down and used in hard pulling. Two experimental tractors dispensed with wheels entirely: one was a huge mechanical screw which wiggled over the ground, and the other a walking robot with disc-shod reciprocating legs. Innovation kept pace with the assembly of each machine and rarely did two tractors from the same maker have more than a family resemblance. A manufacturer could safely call his competitor's latest model a freak. Versatility and turning radius were great talking points, and soon there were short-turn and square-turn models that could make a turn in thirty feet.

The cable system tried a comeback about this time. The British substituted gas or oil engines for steam power on their old rigs, but in France there were more ingenious developments. The "tracteur-toueur automobile Filtz" instead of getting traction through drive wheels running on the ground, pulled itself along by gripping a cable stretched across the field. The more simple and practical "tracteur-truil," of which there were several makes, was designed to combine the advantages of direct traction and cable haulage. This was a tractor with an attached anchor or blocking device and a cable-winding drum at the rear. With this gadget all the power of the tractor's engine avail-

able at a power take-off could be used in hard plowing or other heavy pulling. This idea is in use now in California, where a track-layer, fitted with a winding drum or a winch and cable, pulls large "gopher" (the English say "mole") drainage plows and subsoilers, giant mechanical earthworms which burrow four feet underground.

About 1920 steam made its last stand. Possibly the last important improvement of the conventional steam-traction engine was the Baker steam tractor. This had an automatic magazine self-feed coal stoker and a steam condenser, innovations which cut the water boy out of the threshing crew. It was an excellent machine but it came too late, and its high price limited its sales possibilities. The same was true of the Bryan lightweight steam tractor, an oil burner, built somewhat on the plan of the extinct steam automobile. There were also several modernized steam tractors of British manufacture, including a track-layer, the Sentinel "roadless." There are those today who still dream of the revival of steam as an automotive power. With the development of the small, efficient, high-pressure turbines this may be the step needed to further simplify tractor design.

Though it persisted far longer than might have been

expected, it was soon evident that the large single-cylinder gas engine was unsuitable for tractor service, but anything and everything else was tried. Two large makes of tractors had three-cylinder motors, and in 1918, one maker, strangely adventuresome and modern, brought out an eight-cylinder model called the "Common Sense"—but it had but a single big drive wheel. High-compression engines were not yet perfected. Butane was unknown, but the Germans were pioneering with heavy oil and Diesel tractors over thirty years ago.

Charcoal-gas tractors, pioneered mainly in France, were then, as today, interesting but impractical and inefficient. These machines substituted a stove-like gas producer for the conventional fuel tank, which developed an explosive gas from charcoal or wood. The idea was attractive because the farmer could make his home-grown, winter-cut woodpile furnish his next season's tractor fuel at little cost. In practice, the "*gaz pauvre de bois*," as the French called it, was literally too accurate a name, for charcoal proved to be a poor substitute for gasoline, without economy except in countries where oil fuels are very high-priced or scarce. Contrivances burning charcoal were used in France, Germany, Italy, and Japan throughout World War II. Attachments to convert gasoline motors to charcoal burners were still common sights on the roads of Europe as late as ten years ago. In spite of their theoretical values it is doubtful if wood gas has practical advantages for the American farmer.

By 1924 the tractor mills began to settle down; the cranks and the dreamers had been pretty well weeded out. Only about sixty makes remained, and of these about a fifth, together with a few new ones, are with us today. Such names as Big Four, Flour City, Oil Pull, Hart-Parr, Aultman-Taylor, Buffalo-Pitts, La Crosse, Hackney, Lambert, Pioneer, Mogul, Bull, Happy Farmer, Gray, Best—and many others are but memories. A few can be identified as the progenitors of present models but most of them have gone to the museums and scrap piles.

During the depression tractor designers went conservative—the four-wheeled type becoming the standardized tractor. The complicated freaks disappeared, and not until the coming of the modern general-purpose type was there a pronounced innovation. Many of the old-timers had "modern" features, over a decade neglected, but now restored to favor. Some of the big ones had cabs—not heated and air-conditioned, as they are today, but adequate. Soundproofing and radio equipment are also quite modern. The three-wheeled motor cultivator of twenty years ago, seen a few rods off or in the twilight, could well be mistaken for a general-purpose tractor of today.

When tractors went to rubber there began a new era in design and a spurt in sales. Rubber permitted speed and mobility, easy handling and reduced operating costs. The adaptation of the rubber tire to tractors is one of the most important improvements yet made on farm machinery.

Will the giants come back? Certainly, and much sooner than some think. In fact, they have never been entirely away. A forty-five-foot triple disc, pulled by a 75hp Diesel track-layer, is no watch charm. It seems that in the garden tractor, the "single-team" tractor, and the five-foot combine, the minimum size limits in power farm machines have been reached. There are plain signs that a reaction toward larger units which give more productive capacity to the individual worker has started. It is curious that the large tractor, almost driven from the agricultural field by the lean years of depression, was recalled and saved from extinction by the demands of road building and public works construction, for the alleviation of unemployment which this same depression engendered. The big two-wheeled Tournapull construction tractor, with its nine and a half-foot wheels, is a sample of what to expect. This machine, minus its 36-40, five-thousand-dollar rubber tires, in its basic outline recalls the big two-wheel agricultural tractors, like the old German Stock *motorpflug*, of over twenty years ago.

Some of the designers of the new giants of the fields will borrow ideas from transportation and aviation and solve their problems—not by putting bigger engines in their tractors—but by having more of them. We may expect dual- and maybe multiple-engined farm tractors. This may be the practical solution of the problem of uniting economy of operation with reserve power for emergencies—two or more motors, any of which can be used alone or in combination with the others. Dual-motored heavy trucks are now in operation, some of the largest industrial tractors are of this design, and possibly the first entrant of the type in the agricultural field, a dual-motored tree digger used by nurserymen, all indicate the next revolutionary development in farm power. There is, of course, the alternative idea of having two smaller tractors so designed that they can be united to form one power unit under the control of one operator. This cute idea was used by an Italian manufacturer who, some twenty years ago, produced a two-wheel tractor, two of which could be joined to form one four-wheel drive machine. An inventive Illinois farmer has designed a tandem hitch and control which enables one operator to drive two tractors, discing up to eighty acres a day.

Pipe dreams and air castles these prophecies would have seemed to the pioneers of the prairies—but not today, when dreams are the stuff of which progress is made.

219

THE FARMER TAKES A WIFE

Fashions in courtship and marriage change with the times. The pleasant job of choosing a wife in the old days on the farm was complicated by a good many considerations that we do not bother with today. But this is a pity, for a wife was a wife in those days, and people stayed married. It would be a good thing for the country if farmers could take a step backward and approach marriage as their grandfathers did.

When a farmer buys a cow he looks at her long and carefully, goes over her point by point, and weighs his pocketbook against her virtues and her faults. He should be no less calculating when he takes a wife. A young farmer, whose chief asset is ambition, should keep in mind that he will rise or fall on his choice.

This flint-hearted approach to taking a wife will appear to many, especially the female sex, as a way of saying that a wife should be regarded as a piece of farm equipment. That is quite right. We are going to be realistic about this, as every bachelor farmer should be, and not permit love or sentiment to becloud the

issue. Few farmers can afford love these days. We can back up our judgment by the judgment of wiser men. The Talmud says, "In choosing a wife look down; in choosing a friend look up." An old Czech proverb advises the prospective husband to "choose your wife, not at a dance, but in the harvest field." And Karl Marx (perish his memory) came to the conclusion that "The bourgeois sees in his wife a mere instrument of production." Lord Chesterfield, speaking for the upper classes we presume, said, "To take a wife merely as an agreeable and rational companion will commonly be found to be a grand mistake." Cynics all, no doubt, but realistic.

Romance is only a minor consideration in selecting a farm wife. After all, a farmer can give only a very small part of his time to love, working as he does from sun to sun and then falling into bed dead tired after an early supper. What he should do is to appraise his prospective wife with all his wits about him, and leave love to the idle rich, or the sentimentalist. He will have no time for sentiment in his chosen profession, and besides, if he intends to make any money, he must have a helpmate who will hold up her end in making a fast buck quicker, and in thrift and hard work.

Most farmers, like their cousins in the city, use very slipshod methods in picking a wife. They could do no worse if they pulled a name out of a hat. The eligible bachelor farmer falls victim of a moonlight night, or a dulcet voice, or a sniff of My Sin, never giving a thought as to whether or not the creature in his arms can strip a cow dry or hoist the back end of a wagon. The first female that wants him marches him to the altar. Like their city brothers, they fall for the perfumed butterfly, and marry her, and slowly repent. Farmers don't usually fall in love with the deep-bosomed, wide-hipped, somewhat unimaginative women who make the best farm wives.

How can an ambitious bachelor get the right girl? Our advice is for him to keep clearly in mind what an ideal farm wife should be, slyly canvass his girl friends, choose the one most nearly conforming to that ideal, and ask her for a date. She will take charge of the situation from there on. The thing to remember is *never* to have that *first* date with an undesirable candidate. In this way, he will eliminate the possibility of love complicating his problem, and blinding him, as it always does. He plays safe from the start.

After he has married her, love will likely come along, in the field while she is pitching hay up to him, or in the barn when she whacks Daisy for stepping on her foot. If love does not come along, so much the better; his life will be simpler and more productive without it. He'll have companionship and a helpmate, and what more could a serious farmer want? We'll leave love to the poets and philosophers, and get down to brass tacks, the business of farming.

What are the qualifications of a wife for a young farmer who must make his way? We'll call her the Type I wife, and here are her qualifications:

1. She should be sound of wind and limb, her legs sturdy, and her hands wide and strong.

2. She may be fastidious about her person, but she should not be disturbed by muddy boots in her kitchen, nor by the dogs sleeping under the kitchen stove. She should not mind the breeze from a trench silo, which wafts into the house, nor the continuous parade of newborn pigs and lambs in bushel baskets by the kitchen stove.

3. She should be farm reared. If she has been brought up on a farm she will not be shocked by the little things that are always coming up, like finding a dead cat in the cistern or wheat chaff in the bed. She'll take these things in stride and she'll know how to do things. It takes a woman a long time to learn how to get her weight properly under a bale of hay.

4. She shouldn't have too much education, which is as dangerous as too little. High school is enough, right in her neighborhood. If she goes to college, she'll read books and learn how the other half lives, and she'll likely not be satisfied with life on the farm, always wanting mink stoles and a new Olds 98. It is a great mistake for a Type I farmer to marry a college girl. Comparisons made from books can be a distinct handicap.

5. She must like animals, and understand them, and be willing to pamper them and work all night long during lambing time and when the sows farrow. She should not be afraid of a bull or a mouse.

6. She should love to cook and her greatest joy should be in loading down the table with food and then watching it disappear under the attack of her husband and the hands. She should be thrifty, and emulate the squirrel, filling the cellar with canned goods and the deep freeze with fryers, strawberries, and corn on the cob.

7. She should like being alone. If she is shy and doesn't like people so much the better. She won't pine for the gay crowds, the tinkle of glasses, and the sound of empty laughter.

8. She should be able to bear fine, large, husky sons who can handle a tractor at ten and level off silage at twelve.

9. She should be willing to give up her egg money to help pay the mortgage or to help make the down payment on a new cornpicker. Although she has her mind set on a new washing machine, she agrees a new washing machine doesn't bring in the cash, a cornpicker does.

The Type I farm wife is found in numbers in Europe among the peasantry, where they are an institution. The good ones are grabbed up early by shrewd young farmers; the parents of the less desirable ones have to throw in a load of manure or a cow.

Here in this country Type I is about as hard to find as a good five-cent cigar. They just aren't turning them out on farms any more, for the farmer's daughter isn't what she used to be. Once she gets into high school (and what farmer's daughter doesn't get into high school?), she becomes a drum majorette, or her calf takes first place at the county fair and she has illusions of grandeur, and that spoils her for a good wife. If one can be captured young enough she can be made over by a man who is patient and strong. Once in a while a Type I comes from the Future Homemaker ranks, and there are rare cases where one is born, and nothing can change her. Lucky is the man who finds this rare flower. The ordinary male must put up with the run of the mine, or as a last resort marry a Type II wife, to be discussed later.

Now that we have given the poor but ambitious farmer a score card for a Type I wife, we turn our attention to the Type II wife, a much commoner species. The Type I wife fits into farm life like a hand in a glove; she is the only asset on which the farmer pays no tax. The Type II wife, while possessing virtues of her own and not at all out of harmony in the bucolic scene, adds to rather than fits in. No farmer would list her as an asset—she might be regarded as a companion, a decoration, and sometimes a luxury.

She is most often found in the households of men who have inherited their lands from grandfather, who had a Type I wife. Then there is the occasional individual who started out in life with a Type I wife, who worked herself to death. In his declining years he finds himself with ample means, but lonely. His second choice is usually Type II, and more power to him.

The Type II wife had her counterpart in the old days—the frail, scented lady who painted china and read Ralph Waldo Emerson in the original, and took a girl out of an orphans' home to do the housework. For this reason she was without honor among her neighbors. If she had lived in England she would have been known as the squire's wife. She could not pinch hit for Dobbin when he got the heaves, but she brought sentiment and sensitivity to the farm, and her country gentleman husband could safely love her. This is more than can be said about the Type I wife, for whom love is an unsettling adventure.

The thing to hope for in a Type II wife is that she likes country life and fresh air. Her intelligence and college education are not necessarily handicaps, as they are in Type I. The Type II wife should be able to carry on a conversation with either the hired hand or a banker whose note is due. She should have a good memory for names, because she will find that the bulk of the matters discussed in her circle will be blood-lines. Although knowing the difference between a mare and a horse, a filly and a fillet, Type II wife should know when to be silent in the presence of men. With this blessing alone, some experienced men consider her adequate.

She should look well in blue jeans. It's not good if she runs to hips. She should be seen at horse shows, in jodhpurs, with a crop tucked under her belt in the small of her back. She should not scorn a martini, and, because she will live among men, she should know the difference between a straight and a flush.

Above all, she should take up a hobby, connected with farming, and pursue it to the bitter end of her own energies. This may or may not be profitable. If it is not profitable, the loss will be welcomed by her husband, who takes it off his income tax; if it is profitable, she can brag about the price she gets for a bull, or a filly, or a bitch from an A.K.C. winner.

She likes good paintings, but she paints her own and frames them instead of buying printed classics. She can deliver a calf and once she was midwife for the tenant, whose wife's baby came a month too soon. She hires a strong woman to make jelly but she saves the rose pips, from wild rosebushes on the back pasture hill, to flavor it. She wants a dishwasher, a garbage disposal, and a glass oven, but after dinner she sits with the men, compares a Jersey's butter fat with a Holstein's appetite, and knows when to laugh. She inherited two silver candelabra from her mother and she likes to put new candles in them and use them because they are charming even when she sits down to supper alone with her man.

How does one select a Type II wife? Take your candidate to the fields and the barns. Escort her across a muddy feed lot, lead her through poison ivy, and, poison and all, take her to a dance. She'll complain, to be sure, but if she comes back for more, she's your pigeon. If she's pretty and you love her, so much the better; but watch about the hips.

Now, the reader will see at once the weakness of our advice to the prospective farm husband. What would happen if the Type I farmer makes a goodly fortune and rises to Type II? What if he finds in later life that he can support a Cadillac and country club membership and mink stoles, which is quite possible in our great free country? What of his Type I wife?

He has a problem here. Others have met it in reverse. Many a Princeton man has found it profitable to cultivate the simple virtues of bad grammar and

forget that he knows how to bow from the waist. The farmer comes by these things instinctively and everybody will admire his rugged simplicity and his democratic bearing. His bank account packs enough punch for him.

But his wife is a horse of another color, poor soul, and we don't see how anything can be done for her. She will be much happier going on as she did when she carried water from the well and saved leftovers. She would probably be happier that way. If she isn't, by this time she'll have a daughter her husband can pamper.

We have, too, the annoying situation in which a Type II wife is tied up to a Type I husband. Because the female is stronger and smarter than the male, she can, and usually does, do something about this situation, pulling up herself, her husband, and the farm by the bootstraps into the Type II class. We can always hope things will work out. As they say, there's a lid for every pot.

To confound the cynics and save the nation, we have with us, too, the in-between type, neither Type I nor Type II. She is the ordinary farm girl who takes her calf to the county fair and gets a blue ribbon, and goes to college, too, and dates her boy friend on the next farm.

They go to dances together and they eat hot dogs and drink Cokes at football games and, on some moonlight night in autumn while parked for a spell in the lane, he pops the eternal question. They both know what the score is—hard work, and babies raised by the book, and self-denial until a start is made, and having each other and laughing a great deal and having fun and a full life because they both would rather have a farmhouse on a hill looking out over their own fields than a penthouse on Fifth Avenue. These are the people who make farming the nation's greatest industry, they breed the sons and daughters who staff the professions and trades, pay the taxes, and fight the wars. God bless 'em.

THE FAMILY CEMETERY

Our family cemetery was on a knoll in the south pasture, under a grove of oaks. The first of our family buried there was Eli Riddell, who bled to death from an ax wound in 1790. Eli and two brothers came out to the valley in Illinois after the Revolutionary War to take up veteran land grants. Illinois was a howling wilderness then, and when a man died he was buried on the spot. There was no lumber handy, so Eli's brother Simon made him a coffin out of his bedstead, which he had brought west from Connecticut. They dug a grave under a spreading oak on the knoll. Simon read the burial service. The next day he hewed out an oak slab, burned Eli's name and his birth and death dates on it with a red-hot poker, and set it up over the grave. Eli's widow kept the grave neat and planted a lilac bush nearby.

Ten years later the first church was built at Logan, three miles away, and a portion of the churchyard was set aside as a burying ground. But the Riddells continued to bury their dead by the spreading oak. The ties between the living and the dead were close; a wife wanted to rest near her dead husband, a child among those who had loved it.

It was the custom of members of the Riddell clan to meet the day before Easter to tidy up the cemetery —cut the grass, clean up a year's growth of briers and weeds, mend the fence, and straighten up the leaning gravestones. The women planted peonies and laurel, which in time covered the knoll and invaded the adjacent field. In 1808 six evergreens were purchased from a traveling salesman and planted on the knoll.

Everybody agreed that it was a peaceful spot for a last resting place. The oak threw its shade over the little cluster of graves, and the evergreens swayed in the breeze that always swept up the valley. Young men who came courting the Riddell maids found it a romantic spot on a moonlight night; hunters could always flush a covey of quail from its protective cover, and the first wildflowers appeared there. Small boys became men the night they could walk through the cemetery without whistling.

Some said that the cemetery held the Riddell clan together. The family grew and took up homes in the valley and the cemetery could be seen from every dooryard. The corn and the wheat were planted and harvested and the day's work done within the very shadow of the old oak. Day after day, the Riddell boys, plowing in the field, passed the graves of their ancestors. A tremendous pride of family, its substance and enduring qualities, was engendered.

But time brought its inevitable change. As the family married and new names appeared in the valley, the churchyard cemetery at Logan got more and more of the Riddell burials. By mid-century it fell into neglect, for it was difficult to get volunteers to take care of it. The rail fence rotted and went back to earth, cattle wandered over the sacred soil, saplings and briers grew among the graves. The ever-spreading roots of the old oak and the attrition of time toppled the gravestones.

For more than a generation the cemetery was not used. Then came Lafe Riddell. Lafe was the blackest of a long line of black sheep spawned by the Riddell family. He had gone west after the Civil War, worked in the cow camps and the gambling halls, was a lawman for a time, and never too particular how he made a living. He had china blue eyes, red hair, and a voice like an angel. He was known far and wide as "The Bluebell" because he was always singing or whistling "The Bluebells of Scotland." A friend who came back with him on one of his infrequent visits home said that to hear Lafe sing "Bluebells" by a campfire at night on the prairies would tear the heart right out of your body.

Lafe was a curious combination of harshness and sentiment, hardness and softness, and it was not difficult for the family to understand the strange request he made just before he returned west after his last visit home. He gathered the family about him and bound them to a solemn oath that when he "cashed in his chips" his body would be brought back and laid to rest among his ancestors in the family cemetery. He indulged himself in one of his frequent, short flights of sentiment. "Bury me," he said, "among my forefathers that my ashes may enrich the earth that nurtured me."

Two years later Lafe's old mother received a telegram from a sheriff in Wyoming informing her of Lafe's death and requesting disposition of the body. So Lafe came back, in a wooden box, and the men cleared a spot in the family cemetery, and buried him there. A gravestone of the period, a limestone slab engraved with a weeping willow and a burial urn, was put up. Lafe's mother composed the epitaph, "Sacred to the memory of the pious, amiable and talented Lafayette Riddell." Lafe was amiable, there was no doubt about that, and talented in certain obtuse ways; but only a mother could detect the piety.

Because the stone was new and bright, and Lafe's grave heaved so fresh among the weeds and briers, the family felt obligated to keep it green. The graves and gravestones of the other Riddells who rest there have eroded into common anonymity, but Lafe's stands proudly among the dark tangle, perpetuating his legend and his memory. It is said that at certain times, when the evening breeze plays gently down the valley, the strains of "The Bluebells of Scotland" can be heard, faint and far away.

THE HOMESTEADERS

Life was very simple back in those dear, dead days, when going west was the answer to hope, ambition, and golden dreams. We had no social security to worry about then; no quotas, no income tax, no Communists to complicate our simple lives; no forms to fill out, no red tape to unsnarl, to take us away from our everyday affairs. All we had to do was take care of ourselves and one homestead—nothing much at all.

That was long before they thought of paying farmers not to farm. The politicians of that age had a method which beat any such crude modern scheme all hollow. They simply supplied all the extra farmers with homesteads. And to add a little sporting touch to the deal, they bet the homesteader 160 acres of land against $16.25 that he would starve out within three years.

It worked pretty good, at that. As a means of keeping the citizenry from squandering its time and substance on politics, national finances, and the lack of indoor plumbing in Patagonia, it was a masterful coup. And as a plan for limiting production, it made Mr. Benson's and Mr. Brannan's programs look like conflicting theories of relativity. And it was as simple as the bellyache. I'll never forget the overproduction we never had to contend with on our particular stretch of Wyoming sagebrush forty-odd years ago.

Not that we didn't work hard enough. We did. Sixteen to eighteen hours is a day's work anywhere. That first crop had to be planted in time to mature before the high country's early frost. And before the crop could be planted, the ground must be put in shape for irrigation. Without water, we could not grow anything. We had no money to hire help nor any social planners to tell us when we had put in enough hours for a well-rounded life. All we could do was to go out and start throwing the dirt. Both of us. That was me and Irish—Irish is my wife.

Irish only weighed 110 and had never done any outside work, but she had ambition. She made a top hand from the start. Her busy fingers were in everything from tar-papering the shack to clearing sagebrush and skinning the plow team when I broke out irrigation ditches. The housework? Oh, she managed that, too. Don't ask me how a woman accomplishes her ends. Anyway, a one-room board shack is not much to care for, especially when its occupants only stop there long enough to eat and sleep. And cleaning was simple. A door in each side, plus a Wyoming wind, assures the removal of anything not tied down. There was always a wind. Yes, there was some dust with it, but that got renewed every day. And the baby, being only three months old, couldn't walk out on us just because she was somewhat neglected.

I think there should be a monument to homesteaders' wives set atop the Rocky Mountains. Something like the Christ of the Andes, only on a grander and more imposing scale. Irish was the best 110 pounds of woman who ever wore a pair of Levis.

Even with both of us on the job every waking hour, it was slow going. We had trundled our wagonload of household goods and two jags of new lumber onto the place in March. First, we had to get our tar-roofed shack up. Also, a small barn and a barb-wire corral. That took time. More time was consumed in getting our ditches surveyed so the fields could be laid out to proper advantage.

By the time we actually got started making a sagebrush flat into a farm, we began to see the theory behind that old saw about Rome not being built in a day. The brush had to be chopped out with a grubbing hoe, piled and burned; then the ground plowed and leveled, with all high spots removed and depressions filled to allow the water a free flow. About that time, the water would find a soft spot in a new ditch-bank, presenting us with a few new gullies to laboriously fill and smooth up. We found we could put in a lot of mileage on a small spot.

Along with this, horse feed was scarce and money was scarcer. That meant turning the stock out on the range and working them alternate days. It wasn't a method calculated to do the horses any particular good, but it did enable us to eventually get part of our most promising acres cleared, plowed, leveled, seeded, and ditched for irrigation.

And the horses really couldn't accuse us of selfish-

ness. We went through on grass, too. Well, they call it lettuce, which is practically the same thing. The alkali, bugs, and sundry other blights captured most of our garden that first summer. The lettuce, alone, made a crop. I have never cared much since for lettuce. Neither crisp lettuce nor fried lettuce; I don't even like lettuce in my sandwiches. I'd be just as happy if they never grew another leaf of lettuce—anywhere.

The rabbits helped some, though. There were plenty of rabbits. They served to relieve the tedium of straight lettuce. Then, the following winter, when we changed our diet from lettuce to potatoes, we had rabbits and potatoes. We used them together and separately, stewed, boiled, fried, broiled, baked, roasted, fricasseed, barbecued, and in hash. I also lost considerable zest for the flavor of rabbit meat that winter, especially rabbit with potatoes.

Still, the rabbits were perhaps a good thing. Without them, we might have started in on the prairie dogs and rattlesnakes. There was plenty of both. When we started spreading water, the dogs began moving in all directions; I ran enough water down dog holes that summer to float a battleship.

The snakes hit for the dry spots. It was rather dry around the house. The ones that located this haven rattled their pleasure and sent back for their relatives. We found them in the barn, under the doorstep and in between. Why we didn't get bit still puzzles us. A sudden dry, high-pitched buzz can even now prove my claim to all-time jumping records; I learned to jump forward, backward, and sidewise, all with equal ease, and flatfooted.

Altogether, it was a pretty strenuous summer. Still, we weren't worrying. We had our eyes plastered on that delectable future promised all those with stamina and courage. Our visions embraced waving fields of green alfalfa, quantities of sleek white-faced cattle scattered over nearby hills, a big rambling house sprawled under some future cottonwoods and fully equipped with all modern comforts and accessories.

We drove a team and wagon twenty miles to the river, one Sunday, to get our start in cottonwoods. The load of sprouts we brought home and planted would have sheltered a lot of house if the alkali hadn't burned up all but three of them. I guess the Lord figured those three would be enough to shelter all the house we'd have for some time. If that's the way He figured, He was right.

The alfalfa did better. There must have been at least half of it that pulled through. The Russian thistles, which filled in the bare spots, made it look like quite a pile of hay when we got it stacked up alongside the corral. The fine white-faced cattle that ate our grain, unfortunately, belonged to someone else. It was all open range around us. We had neither time nor money to fence until midsummer. By that time, we didn't need a fence. Irish got to be quite a cowpuncher, chasing those cows back to the great open spaces. I think that must have been where she learned to swear.

On those forays Irish rode a locoed mare, appropriately named Blaze. She was a splendid saddler and a wonderful cow horse. Unfortunately, she had been poisoned by loco weed previous to our association with her. The disease hadn't affected her physically, but had left her a trifle eccentric in behavior. She hated to work in harness, showing her displeasure by balking, running away, and chewing on her teammate. She absolutely refused to be led by the halter and frankly hated automobiles. When an occasional car would pass her along the narrow prairie road, she would immediately lay back her ears, bare her teeth, and race after it at a dead run, as though determined to destroy any such stinking threat to good, honest

horseflesh. When ridden to town, she would invariably put on a show upon being remounted. Immediately upon being untied from the hitch-rack, she would start tossing her head, rearing and side-stepping in a circle like a green bronc about to come unhinged. The rider had to mount on the fly. And the moment he hit the saddle she would leap the length of herself and tear off in all directions as though escaping from the environs of hell. Irish always got as much fun out of it as the mare did, judging from the way she usually chose the mare to ride when going to town.

Blaze was with us through our entire seven years on the homestead. During the period of the full moon she was always more unconventional than at other times. But always in the work she liked, handling stock or jogging the trails, she never shirked or let us down. We thought lots of her. We have often hoped she lived out her allotted time with the neighboring rancher who bought her when we moved away.

One nice thing; it was a light job to get the year's harvest under cover before winter. The potatoes were small enough to handle easily and the rabbits furnished their own accommodations. Wood was free for the getting. I only had to haul it fifteen miles from the mountain. Our water supply, after the canal was shut off for the season, was a mile-distant lake. Just a refreshing drive with a couple of barrels in the wagon each morning. We sure had no pie-in-the-sky fireworks that first winter.

The first cold snap let us in on a big joke the sun had been preparing for us during the summer. Helped by the hot, dry winds, it had opened up every crack in the shanty. We covered up all we could find, but we missed a lot. Quite a lot, in fact. An average Wyoming blizzard will disclose holes that no human eye can detect. We stuffed rags in the cracks till the walls looked like a mattress the moths had been working on. The wind would eventually work them out again, but that was all a part of the game.

We had another game we played a lot that winter. During the big blizzards the wind would drive snow through the keyhole in the door to form a long, thin drift out across the floor. We bet on the length of the drift in the morning. The loser had to build the fire. We never bet on the drifts that fell across our bed, though. That was too intimate to be good sport.

We invented a number of similar entertainments to amuse ourselves; we bet on the depth of ice in the water pail to see whether I hauled water or Irish melted snow in the washtub; we devised new ways to cook rabbits and potatoes; and we figured plans for a windproof house. We were mostly our own company. We had only one reasonably close neighbor. And town—two stores, a restaurant, and pool hall—wasn't particularly alluring even had our finances and love for riding a lumber wagon all day in the cold been stronger.

It was that winter that we burned up several years' hoarding of favorite old magazines. Our woodpile ran down to a splinter during the tail end of a spring blizzard, and I couldn't tackle fifteen miles of unbroken drifts until the storm broke. To eke out our scanty heap of wood, we kissed our treasured back-number library good-by. It would surprise you what good fuel they made when rolled and bound with haywire.

However, the seasons have a way of wheeling along. Spring arrived with a lush mellowness, as if trying to atone for frostbites and gloomy skies and rabbit stew. It lifted our spirits accordingly. When the frost went out, the Reclamation Service gave me a job cleaning ditches.

Our land was on a U.S. Reclamation Project, where the desert is supposed to blossom like the rose and milk floweth through outcroppings of pure honey. Providing, of course, one is able to pay for construction costs, yearly water bills, drainage, replacements, living expenses, taxes, and other necessities.

There were a lot of jokers in the deck, most of them wild. We figured that out later. Right then, we were too busy gloating over our chance to earn some real cash money. Some of this new wealth bought us a milk cow and a few chickens. Our epicurean tastes went up immediately.

That was the spring one of the big sheep outfits range-lambed near us. They gave us a dozen or so bum lambs. It looked liked a bonanza. We had fresh milk and the lambs were free. Combining the two should set us up in the sheep business at no cost save a little effort. The lambs, unfortunately, didn't seem to take kindly to a two-legged parent. Perhaps their sense of family honor was offended. Anyway, it was only by dint of a box behind the cookstove, some maternal hovering during the long night hours, and considerable uncensored language, that we managed to bring five of them through to pasture age.

We got the range cattle fenced out that spring, and more land to crop. Yet, our particular area of desert failed to exhibit any of the advertised Garden-

of-Eden aspects. Instead, it began to go seepy. Much of such land is heavily impregnated with alkali. Under steady irrigation the soil will absorb water until the underground formation brings it to the surface. There it will seep out, bringing the alkali with it, to form a white, incrested bog. A skimpy form of greasewood will grow in it, if it isn't too strong. Unfortunately, there wasn't much future in the greasewood business at that particular time.

Our crop was starting out pretty good when the grasshoppers came. They came in platoons, regiments, and swarms, organized and free-lance, regulars and guerrillas.

We got some turkeys to eat the hoppers, but the coyotes moved in to eat the turkeys. I did get a few coyote hides, but was careful to not let it go any further. I was afraid they might taste like rabbits. Then in the midst of the grasshopper campaign, Irish began to complain about feeling poorly.

It had something to do with what was locally known as a blessed event. This was what caused her to shove me out on the cold floor at three o'clock one morning, with orders to hightail for a doctor. I hightailed. My saddle horse took me several miles to a car, then the car went on for the doctor. The doctor, the car, and myself all arrived neck and neck with the stork. I knew by her sob of relief that Irish had been pretty scared, but I never knew till long afterward just how scared she actually had been.

Things didn't work out so well a couple of winters later. She had quit making marks on the calendar again, and we were looking forward to its arrival in the spring. Along late in midwinter, we were wrapped up in a thirty-below blizzard when something went wrong. We never knew what. Irish went to bed, feeling upset. As the house was puckered up in its customary stormy night chill, I soon followed.

We lay there listening to the shrieking wind and the roof boards popping with frost, when—Bam! Glass tinkled merrily over the floor. The intense cold, so suddenly contracting the lamp chimney after the light was out, had shattered it into a thousand frag-

231

ments. Luckily, we had a spare in the cupboard. We congratulated ourselves on this and went back to sleep.

To sleep, yes, but not sleep broken by dawn. In the middle of a balmy springtime dream, I found a determined elbow prodding me in the ribs. Irish's voice shattered the rest of my coma. She was going to be sick, she said, and it was time for all good men to come to the aid of the party.

I tried to argue the matter. It was weeks too soon; some minor disorder had needlessly alarmed her; and the floor was cold. But she soon set me straight. She wanted a fire, some hot water, and a light. And she wanted them now! The argument was over.

Thanking my guardian angel for that extra lamp chimney, I got a fire going, broke the ice in the bucket and filled the kettle. It was 2 A.M. and the storm was swooping down fiercer than ever out of a forty-mile gale. To go for a doctor was out of the question. Anyway, there wasn't time. I rolled up my red flannel undershirt sleeves and tied a flour-sack apron around my Levis.

Then, as I loped madly about, trying to round up everything she thought we were going to need for the main act—blooie! Away went the second lamp chimney. I guess it had heated up too quickly after its long cold storage.

Still, it takes more than a busted lamp chimney to stop a rising young obstetrician out to do or die on his first case. The stable lantern was still in commission. It was a bit blinky and had the habit of withdrawing within itself at sporadic intervals, but it represented a light. With it swinging by the bail from a bedpost, I took all three degrees in midwifery in about thirty minutes. They were long minutes.

I wish I might write a more happy sequel to that long, bitter night. But the little chap found it too harsh a world, improperly prepared as he was to face it. Perhaps an incubator and professional attention might have saved him. We'll never know. We are sure only we did the best that knowledge and circumstances permitted.

Life and death in a day. A scar for time to heal. I built the tiny casket myself. Our wholehearted neighbors gave their aid willingly and generously, coming as soon as they heard. We dug the grave up on the hill beyond the house. There he lies, a bitter-sweet memory of a black, storm-swept night.

Those neighbors of ours! I would like to speak of them more fully, only I know no words of mine could ever do them justice. Their time was as limited as their worldly goods, and they had little opportunity for social amenities, but in case of trouble or need, they gathered from all directions, hurrying through the sagebrush on horseback or in wagons, buggies or limber-jointed T-Models. Distance was no object, nor was weather. A neighbor in distress was a call that knew no obstacles. It brought out everything from physical assistance to grandmother's bedspread from the bottom of the old cedar chest. Whatever they had was offered freely, even eagerly, without stint or question.

Everyone turned to and did what there was to be done without stopping to worry much whether he would be able to handle it or not. He usually had to handle it.

Like the time our cow bloated on alfalfa. She had busted through the fence and stowed away a good load before Irish noticed her. I was on the mountain after wood that day. Irish was alone with the kid. By the time she got the cow to the corral, the old glutton was swelled up like a politician over his first seat on the gravy boat. Green alfalfa works fast. The cow went down a moment later and started rolling her eyes. It was serious, for she was the only cow we had.

Now, the usual procedure is to stick the animal with a trocar, forward of the hip bone, thus letting out the gas. Alas! we had no trocar. But trust a woman like Irish to figure out a substitute. Irish thought of the butcher knife. It resembled a trocar about as much as a scythe does a razor, but it had a point and was sharp. She carved a lot of cow, and probably punctured a lot of things not in need of puncturing, but she released the suffocating gas. Moreover, the cow survived both the ailment and the operation.

Most of our furniture was the product of our imagination. We cobbled our own shoes and shod our own horses. We practiced home barbering and made our own clothing. I even made myself a pair of pants one spring, a patch at a time. As a matter of fact, patches might be worked into a coat-of-arms for homesteaders. But for patches, tin cans, and haywire, it's doubtful if the Great White Father would ever have been able to settle half the territory he hijacked the Indians out of.

And you can't possibly underrate baling wire, that priceless commodity, the supply store and repair kit of every homesteader. Without it, there would have been few complete pieces of machinery, harness, vehi-

cles, or furniture. It served as nails, bolts, rivets, and clamps; safety pins, buttons, hooks, and rings; handles, bails, bands, splices, and welds; rope, leather, wood, iron, and what have you. It often took the place of the entire original object. A wonderful material, indeed! We called it Mormon Whang.

That second season showed us gaining a little ground. I found more work with the Reclamation Service on some new construction. The good hundred-per-cent dollars they handed out each month answered a lot of embarrassing questions.

It also furnished a few complications. A man has to be considerable of a stepper to farm an irrigated homestead, still in the making, while working elsewhere. I swapped my bed for a lantern and still couldn't keep up. The new acreage we had laid out shrunk a half by seeding time. And the crop from that didn't burst any barn seams.

We did have enough to winter our stock, though, by counting forkfuls and sorting the manure carefully. We had managed to get our house lined in the meantime. Also on the black side of the ledger were a pile of vegetables—mostly potatoes—some husky lambs, a few desert-trained roosters of the mustang type, and a pig which we later fattened on potatoes.

Anyone who has never eaten a hog fattened solely on raw potatoes has missed an interesting gastronomical experience. It made pretty good sausage, though, if ground fine enough and mixed with plenty of mutton. And it did help break the monotony of potatoes.

Anyway, we came out for the third round, still contending we weren't whipped. We even had enough nerve to buy a bunch of cows on credit. Or maybe it was our creditor who had the nerve. In either case, we felt good about it. That little herd looked wonderful. So did our first calf crop. Rainbows started shooting up all over the sky.

But it didn't last. The seep was creeping steadily down across our best land, taking the alfalfa as it advanced. That cut our productive acreage in half, leaving us the half that hadn't yet been gotten into production. I think our corps of Reclamation Engineers was the forerunner of the New Dealers' cropless farming idea just a little ahead of its time. They were full of experimental bubbles that usually burst on some plodding homesteader's bowed head. It helped add that little thrill of "what next?" to an otherwise humdrum life.

And this being jerked backward when we were all set for a forward spurt, gave us plenty of new things to think about. Primarily, it meant a two-year job getting the ruined acres cleaned up and back into crop. It requires at least one season of intensive cultivation and irrigation to wash and air a heavy accumulation of alkali out of the soil enough to fit it for growing anything. Meanwhile, we had a bunch of cows that figured on doing a lot of eating that winter. They discovered their mistake before spring. That is, the ones who were still interested.

These repeated setbacks sent me back on the trail of pay checks, leaving Irish to work the farm. Even today the occasional rare sight of a female with a shovel in her hands brings memories of faded, overworked women trying to keep slender crops alive while husbands sweated out another grubstake on distant jobs. The whine of raw March winds or the savage lash of midwinter blizzards recalls pictures of wind-whipped, bonneted figures struggling with hayforks and frozen water troughs. Time hasn't erased the haunting loneliness of eyes searching the seldom traveled trails winding across dun-gray sage flats. And ever the bitter alkali curling the soap in washtubs and turning skins into a fair imitation of rusty iron; or, as dust, sifting through every crevice in unfinished board shacks to make mockery of limited attempts at beauty and homey comforts.

Still, we lived through it. I guess we didn't know any better. There were no social planning wizards to show us the error of our ways in those benighted times. Neither were there any feather beds set to catch us when our knees wobbled.

And we did make progress, in kind of a stubborn, accumulative sort of a way, until we could look back with a grin of self-satisfied amusement at the long-odds bet we won from Uncle Sam. Things usually worked out like that, back there, when life was simple.

SPAN OF LIFE

It was spring and Jesse Metzger's bride was on her knees in the kitchen garden, setting onions. The rich, dark earth still held its winter chill and there was some old, tired snow on the north side of the gully beyond the barn. But the sun was warm, and a few pink fingers of rhubarb had thrust up through the leaf mulch put on last fall. Mrs. Metzger was pushing the season a little, but onions could stand it, and fresh green things out of the garden were very good after a winter of salt pork and canned tomatoes.

When the wayward spring breeze shifted from the barn, she caught the ammonia tang of fresh manure and heard the regular thump of a pitchfork against the wooden sides of the gravel wagon. Her man was taking the last manure out of the feed lot, hauling it to the ten acres along the creek, where he would have corn this year. This would be their first year on their new farm. There were mortgages on the land and on the team, but they were young, this was their honeymoon, and they would raise a family here, pay off the debts, and lay something by. It was the year 1898, corn was twenty-five cents a bushel, and for thirty-five cents you could buy enough calico for a dress.

There were ninety-six acres in Jesse Metzger's farm. "It belonged to an old maid who had tenants on it for a good many years," says Jesse. "It was pretty well run down and I got it for forty dollars an acre. The house and barn were pretty good and it was only two miles from Felicity. There was a grocery at Felicity, two blacksmith shops, and our church. We belonged to the New Lite Church. There ain't very many of them around any more. The New Lites just kind of dwindled away and we went over to the Methodists. As far as I can see, there's no difference."

Jesse had saved enough, working on his father's farm in neighboring Brown County, for the down payment on his farm and a few secondhand tools. He had a pretty good team of horses, a spike-tooth A harrow, a breaking plow, a one-horse, two-shovel cultivator, and an old wagon with a gravel bed, a hayrack, and a grain bed. Mrs. Metzger's parents gave her a cow with calf and a dozen hens and a rooster for a wedding present, and Jesse had a sow with a litter of eight pigs. They had a new cookstove. The remainder of their furniture was secondhand and gifts from relatives; they hauled it all over from Brown County in the grain wagon.

On the second Saturday after they moved in, Mrs. Metzger had saved six dozen eggs and two pounds of butter. She and Jesse drove to Felicity for their week's groceries and she sold the eggs for fifty-four cents and the butter for forty-five cents. She took a dime of this and dropped it in an old sugar bowl on the top shelf of the kitchen cupboard. That was the way it was; you couldn't get ahead unless you saved a little. After fifty-six years of married life, the same sugar bowl is on the same shelf in the same cupboard in the same kitchen. It has never been quite empty.

That first year Jesse planted ten acres of corn by hand. He plowed it three times with his one-horse, two-shovel plow, laying it by when it was armpit high. He had planted pumpkins in the corn and when he came to a vine across the row, he went out ahead of the horse and laid the vine along the row. It was hot in that cornfield in the July sun.

The tenant before him put in twenty acres of wheat. He had no binder, but he traded work with a neighbor, who cut the wheat. Jesse shocked it himself. His neighbor unhitched at suppertime, but Jesse was far behind and he kept right on working until after dark, and finally had all the sheaves up and capped. His wheat was pretty good for those days, eighteen bushels to the acre, and he got his first real money from the farm when he sold it for eighty cents a bushel, hauling it to a barge on the Ohio River, two miles away.

In July came the threshing ring. Jesse and Blanche, that's Mrs. Metzger, would get up early, do the feeding and have breakfast, and by the time the dew was off, they would be jolting over the country road. Blanche would get off at the house and join the other women in the kitchen, and Jesse would pick up a pitcher and put on his first load. There were eight of them in the ring, and that was eight moves, and eight big threshing dinners, and sweat and dust and coming home at darkness and doing the feeding and milking and falling into bed dead tired. But it was something to look forward to, the best time of the whole year. All the women worked and talked at the same time, and the men tried to outdo each other

at the table, and bragged a lot about their hogs and their corn, and cussed the county commissioners because they neglected the roads and the bridges.

When the corn was cut and in the shock Jesse borrowed a one-horse drill and put the ten acres in wheat. He had traded work with a neighbor and with an extra hand who came out from Felicity every morning, he had got off his hay and his mow was full. Blanche helped him one day, loading the wagon while he pitched from the ground. She mowed it away, too. He hadn't liked her in the mow, for it was hot and dusty, but he did want to save all the hay he could. Sometimes he thought she worked harder than he did, for she had the cellar full of canned stuff, and had made ten gallons of sauerkraut, dried apples and corn, and when they butchered that year she worked late every night for a week, putting up sausage in jars, making scrapple, and pickling the feet and ears. She had done all the work in the garden and had a heap of food in the cellar she had raised herself, although Jesse did plow the potatoes once or twice.

"She didn't complain," says Jesse. "Women always worked like that—they didn't know any other way of living. They wouldn't do it today. Why, most of my neighbors don't have a garden any more. It's easier to buy cans at the grocery."

In September Jesse and Blanche spent the better part of a day at the Georgetown fair, the first time they had been away from the farm, except to go to Felicity to church, and for their weekly groceries. Blanche was very proud of a quilt she had made the winter before, and everybody said it was pretty enough to take a prize at the fair. She had sent it over by a neighbor, and she was anxious to see if she had won a prize. Sure enough, when she and Jesse walked into the pavilion, they saw the quilt display, and pinned to Blanche's quilt was a blue ribbon. She put the two-dollars prize money in her sugar bowl.

They met some of their old friends and kinfolk from Brown County and talked a lot and caught up on what had gone on since they left. At noontime Jesse watered his horse, gave him a sack of hay and three ears of corn out of the boot of the buggy, and he and Blanche took their basket of lunch and ate with some of their friends under a tree. In the afternoon Jesse bought a bag of hot peanuts and two cigars, which cost him a total of ten cents. Right after the balloon ascension he hitched up and they started the twenty-four-mile trip home. Old Daisy, who was more at home drawing a plow than a buggy, jogged slowly along, raising a lot of dust with her big feet. Blanche and Jesse felt tired and happy, and dozed a little from time to time. It was dark when they pulled into the barnyard and the feeding and milking had to be done, and supper prepared. It was nine-thirty when everything was finished, and they went straight to bed. After all, they had been up since four-thirty that morning, and had driven forty-eight miles at a slow horse-and-buggy pace.

Day in and day out, it was toil, getting up by lamplight, doing the milking by lantern light after the day in the fields. How welcome was the rare recess from work, a part of a day when it rained, a whole day when the corn was laid by. One Saturday afternoon Jesse and four of his neighbors borrowed a seine and went down to the Ohio River and seined a backwater, bringing home a tubful of carp and catfish. He went hunting a time or two and once got so many rabbits that he and Blanche gave a rabbit supper. By this time they knew everybody in the neighborhood and waved at every passing buggy and wagon on the Felicity road that passed their farm. They had made some good friends and life was pretty wonderful and satisfying and full.

Jesse saved out ten bushels of his best wheat, and when it had dried out well, he and Blanche took it to the mill on Bullskin Creek to have it ground. The old stone burrs turned out a fine dark flour. "Blanche made the best salt risin' bread in the county," says Jesse. "The stuff we buy now ain't got no more flavor than a newspaper."

When the days shortened and the first frosts came, work slackened in the fields, and Jesse and Blanche felt they had earned a day or two off, and besides, they needed some things for winter. A neighbor drove them down to the landing on the Ohio and they took the six o'clock boat to Cincinnati. It was a four-hour trip and they went to the Pioneer store and each got two suits of heavy underwear. Jesse bought a heavy pair of felt boots, with rubber soles, which cost him two dollars. Blanche got gingham and calico for two dresses. They ate lunch in a restaurant and took the horsecar out to Blanche's sister in Mount Auburn, where they stayed the night. They talked about the trip all winter—it was quite a splurge for them, and both of them secretly wondered if they hadn't spent too much money, being in debt as they were. The trip cost twelve dollars, including their purchases.

They went to church every Sunday and that winter they traded oyster suppers around the neighborhood. A half-dozen families chipped in for a gallon of oysters, and the host furnished the milk and the crackers. They gathered at suppertime on Saturday night, hitching their blanketed horses around the fence in the barnyard. The women spent most of the time in the kitchen; the men sat around the hot stove in the living room, smoking their Saturday night cigars and discussing a new check-row cornplanter, which one of them had just bought, and the relative merits of William McKinley and William Jennings Bryan, the silver-tongued orator.

Right after Thanksgiving, Jesse loaded three fat hogs in his grain bed and he and Blanche hauled them over to the Parker farm, where they had a butchering. Four families had teamed up and that day they killed, dressed, and hung eleven hogs. The eleven white carcasses hung in a row in the frosty moonlight, cooling out for the next day, when they would

be cut up. The four families were on hand early the next morning, the sausage was stuffed, the lard rendered, and the offal trimmed and divided. Jesse took the sides, hams, and shoulders and gave them a salt and sugar cure he had learned from his father. Blanche put up part of the sausage and pickled the feet and made scrapple. That was their meat for the year, barring an occasional chicken, or a piece of beef when a neighbor butchered a calf. That was the thing to do —put up your own meat. Butchering was as much of an occasion as threshing—not work at all, but fun.

In those days you could hire a good farm hand for twenty dollars a month and keep. He worked from sun to sun when need be, and all day on Saturday, too, during the haymaking and harvesting. Other times he wanted Saturday afternoon off, and feed and pasture for his horse. On Saturday afternoon he took off to Felicity, where he raced his horse up and down Main Street. Saturday night he went courtin', taking his girl to a church ice cream social, or, during the winter, to a revival meeting at a country church. He saved his money, bred his mare, and in four or five years had a team and enough money to buy some secondhand tools. Then he started on shares for himself. That was how Jesse got his start. Unless you inherited a farm, or married one, you started that way. It was hard work and self-denial for long years, but it was possible in those days.

A brave new century dawned and with it came a little war with Spain, the assassination of the President, and a stirring in the minds of men. The pioneer days were over and that explosive energy which had carried the American farmer across a continent was now turned to the arts of living, to making life easier.

Jesse and Blanche, with a son added to the family, took the first decades of the new century in stride. Changes and better things came slowly and imperceptibly, prices got a little better, sugar and coffee and winter underwear cost a little more, a two-row corn-planter came out and a two-horse cultivator, and hours in the field were cut down considerably. But these were little improvements in old familiar things, expected and accepted.

It was not until the twenties that the accelerated pace of the new era began to push Jesse around. The din of gasoline tractors echoed across the fields to him, walking quietly behind his sweating team. At the blacksmith shop his neighbors disturbed him with talk about a hybrid corn, which they said produced unheard-of yields.

But Jesse is a cautious man, not one to take up with a new thing just because it is new, or go off half-cocked. "It's just a flash in the pan," he said to himself, and went on with his old open-pollinated seed. He always saved all his own seed corn, large, fat, hard ears, and he just couldn't bring himself to sell it for horse corn and go out and buy the new seed at fancy prices. "I want to see a hundred bushels to the acre before I believe it," he said.

Then one year he ran out of seed corn and had to have some quick to finish his planting. He went to the seed dealer in Felicity; the only seed the dealer had was a bushel of hybrid and Jesse had to take it. His hybrid corn made sixty bushels to the acre that year, his old corn barely forty.

Then, in the fall of 1932, working too long and too late to be careful, Jesse lost a hand in a corn shredder. The next months were tough for him. "I thought I was done for," he says. "Couldn't see how I could do

my farming with one hand." But he stuck to it and worked things out and learned how to get along. His neighbors say Jesse Metzger does more work with one hand than most people do with two. "He doesn't complain; never did," says Blanche. "The only thing he can't do with one hand he could do with two is button up his shirt sleeve." Jesse says that the loss of his hand was somewhat a blessing in disguise. "I couldn't manage a team very well with one hand," he says, "so I teamed up with my brother-in-law and we bought one of the first tractors in the county. I found out that machinery could save backache."

It was when his son, Wayford, came back from college that Jesse fully realized that progress had come to the farm. When the children were still in diapers he and Blanche had planned a college education for them. "It was just natural that we would want better for them than we had," he says. "The more you can use your head, the less you have to use your back."

Wayford brought back from school a parcel of new ideas about farming that sometimes astonished, sometimes frustrated Jesse. Wayford calmly but firmly set out to modernize both his father and the farm. For one thing, he persuaded his father to more than double his fertilizer.

Jesse had brought with him to his farm an abiding faith in manure. His father and his grandfather, from a solid Pennsylvania Dutch county, believed that the panacea for all ills of the land was more manure. Jesse was like that, too, until Wayford began to talk straight nitrogen and three and four hundred pounds of mixed fertilizer to the acre. Jesse always used a little dab of fertilizer ever since he had been bested three years in a row by his neighbor. "That was soon after the First World War," said Jesse. "My corn always beat his, but he started to use a little fertilizer—maybe 150 pounds—and he beat me three years in a row. If I'd had enough manure, this wouldn't have happened, but I didn't and I took to using a little fertilizer. Never could see laying out that much money until Wayford talked me into it. We tried a part of a field one year. That convinced me. Now we put on 200 pounds of ammonium nitrate and 33 per cent nitrogen, and plow it down. Then we put down 450 pounds of 8-20-20 to the acre when we plant. Best corn crop I ever had with manure was sixty bushels. We get close to a hundred now, and this land isn't the best."

The fields and barns on Jesse's farm slowly and

imperceptibly took on the new look, but life within the farmhouse followed the old accustomed ways. The supper by lamplight, the family gathered around the base burner on winter evenings, the bucket of water brought from the dooryard well on the kitchen table. Mrs. Metzger walked to the neighbors to borrow a cup of sugar—and sat for an hour, in housewife's small talk. The family went to Sunday school and church and Blanche baked a cake for the social.

Then the telephone lines reached out to the farms and hamlets of America to change the way of life, to end the isolation. They leaped the bad roads and the distances; it was the telephone bell that tolled the end of an era.

Mrs. Metzger agrees that the telephone marked the end of the good old days. "We stopped going to see our neighbors," she says. "It was too easy to step to the telephone and talk to them. We quit visiting back and forth, and the oyster suppers petered out and we didn't go to church as much as we ought. People dropped off being neighborly, but we kept the old party line buzzing."

The telephone was the foot in the door, the forerunner of all the gadgets of the machine age. "They put in a power line from Felicity after Roosevelt came in," says Jesse, "and I wired the house. I got my first automobile then, and the county filled up the holes in the pike and put some tar on it. We breezed into Cincinnati to see a movie when we wanted to and my wife talked me into a radio. Then we got a milking machine and we put water in the house. There's hardly anything around the place now we had when we moved here."

When Jesse set up housekeeping and farming, he had a bottle of Sloan's Liniment on the ledge back of the horse stalls, a box of rat poison out of reach under the eaves of the smokehouse, and a few odds and ends of arnica, witch hazel, and laxative pills on a shelf in the kitchen besides the clock. For many years he needed nothing more from the chemist or the druggist.

"Then, all of a sudden," he says, "the bugs came and our stock got diseases we never heard of before, and the milk inspector said we had to keep the flies out of our cow barn. A lot of fancy poisons for rats came out and we had to inoculate our legumes and we had to spray five or six times to get an apple crop. We had to spend money on things we never spent on before, and we couldn't keep up with the new ones.

"We were a lot happier then, too, because we didn't see so many things we wanted and couldn't have. There are so many temptations in a store today you can't get out until your pocketbook is empty. We didn't have social security then and if we didn't fix ourselves up for old age we'd land in the poorhouse and we all knew the county poorhouse.

"If our only pleasure had been in making money we wouldn't have had much pleasure. We had to get our fun out of other things. Why, I got more pleasure out of having a couple of barrels of potatoes in the cellar and a half-dozen hams hanging in the smokehouse than a lot of money in the bank. I'd raised those hogs and fattened them and butchered them, and I saw the potatoes pushing up out of the ground in the spring. Anybody who hasn't grown his own stuff doesn't know how it feels. I wouldn't want to work in a factory and draw a check on Saturday night and take it around to the grocery and buy canned goods. Food wouldn't taste the same. You've got to live with it and raise it yourself.

"We didn't need much money in those days. Not even to get started farming. If you were willing to work everybody helped you and pretty soon you had the mortgage paid off. Now, with farms getting bigger and bigger, the little man hasn't much of a chance. Big farms you can't work yourself are a bad thing for our country.

"I made out fine on a small farm; paid off the mortgage, educated two children, and saved money. Not much during the depression, but a little; and I really made money during the war. Now my son is with me, and two families have to make a living here. We started a dairy ten years ago, and we've done all right. We get more tonnage from thirty acres than we used to get from the whole farm, and we keep six times the number of cattle. But it's getting harder and harder every year—we spend just as much, and we are getting less and less for our milk and hogs.

"Farmers have always kicked about taxes and the high prices in stores. I kick, too, but when I think of the roads we have now and the help we get from the county agent, I guess I shouldn't kick. I don't know what we would do without radio and electric lights and the milking machine. Life is a lot easier than it was and that costs money."

When Jesse reached voting age he conscientiously went to the polls and put an X under the Eagle, because he was a Republican and his father and grandfather before him had been Republicans. He was mainly interested in the county commissioners—the only time he ever scratched his ballot during those years was when a Republican commissioner refused to do something about the road in front of his farm. The national government was the President and a mass of men he never knew, called Congress. Once in a while there was a William Jennings Bryan or Theodore Roosevelt who became real people, but the issues of the national government were as foreign as Russia.

Today Jesse Metzger doesn't care who his county commissioners are, but he knows that Henry Wallace ordered him to plow down his pigs, and he says Eisenhower has the best foreign policy, and he almost got into a fist fight over McCarthy.

"The government has taken away all our freedom," he says. "They have a picture of my farm and they know what I got in every field, and there's a milk inspector out here every whipstitch telling me what to do. They let us alone in the old days.

"Maybe I'm getting old and slowing down, but with all our machines and motors and automobiles, we never seem to have enough time to just sit and rest and think, like we did when I was a boy. The things that we enjoyed then were being neighborly and helping each other. We had to find our pleasures in ourselves and our friends. Now we depend on television and the movies. Not much heart in our pleasures

"Life is easier, though, for we don't have to use as much muscles as we did, but I would rather take it a little slower, and live longer. I've lived a full span of life—I'll be seventy-seven my next birthday—and I don't see that we're any better off today. As I said before, I think Blanche and me were happier when we were young because there weren't so many things to want. It's wanting what you don't need that makes people unhappy."

MOUNTAIN WOMAN

Martha Stark raised nine children in a three-room clapboard cabin on a thirty-five-acre farm in the high hills of southern Kentucky. She is eighty now, a widow for sixteen years, and she lives alone in a house she came to as a bride. She gets around well and on good days will walk the mountain paths to visit a son who lives across the valley. Several years ago, from her first old-age pension check, she bought herself a set of teeth. They are a little loose and she doesn't dare smile as wide as she might. She is lean and bony and wears her hair in a tight bun on the back of her head. Her eyes are china blue, like her Scotch-Irish ancestors.

When Martha Stark is asked how nine children were clothed and fed and schooled on two acres of corn and beans, a few half-wild sheep on the mountain, and a flock of geese which wandered up and down the branch, she tells you, "You would have to do it yourself to know how."

When John Stark married Martha Lennox in 1898, he took her to a lonely two-room log cabin on Spring Branch. He had thirty-two acres, a mule, a dozen or so sheep, a hillside plow, and a mudsled which he had made himself. There were several strips along the branch, a little more than an acre in all, which were level enough for a crop, and about an acre on a cleared hillside where he planted corn and beans and pumpkins and a garden. Martha's mother had given her a pair of geese and a setting hen with fifteen eggs under her. In the house were a homemade bedstead, three hickory split chairs, a table, and an odd collection of pots for the fireplace. There was a cornhusk mattress on the bed and two quilts which Martha had pieced herself during the three years that John came over the mountain to court her.

That first fall when the corn was picked, John loaded half of it on the mudsled and took it to the mill at Indian Bottom, eight miles away. The other half of the corn went into a pig which a neighbor had given him for a week's work cutting fence posts. Martha combed and carded the wool from the sheep, carried it to her mother's loom, and made a strip of cloth for their winter clothes. She sewed these by hand—dresses, shirts, pants, coats, everything from the same strip of cloth, scratchy and rough, but durable and warm. She plucked the geese and made their first pillow and used the fat from the hog to make lye soap, using ashes from the fireplace to make the lye. Their diet, day after day, was corn meal mush, beans and fatback. That winter John made fifteen dollars working in a sawmill. They spent four dollars on a wooden pump for the well and the remainder on salt and thread and odds and ends. "It just slipped away," Martha says. "We spent it all and I can't remember for what. That's the way with money."

Then the children began to come. The corn rows were pushed a little further up the hillside, and even the patches on John's overalls were patched. Months on end there was no money in the house; it was either borrow, barter, or trade. John helped a neighbor put up a chimney and brought home a ham. Martha could make the best soap on the branch—white and hard and clean-smelling. She traded a bar here and a bar there for salt or a jug of sorghum or the rare luxury of coffee.

When the lumber companies began logging off the mountains John got work with his mule, snaking the logs down to the river and then when the spring freshets came, floating them to the mill at the railroad, twelve miles away. He added a lean-to kitchen to the house and covered the logs with clapboards. He cleared a little more land on the hill, put in more corn. When he had enough extra to make a run of corn whiskey he and two of his neighbors bought a length of copper tubing and set up a still in a dead-end hollow near a spring. Working at night so that the smoke would not give them away, they jugged the clear moonshine and brought it down to their cabins.

"We all took a sip in the morning and just before we went to bed," Martha recalls. "The kids too—and we never had any colds or stomach trouble."

For many years John made his own shine, unmolested and untroubled. It was like a crop, a part of the family diet. Sometimes he sold a little or traded some to a neighbor who was short. But he wasn't in the business and he couldn't understand why you couldn't make your own beverage the same as you could grow your own corn for meal. After a while the revenuers came. They snooped around, arrested a neighbor up the branch, and discouraged John.

"They never did catch my man," says Martha. "He traded off his worm and bought his shine. You could get a jugful for a quarter in those days. I'd like to have some regular, but they put lye in the stuff they make now, and we don't drink it any more. They take it to Cincinnati where they'll drink anything."

Shoes were the biggest clothing problem for the growing family. Martha's uncle was a shoemaker, but he lived at Indian Bottom, a good day's travel from Spring Branch. Once a year John loaded his family on the mudsled and with two calf hides he had tanned himself, paid Uncle Hugh a weekend visit. Uncle Hugh took the boot sizes of the family and a month later the work was done. A pair of boots lasted a year or more. They were boots, not shoes, and sometimes as a special favor Uncle Hugh put on copper toe-plates for the boys.

The children attended school at Jeremiah, a village two miles from their cabin. If they managed three or four days a week they did well. Often in winter the hill trails were too difficult, and in the spring and fall they missed whole weeks, helping with the farm work. Truant officers and school buses were unknown to them, and if they acquired a working acquaintance with the three R's at the end of their short school life, they were contented. There were few who knew more than how to "cipher" and spell out the Bible.

They learned more on the mountain and in the fields than they did from the teacher. As soon as they were old enough to walk they scoured the mountains for nuts in the fall, sassafras root in the spring; they gathered blackberries, wild grapes, papaws, and "poke greens," a salad made with dandelions, pokeweed, and water cress. They trapped and hunted small game at all seasons. They held the wicks while their mother poured the candles and carried the lead pot from the fire when their father poured the bullets for his long rifle. They learned to shoot straight and fear strangers and how to fight "rough and tumble." They joined their elders in a dipper of moonshine before bedtime. Those that survived were tough and resourceful. They became self-sufficient like their parents; they knew how to endure privation, how to "git along."

This was the way of life for a hundred years after the wild game had vanished, and a living had to come out of the thin soil. No new blood came in, for the soil was giving up its maximum, and would support

no more. A young man went to the cabin up the branch for his bride; when his children were ready for marriage, they too went up the branch. It was easier than walking miles, all uphill, to the next branch to court a girl who might ultimately refuse the honor, or whose brother might take a shot at you because all strangers were suspect. So there was inbreeding from the start; today everybody is a cousin, and the same Old English names of Adams and Collins and Caudill crop up all over the Tennessee and Kentucky mountains. The inbreeding produced an annual crop of idiots, and undernourishment contributed much to the decline of the stock. By the turn of the nineteenth century the Kentucky and Tennessee mountaineers were tagged with a stigma—they were hillbillies, and hillbilly is not a complimentary name. They settled into a pattern, tall, lean, hawk-nosed, thin-haired, stooped, and they talked with a drawl in a language which smacked of Chaucer and the King James Bible.

The long rifle was the law. If your neighbor stole your pig or violated your daughter, you took your squirrel gun off the mantel and went gunning for him. Family feuds went on into the third and fourth generations—the Hatfields and the McCoys exterminated each other. Breathitt County was known through the land as Bloody Breathitt; it was indeed a foolhardy stranger who allowed the sun to set on him in the Breathitt mountain.

Martha does not like to talk of those years, and the privations of her family. "It was easier for my grandfather," she says. "He could shoot the winter meat in one day on the mountain."

Many of the old arts of self-sufficiency had been lost; no longer would mountain people spend weeks at the salt licks. No longer were young girls willing to sit hour after hour at a loom, weaving the cloth for the family. Those things that must be bought cost more, and the list of those things one wanted grew faster than the means to buy them. As the new way of life pushed in from the outside world, the young people went north to the cities, for their home hills offered them less and less. When a cabin burned it was not rebuilt; hillside cornfields went back to briars and weeds. The mountains were losing their people.

In 1910 the railroad came. John Stark got a job laying track and later when the mines opened he became a miner. The hours were long and the pay low, but it did bring in cash. Coffee replaced sassafras tea as a hot beverage and brown cane sugar took the place of sorghum molasses. Martha remembers her first calico dress—and the first oranges John bought for the kids' Christmas.

But the money could never keep up with the children. Eight of them came along in twelve years. The four double beds just about filled the two rooms in the cabin, and ten hungry mouths had to be fed from the little corn patch and the kitchen garden. That calico dress lasted her for seven years for she wore it only to church and funerals.

No one could afford to be ill. The doctor was fourteen miles away and he charged fifty cents a mile, going and coming, for a visit. A midwife brought Martha's children and homemade potions and ointments had to take care of the day-to-day illnesses. One of the boys broke a leg and that cost them twenty-five dollars, which they were two years in paying. Bad teeth stayed in until one got the courage to have them pulled with a pair of pliers. One just wore out the measles and whooping cough and drank moonshine for all the common ailments. The weak died and the strong survived, all a little undernourished, a good deal overworked, and one was always tired. Life was serious, with no relief except the Sunday church, where the preacher scared you half out of your wits with his threats of hell-fire and damnation. But there one could forget the hard life—let himself go; and the shouting and carrying on at the winter revival meetings were something to look forward to.

Martha Stark is a Baptist, and an ardent one. Her great-grandfather brought a Bible in his saddlebags when he came north out of Carolina. Religion, as an emotional outlet, is strong in these hills. In the early 1800's a powerful evangelical group of Baptists in North Carolina undertook to bring the Bible to the "heathen" settlers in the Kentucky and Tennessee mountains. This was the Roaring River Baptist Church, and its missionaries prayed and baptized and exhorted their way into every nook and cranny of the mountains. The Baptist Church is predominant, the hard-shell, shouting Baptists who believe in instantaneous conversion, hell-fire and brimstone, and infant damnation.

The mountain people attend church as people of the cities attend the theater or the races. It is their recreation, their promise of better things to come. During the annual winter revival meetings the countryside turns out for an emotional binge seven nights a week, attending meetings in their own and neighboring churches, walking miles over the mountain trails. They shout, are seized with frenzies, speak in unknown tongues. Preachers are measured by the volume of their exhortations, by the very violence of their appeal. The best are those who leave their audience trembling and terrified at the prospect of an eternity in hell. Many of them are adept at mass hypnotism; these are the prophets and leaders of the mountain people.

Martha never misses a meeting. Her church is one of the few remaining ties with the old way of life. That life may have been more difficult, but at least she was familiar with her problems then, and had her own way of solving them. She is ill-fitted for the new life of the juke box and store-boughten dresses and frozen foods. She accepts her old-age pension check, for she must live, but it violates all her age-old principles of self-reliance and independence. That is why Martha Stark will never leave her tumble-down mountain home—until she joins her husband in the cemetery down the branch.

THE COUNTRY DOCTOR

A product of an early Midwest medical school, he came to our little village in the hills of southern Ohio and hung out his shingle. His name was Alonzo Adams, and he was in his mid-twenties. He grew a beard, and people were soon calling him "Old Doc," a name he carried for sixty years.

He was the first doctor in our part of the country. Before he came we got along with a midwife, home remedies, and prayer. We survived.

Men were kicked by horses and laid low by falling trees; they cut their toes off with axes, froze their fingers and ears, and were poisoned by contaminated water and unrefrigerated foods; they were bitten by snakes, got rheumatism from exposure, and suffered from gastric troubles brought on by lack of proper food, but somehow they got well again.

The cure for all ills was the brews and potions passed down from ancestors, and the old reliables, castor oil, Epsom salts, and arnica. They used whiskey and a wad of tobacco for disinfectant. Sulphur and molasses, followed by dandelion greens and sassafras tea, were sovereign spring remedies for phlegms accumulated in the body during the winter. Most ills were worn out, or they wore out the victim.

When a doctor came to a community he was promptly challenged by these home remedies, and Old Doc never quite conquered them. Naturally, he was called only when old home remedies failed and, of course, for accidents. He had to be wise and patient in substituting science for the bark of the sassafras root. He soon learned that he could not be a person, for there was really no place in the community for a person of his mythical and actual gifts. He was both at the top and the bottom of the social order, more important than the banker in time of trouble, less important than a hired hand when it came time to pay the bills. He was more an institution than a person, and few thought of him as a man with the emotions of an ordinary person. Old Doc observed the vows of his calling faithfully. What he knew about the private lives of the people in his community would have sent most of them to jail. They took their intertwined spiritual and domestic problems to him along with their ailments, and found a wise counselor.

His fee for a house call was two dollars when he came to our community, and when he died sixty years later his fee was still two dollars. A house call might take him two blocks down the village street on a pleasant summer afternoon; it might take him twenty miles into the country in the worst blizzard of the winter.

While Old Doc practiced his profession without the multitude of scientific refinements we have today, he did surprisingly well with his simple drugs and tools. He was a good diagnostician of the mind as well as the body, and was not above psychological tricks if he thought they were needed. He regularly sold, for a dime a bottle, "the best cure for sore throat in the country." It was a six-ounce bottle of common salt solution, colored red, and was used as a gargle. If asked what it was, Old Doc lowered his voice mysteriously and said, "Sodium chloride and H_2O."

He was versatile, too. He pulled teeth, examined the eyes for glasses, and occasionally ministered to a sick cow or horse. His favorite remedy was a vile mixture of quinine, iron, and strychnine, which he called Q.I.S. Sometimes calomel was substituted for the strychnine. It was a sort of shotgun mixture good for most anything that came along, could do no harm, and tasted vile enough to satisfy the most rabid hypochondriac. Most of his emergency surgery was performed in the field or on a kitchen table. His surgical kit contained a saw, two or three scalpels, a pair of forceps, and a needle with a length of catgut.

He might have laid by a fortune, for he never had time to spend money, if he had collected only a modest percentage of what was owed him. The grocer and the hardware store were paid when the hogs were sold in the autumn. Old Doc was paid out of conscience money. He rarely collected his five-dollar fee for the birth of the first child; it was only after the second came along that the embarrassed father paid his old bill. He was paid in odd ways, too. The very poor were the best pay, for they put a bag of potatoes or a couple of fat hens in the boot of his buggy when he left, and often at Christmastime a ham or a barrel of apples came his way on a bill he long since had written off. He never billed his creditors. He never married; never no time for courting.

Joe Wilson, some thirty-five years old and a well-to-do farmer, went to Old Doc for a birth certificate. He wanted to take his family to Europe and needed records for his passport. Old Doc looked up his records, wrote out the certificate and handed it to Joe. "How much do I owe you?" asked Joe. It was then that Old Doc came as near as he ever had come to dunning a creditor. "You don't owe me anything for the certificate," he said, "but you're not paid for yourself yet. Your father forgot the item when you were born."

Old Doc's sole heir was a nephew in Pittsburgh. His biggest legacy was six ledgers recording three score years of service and more than $100,000 in unpaid bills, some almost sixty years old. He left also a modest house in the village, 120 stony acres and an old farmhouse two miles out, and three old horses.

He kept two horses in a stable back of his home, a light cart for summer use, and a staunch, closed buggy for the bad season. People said he wore out a horse a year galloping over country roads in a sea of mud to bring a baby, or tie up an artery. His horses and the stable were cared for by the village dolt, Henry Carr, who slept in a room in the stable and was always on call. When Old Doc died, Henry got his bank account—$325.76.

Old Doc passed away during the peak of a flu epidemic. It was not the flu that took him, but at eighty-six, two days and nights without taking off his clothes and with no food except coffee was too much for his aging heart. He came in early one morning, fell asleep in his chair in his office, and never awakened. He has the finest marble monument in our cemetery, put up by his faithful friends who never thought to pay him in life, but opened their purses when he died. His funeral was the largest in the history of our village.

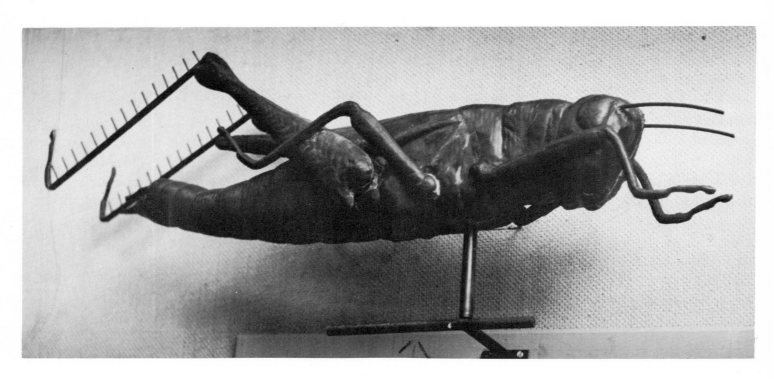

THE PLAGUE

The summer was very hot. Dry, hot winds blew and there was no rain.

One day when Pa came in to dinner he said, "The grasshoppers are hatching. This hot sun is bringing them out of the eggs and up through the ground like corn popping."

Laura ran out to see. The grass on the knoll was hopping full of tiny green things. Laura caught one in her hands and looked at it. Its wee, small wings and its tiny legs and its little head and even its eyes were the color of the grass. It was so very tiny and so perfect, Laura could hardly believe it would ever be a big, brown, ugly grasshopper.

"They'll be big, fast enough," said Pa. "Eating every growing thing."

Day by day more and more grasshoppers hatched out of the ground. Green grasshoppers of all sizes were swarming everywhere and eating. The wind could not blow loud enough to hide the sound of their jaws nipping, gnawing, chewing.

They ate all the green garden rows. They ate the green potato tops. They ate the grass, and the willow leaves, and the green plum thickets, and the small green plums. They ate the whole prairie bare and brown. And they grew.

They grew large and brown and ugly. Their big eyes bulged and their horny legs took them hopping everywhere. Thick over all the ground they were hopping, and Laura and Mary stayed in the house.

There was no rain, and the days went by hotter and hotter, uglier and uglier, and filled with the sound of grasshoppers until it seemed more than could be borne.

"Oh, Charles," Ma said one morning, "seems to me I just can't bear one more day of this."

Ma was sick. Her face was white and thin, and she sat down tired as she spoke.

Pa did not answer. For days he had been going out and coming in with a still, tight face. He did not sing or whistle any more. It was worst of all when he did not answer Ma. He walked to the door and stood looking out.

Even Carrie was still. They could feel the heat of the day beginning, and hear the grasshoppers. But the grasshoppers were making a new sound. Laura ran to look out at them, excited, and Pa was excited, too.

"Caroline!" he said. "Here's a strange thing. Come look!"

All across the dooryard the grasshoppers were walking shoulder to shoulder and end to end, so crowded that the ground seemed to be moving. Not a single one hopped. Not one turned its head. As fast as they could go, they were walking west.

Ma stood beside Pa, looking. Mary asked, "Oh, Pa, what does it mean?" and Pa said, "I don't know."

He shaded his eyes and looked far to west and east.

"It's the same, as far as the eye can see. The whole ground is crawling, crawling west."

Ma whispered, "Oh, if they would all go away!"

She kept on watching the grasshoppers walking by. There was no space between them and no end.

Grasshoppers were walking over Carrie. They came pouring in the eastern window, side by side and end to end, across the window sill and down the wall and over the floor. They went up the legs of the table and the benches and Carrie's high stool. Under the table and benches, and over the table and benches and Carrie, they were walking west.

"Shut the windows!" said Ma.

Laura ran on the grasshoppers to shut it. Pa went outdoors and around the house. He came in and said, "Better shut the upstairs windows. Grasshoppers are as thick walking up the east side of the house as they are on the ground, and they are not going around the attic window. They are going right in."

All up the wall and across the roof went the sound of their raspy claws crawling. The house seemed full of them. Ma and Laura swept them up and threw them out the western window. None came in from the west, though the whole western side of the house was covered with grasshoppers that had walked over the roof and were walking down to the ground and going on west with the others.

That whole day long the grasshoppers walked west. All the next day they went on walking west. And all the third day they walked without stopping.

No grasshopper turned out of its way for anything.

They walked steadily over the house. They walked over the stable. They walked over Spot until Pa shut her in the stable. They walked into Plum Creek and drowned, and those behind kept on walking in and drowning until dead grasshoppers choked the creek and filled the water and live grasshoppers walked across on them.

All day the sun beat hot on the house. All day it was full of the crawling sound that went up the wall and over the roof and down. All day grasshoppers' heads with bulging eyes, and grasshoppers' legs clutching, were thick along the bottom edge of the shut windows; all day they tried to walk up the sleek glass and fell back, while thousands more pushed up and tried and fell.

Ma was pale and tight. Pa did not talk and his eyes could not twinkle. Laura could not shake the crawling sound out of her ears nor brush it off her skin.

The fourth day came and the grasshoppers went on walking. The sun shone hotter than ever, with a terribly bright light.

It was nearly noon when Pa came from the stable shouting: "Caroline! Caroline! Look! The grasshoppers are flying!"

Laura and Mary ran to the door. Everywhere grasshoppers were spreading their wings and rising from the ground. More and more of them filled the air, flying higher and higher, till the sunshine dimmed and darkened and went out as it had done when the grasshoppers came.

Laura ran outdoors. She looked straight up at the sun through a cloud that seemed almost like snowflakes. It was a dark cloud, gleaming, glittering, shimmering brighter and whiter as she looked farther into it. And it was rising instead of falling.

The cloud passed over the sun and went on far to the west until it could be seen no longer.

There was not a grasshopper left in the air or on the ground, except here and there a crippled one that could not fly but still hobbled westward.

Pa leaned in the doorway and said, earnestly, "I would like someone to tell me how they all knew at once that it was time to go, and how they knew which way was west and their ancestral home."

But no one could tell him.

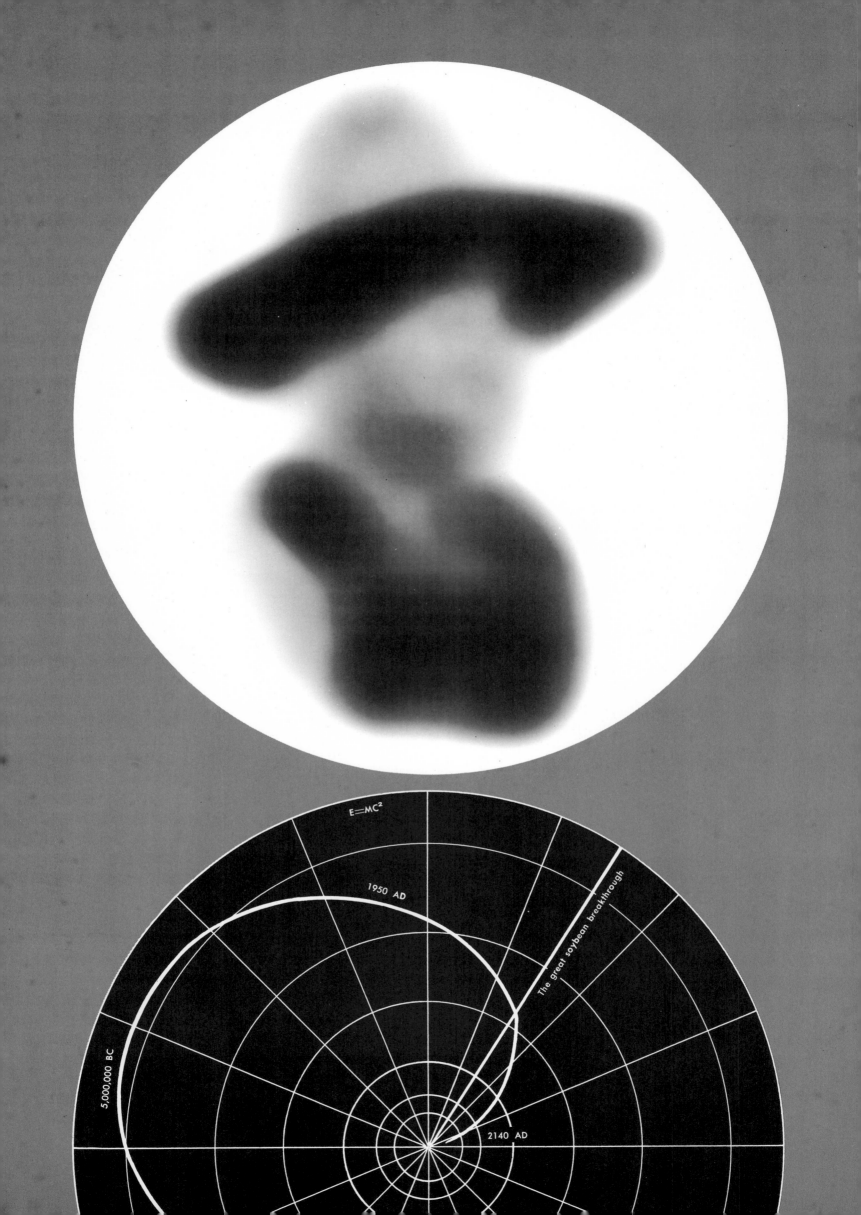

THE LAST FARMER

This is good-by. Soon it will all be over and they will speak of the farmer along with the dodo, the passenger pigeon, and the giant ground sloth. Now that the end is near, I feel the need to leave some sign of my passing—if only this good-by.

For many, many years I and my fathers before me have lived here on this preserve, The Farmer's Refuge, so that modern man, who long ago outgrew the need for farmers, could see what a primitive was like, and how he lived. The Preserve Committee felt that the farm was a link between the twenty-second-century culture and what they called the production-for-subsistence life of earlier man. I believe that they intended to continue supporting this farm as an educational institution forever. I thought that I should live out my life here and see my son take over—until that terrible moment this afternoon.

As soon as I saw the headline, I felt as if I had heard the voice of doom. "LAST FARMER TO GO," it said.

I had seen stories about me in the paper before, but they had almost always been in the feature section. Once, back in June, 2133, there had been a front-page story on my marriage, but that was a pretty story. The headlines had read, "STATE MATES OUR FARMER," and the story had started, "Heigh ho the derry oh, our farmer takes a wife. . . ." But most of the stories, as I say, had been picture features showing what a farmer looked like and how I practiced the lost art of planting. I clipped all these stories for my scrapbook. Never, had there been anything terrifying like this story, "LAST FARMER TO GO."

The Farmer Wardens had tried to keep it from me. I know that they did it out of kindness—and I am grateful for their compassion—but I was bound to learn about it sooner or later.

I was cleaning up after a picnic when I found out. You see, they let folks picnic here so that they will leave bottles and cans and papers around. The scientists feel that it may be necessary for my survival since all of my ancestors have cleaned up after picnics as far back as there is any record of farmers as a group.

Well, as I say, I read of my doom in a paper left in the picnic mess. It was a terrible shock. At first, all I could do was to sit and stare at the headline trying to adjust myself to the stunning news. There was a long article below, but I couldn't bring myself to read it just then. I put the paper in my pocket and hurried back to do the milking. There was a much larger audience this evening and I remembered that for several days I had been dimly conscious of the increased size of the crowd. They all looked sad, I thought, and I'm sure that I even saw one dab at her eyes.

Performing with the cows always has a calming effect on me. After it was over, I sat down quietly and read the whole article. Not only did it tell of my end, but it gave a fairly complete history of farmers. I can see now that extinction was inevitable. And I know now why father couldn't bring himself to tell me the whole story of our past.

Father *had* told me quite a bit of our history; of how, back in the dim past, most men had been farmers. I recall exactly how he said that, as though he expected to be contradicted and knew that he couldn't prove such a ridiculous statement. He repeated it angrily, "Most men were farmers in those days," and pounded the table with his fist. He also told me that centuries ago, sometime between the first fumbling attempts to harness the atom and the beginning of interstellar flight, man became aware that the farmer was disappearing. All of this was told in greater detail in the newspaper article.

The article also gave many facts that I had either never heard or had forgotten. For example, it said that as early as the middle of the twentieth century, men were beginning to predict the end of the farmer.

At that time, their forecasting efforts were based on the simplest form of arithmetic. They knew that in 1920 there had been 6,448,343 farms each averaging 148 acres, making a total of 954,355,000 acres of land in agriculture. They also knew that by 1950 there were only 5,382,162 farms, but each had grown to an average size of 215 acres which made a total of 1,157,165,000 acres of agricultural land.

In working with these figures, one fellow, Blackenschultz by name, made the first stab at prediction. It was easy to see that the U.S. was losing farmers at the rate of 35,539 a year. Blackenschultz simply divided the number of farmers counted by the census taker in 1950 by the number who were leaving farming each year and arrived at the figure 151.44. He added

151 years to 1950 and came up with the year 2101 as the last one for the farmer. Carrying the number to two decimal places was very shrewd; 44/100ths of a year was 160.6 days. This figure made it possible for him to predict that the last farmer would disappear at twenty-four minutes past two in the afternoon of June 9 in the year 2101. That twenty-four minutes past two gave his prophecy a terrible feeling of exactness that made people believe it even though others came out immediately with contradictory dates.

As a matter of fact, Blackenschultz's computations had just appeared in an obscure agricultural journal, *The Farm Quarterly,* when John H. Bennourse came out with a much more conservative estimate. Bennourse began with the growth in farm size, which was figured at 2.23 acres a year and, using this growth rate as a start, he estimated that the number of farms would be cut in half every 96 years. At this rate, in the year 3870 there would be but eight farmers left. And here is where Bennourse showed his genius. "It is reasonable to presume," he said, "that two of these farms will belong to Texans and that during the year one of them will lose his farm to the other in a game of poker. Three of the farms certainly can be expected to belong to widows. Since there will then be so few farms, there will be one farm management company which will manage all three of them; in effect making them into one farm. The rest of the farms, one can

easily suppose, will be suffering from an unfavorable corn-hog ratio and so will be taken into a giant vertical integration. Therefore, I predict, that next year will see the consolidation and extinction of the farmer."

While these men were arguing as to just how soon farmers would squeeze each other out, Gail O. Wellsbraith came up with a third estimate based on how soon superhighways and subdivisions would use up all available land. Wellsbraith claimed that even if all of the agricultural land were consolidated into a single farm in 3871 as Bennourse insisted, it would be neither a very large farm nor would it last very long because —according to *his* figures—by 3873 the entire earth's surface would be covered with concrete roads and ranch-type houses with handkerchief-sized lawns. Wellsbraith left himself a big out, however. "If they begin planting high hedges to screen the picture windows," he said, "they'll use more land and that will shorten the time. If, on the other hand, there should be a swing toward the duplex, it could add as much as a hundred and fifty years to the process."

One economist, Milo Paarlbutz, postulated a quicker, more rugged end for farmers based on what he called the *law of the geometrical growth of the ideal staff.* This law was based on two theorums: (1) the importance of an administrator is measured by the size of his staff; and (2) every government worker is convinced that his efficiency would be vastly im-

proved by having one or two helpers to free him for more important work. On the basis of these two assumptions, Paarlbutz predicted that by 1997 the United States Department of Agriculture bureau-agricy (a term he coined) would exactly equal the then number of farmers. From here on, any slight ripple in our economy might endanger this whole structure. Should this happen, he felt, the bureau-agricy would abolish the farmers to protect their own.

It was about this time that a member of the primitive church—The First Church of Cybernetics—fed some of this data to a thinking machine, one of the ancestors of The Great Machine. I should explain that this was the age when fertilizers had reached the just-throw-on-a-handful-and-jump-out-of-the-way stage. When the machine received the data, it gulped, shuddered, thought for a moment, shrugged its transistors, and began clicking out questions. The first one it asked was, "Have you thought where you are going to put the surplus commodity bins in fifty years?" It glowed for a moment and then wrote, "This will take space, space, space. What about parking lots? What about amalgamating with Australia and Canada? What about drive-in movies? What about acceleration and retarding factors? What about something to eat?"

Before the Cybernetic Shaman had agreed upon answers to these questions, the great soybean breakthrough occurred, changing the whole problem. Soybean production occupied 93 per cent of all agricultural land, for man had already learned to convert soybeans into satisfactory substitutes for milk, cream, butter, lard, soap, steak, jello, hamburgers, corn flakes, linoleum, pressed duck, chewing tobacco, and blood.

Then, suddenly, dramatically, they learned how to make soybeans out of nitrogen, in the form of urea, and corncobs. Then, just as dramatically, they learned that corncobs weren't absolutely necessary.

After that—who cared what happened to the farmer: We would have disappeared within a decade had not the Eleanor Roosevelt Foundation organized the Society for the Prevention of the Extinction of the Farmer and arranged that we, my family, the last of the farmers, be made a trusteeship of the U.N.

And so we have lived here on this plot of land, father and son, generation after generation, for the past 172 years. We have grown used to people watching us, their noses flattened against the glass enclosure, as we went about our chores.

Each week they have watched us eat the products of the farm to demonstrate their uses, though, of course, we have *actually* lived on pelleted, irradiated nitrochlore like everybody else. As a matter of fact, I even developed a depraved taste for sirloin steaks when I was a youngster and worried Mother terribly by asking for them between our public farm meals.

Occasionally, one of us would decide to leave the farm. My brother did that, but later I saw him looking longingly through the glass, hoping to get back in. Once, I climbed on top of the silo and looked out onto the world that supported me. It was evening and the city, under its great protecting dome of plastic, glowed and twinkled. Rockets were rising with a magnificent rush through the transport chutes out through the dome into space. Luminous, hovering mobiles darted about like amoebae in a lettuce leaf broth. How could man have done so much, I wondered. For a moment

my eye fell on a young bean plant sprouting there
the cement rim of the silo; rootlets probing each
minute crevice, firm translucent stem hoisting up the
two bean halves, growing toward the light. I decided
never to leave.

I have been happy here. Recently, I felt that I was
on the verge of solving one of our ancient problems—
how to get the first cutting of hay in before it was
rained on. We worked hard all of our days and in the
evenings we used to sit and amuse ourselves with a sort
of a patience game my great-great-grandfather invented called Converting to New Parity.

I know that it is sacrilegious of me to think this, but
I believe that our life would have gone on in this
happy way forever if one of the Praying Mentors had
not come across the early texts of the farmer disap-
pearance problem while going through some early
scrolls. He and others of his sect reverently considered the data. They asked the venerable Head if this
might not make a suitable offering to The Great
Machine. At first he took a very matter-of-fact view
of the entire matter. "But the farmer disappeared a

hundred years ago; it would not be fitting to ask
It a question which was long ago answered. Do you
doubt that The Great Machine would know the date
on which the farmer disappeared? Have you no
faith?"

But one of the Mentors, whose argument is so re-
fined that it is claimed he can even polish breath, said
gently, "Can it truly be said that the farmer is extinct
when a farmer still lives and farms?" The Head
granted them permission to feed The Great Machine.

When they fed in the information, Its lights twinkled appreciatively, Its feedback mechanism went into
operation, and Its memory tapes whirred. In the awful
hush, the benign clatter of Its keys was heard and It
gave forth an answer.

And when The Great Machine speaks, man must
obey for It is never wrong.

And so I must go, for It said that farmers would
disappear when the year 2140 was sixty days old.
That would be on February 29th of this year.

Good-by, friends. Tomorrow is Leap Year Day
for me.

255

Acknowledgments

Editorial assistants, members of the staff of *The Farm Quarterly:* Aron Mathieu, Fred Knoop, Grant Cannon, Charles Koch, John MacCallum, Hilda Carberry, Martha Ransick; production, James Rosenthal, Jack McCain; layout and design consultants, Noel Martin and William Leonard.

Articles: The Hucksters, George Fichter; Sweet Music, John Goodwin; The Last Buggy Factory, George Laycock; Livery and Feed, Seth Thompson; Groceries and Notions, James David Frye; Wild Honey, Ewart A. Autry; The Old Oaken Bucket, Samuel Woodworth; Pennsylvania Barns, Henry Kauffman; They Set a Good Table, Alberta Wilson Constant; Of Horses and Harness, Charles Koch; The Family Cow, Ben Brown; Ice Harvest, Haydn S. Pearson; Lillie Cooks for Threshers, Joanne Belle Pierce; The Winter Woodpile, Stoyan Christowe; Go Fetch the Cows, Jean Bell Mosley; The Moon and Andy, John H. Durrell; Johnny Appleseed, Robert Price; The Christmas Program, Marion C. Seddon; Christmas on Dutch Fork, J. M. Eleazer; There Were Giants in Those Days, Archer P. Whallon; The Homesteaders, Glenn R. Vernam; The Plague, Laura Ingalls Wilder; The Last Farmer, Grant Cannon. All other articles written and edited by R. J. McGinnis.

Illustrations: Jacket, R. J. McGinnis. 2, F. Knoop. 8, F. Knoop. 11, McGuffey Reader. 12, W. Homer—Brown Bros. 13, J. Clark. 14, 15, 16, Brown Bros. 17, Warshaw collection. 17, label. 18, K. Ruohomaa. 20, U. S. Post Office Dept., 21, J. Clark, 23, Brown Bros. 24, 25, Pug Dailey. 27, Ohio Historical Society, 28, Brown Bros. 29, Ohio Historical Society. 30, McGuffey Reader. 31, McGuffey Society. 32, 33, McGuffey Reader. 35, R. Mortland. 36, Tobacco label—Ohio Historical Society. 37, Brandy label. 38, D. Timmerman. 41, R. J. McGinnis. 42, F. Knoop. 43, K. Pazovski. 44, J. Clark. 45, Brown Bros.—J. Clark. 46, K. Pazovski. 47, F. Knoop. 49, Brown Bros. 51, Warshaw Collection. 52, G. Peterson—Shostal. 54, Brown Bros. 55, V. Fisher. 57, Mercury Pictures. 58, F. Knoop. 59, G. Anderson—A. Devaney. 60, V. Fisher. 61, F. Knoop. 62, V. Fisher. 65, McGuffey Reader. 66, 67, F. Knoop. 68, Brown Bros. 69, T. Godsey. 70, Mercury Pictures. 71, R. J. McGinnis—F. Knoop. 72, 73, 74, 75, R. E. McGinnis. 76, J. Clark. 77, V. Fisher. 78, T. Godsey. 80, W. Rittase. 81, M. Ahlers. 82, Farm Security Administration. 83, C. LaTour. 85, G. Hoxie. 86, V. Fisher. 87, K. Pazovski. 88, R. J. Lewis—J. W. Stair. 89, H. Kauffman. 90, Brown Bros. 91, Farm Quarterly. 92, L. Gardner. 93, V. Fisher. 94, J. Latta. 96, J. C. Allen & Son. 98, F. Knoop. 99, M. Peterson. 100, W. Rittase. 101, J. Munroe. 102, E. Armstrong. 103, Standard Oil Co. 105, McGuffey Reader. 106, J. C. Allen & Son. 108, Ohio Historical Society. 109, V. Fisher. 110, R. J. McGinnis. 113, J. Munroe. 114, H. McLaughlin. 115, J. Clark. 116, 119, Farm Quarterly. 120, Shostal. 122, Yankee Magazine. 123, Standard Oil Co. 124, R. J. McGinnis. 125, Brown Bros. 126, R. J. McGinnis. 128, T. Godsey. 129, V. Fisher. 130, K. Pazovski. 131, K. Ruohomaa. 133, Brown Bros. 134, R. J. McGinnis. 135, Brown Bros. 136, J. Clark. 138, J. Munroe. 139, K. Pazovski. 140, Standard Oil Co., R. J. McGinnis. 141, U. Oklahoma Press. 142, J. McManigal. 143, K. Oeser. 144, 145, R. J. McGinnis. 146, K. Keller. 149, C. LaTour. 151, U. S. D. A. 153, Farm Quarterly. 154, R. J. McGinnis. 155, M. Ahlers. 157, McGuffey Reader. 158, R. Goodman. 162, F. Knoop. 164, K. Pazovski. 165, 166, 167, 169, Ohio Historical Society. 171, Dr. R. Shaw. 173, G. Cannon. 174, U. S. Army Air Force. 177, J. Clark. 178, G. Hoxie. 179, M. Ginaven. 181, McGuffey Reader. 182, R. Goodman. 183, Ohio Historical Society. 184, 185, R. Goodman, 187, V. Lapham. 188, 189, Brown Bros. 190, R. J. McGinnis. 192, J. Munroe. 193, Brown Bros. 196, M. Smith. 199, R. J. McGinnis. 200, Bettmann Archive. 202, Brown Bros. 203, F. Knoop. 204, 205, Brown Bros. 206, J. C. Allen & Son. 208, Farm Quarterly. 209, F. Knoop. 211, McGuffey Reader. 212, 213, C. Mansfield. 214, Caterpillar Tractor Co. 215, Massey-Ferguson Co. 216, Carr Scott Co. 217, Avery Co. 218, Baker Co.—Massey-Ferguson. 219, Caterpillar Tractor Co. 220, Joe Munroe. 223, F. Knoop. 224, 226, K. Pazovski, 227, C. Whisnant. 228, G. Vernam. 229, Library of Congress. 231, G. Vernam. 233, A. Rothstein. 234, Library of Congress. 236, R. J. McGinnis. 238, Farm Quarterly, 240, 241, R. J. McGinnis. 242, K. Pazovski. 245, R. J. McGinnis. 246, Brown Bros. 247, R. J. McGinnis. 248, K. Pazovski. 249, U. S. D. A. 250, F. Eichenberger. 252, F. Knoop. 253, M. Ahlers. 254, Ansco. 255, Standard Oil Co.